Taboo Subjects

Taboo Subjects

Race, Sex, and Psychoanalysis

Gwen Bergner

University of Minnesota Press
Minneapolis • London

Chapter 1 was previously published as "Who Is That Masked Woman? or, The Role of Gender in Fanon's *Black Skin, White Masks,*" *PMLA* (1995): 75–88. Chapter 2 was previously published as "Myths of Masculinity: The Oedipus Complex and Douglass's 1845 *Narrative,*" *Discourse: Journal for Theoretical Studies in Media and Culture* 19, no. 2 (Winter 1997); reprinted with permission of Wayne State University Press.

"Bill of Rights" by Maria P. P. Root reprinted with permission of the author.

Published by the University of Minnesota Press
111 Third Avenue South, Suite 290
Minneapolis, MN 55401-2520
http://www.upress.umn.edu

Library of Congress Cataloging-in-Publication Data

Bergner, Gwen S., 1963–
Taboo subjects : race, sex, and psychoanalysis / Gwen Bergner.
p. cm.
Includes bibliographical references and index.
ISBN 0-8166-4067-X (hc : alk. paper) — ISBN 0-8166-4068-8 (pb : alk. paper)
1. American literature—History and criticism. 2. Racism in literature.
3. Psychoanalysis and literature—United States. 4. African Americans in literature.
5. Race relations in literature. 6. Miscegenation in literature. 7. Taboo in literature.
8. Race in literature. 9. Sex in literature. I. Title.
PS169.R28B47 2005
810.9′3552—dc22

2004022000

Printed in the United States of America on acid-free paper

The University of Minnesota is an equal-opportunity educator and employer.

12 11 10 09 08 07 06 05 10 9 8 7 6 5 4 3 2 1

For my parents,
Renée K. Bergner, M.D., and
Arthur Bergner, M.D.

Contents

Acknowledgments

This book has been a long time in the making, and I have many people to thank for advice, suggestions, and support. I am grateful for my friends and family members who, though not specifically named here, have nonetheless enriched this work and sustained me.

I began this project while in graduate school and, from this period, I am particularly grateful to Diana Fuss, who was a generous reader and a great resource. I deeply appreciate the unfailing support Arnold Rampersad granted the project as it was taking shape. Valerie Smith provided crucial encouragement and insight; her integrity, professional generosity, and personal warmth continue to inspire me. I am indebted to Kim Benston for many ideas that contributed to the initial conception of this project and for his unselfish gifts of time and support. He remains a model for me both as a person and a scholar. For their critical influence and gifts of time, I thank Thomas Keenan, Wahneema Lubiano, Toni Morrison, and Andrew Ross. I benefited greatly from the friendship and intelligence of Tracy E. Brown, Audrey Fisch, Janet Gray, Erin Mackie, Gayle Wald, and Dana Nelson. I thank Sharyn Barson for her sustained insight and understanding.

I would like to thank my friends and colleagues from Middlebury College, especially Holly Allen, Michael Newbury, and Timothy B. Spears, for their personal and intellectual companionship during the year I taught there.

At West Virginia University, I have found a professional and personal home. My colleagues are caring teachers, committed citizens, and inspiring researchers. For their friendship and help with everything from prose to plumbing, I am especially thankful to Timothy Dow Adams, Dennis Allen, Laura Brady, Jonathan Burton, Elaine K. Ginsberg, John Lamb, Brian McHale, Ethel Morgan Smith, and Timothy Sweet. Our graduate students have challenged and engaged me in the classroom and out; they have gone on to become valued colleagues. Among these, I thank especially Brenda Boudreau, Kelli Maloy, and Dan Tripp. I have enjoyed important institutional support from West Virginia University, especially through generous funding that allowed me to work on this book over several summers.

I owe thanks to several people who made it possible for me to publish sections of this book in earlier versions: Domna Stanton, the editorial staff, and the anonymous readers of *PMLA,* and Christopher Lane and the editorial staff of *Discourse.* The editors of these journals honed my language and clarified my arguments; from them, I learned much about writing.

My gratitude goes to Richard Morrison at the University of Minnesota Press for his confidence in the project and his efforts to shepherd it through publication. I thank Samira Kawash, who served as a reader for the manuscript, and Jean Walton, whose brilliant work on race and psychoanalysis influenced me long before she served as a reader of the manuscript for Minnesota. Jean's meticulous but sympathetic reading of the manuscript as well as her suggestions for revision have guided and buoyed me during the most recent stages of writing.

In truth, my debts extend back even before graduate school to my undergraduate years at Cornell University. When I went to Mary Jacobus for help devising a paper topic on *Wuthering Heights,* she told me to read Freud's *The Uncanny.* That was the beginning of everything. But even before that, Molly Hite's course on twentieth-century women writers had helped me make sense of my world and my intellectual interests. When I couldn't decide on a major and decided to take time off from school, Molly's staunch confidence in me saw me through. Laura Brown, Ann Kibbey, Biddy Martin, and Timothy Murray were especially influential teachers.

The love, patience, and good works of my friends Karin Bloom and Tracy Tomasi have served as a continuous reminder of what is most important in life and outside of academia. They have encouraged me to finish this project.

Most of all Catherine Gouge's absolute faith in this project served as the grounds for its completion, and her game companionship enlivened the last leg of the writing process. I am grateful to my family, who made this choice of life's work possible. I hope that this book honors, in some way, my grandparents, David and Lee Bergner and Richard and Suzanne Kirsch. I cannot hope to match the example of service set by my parents, Art and Renée Bergner; their influence undergirds this work. Along with my sister, Kim Bergner, and her family, they have always expressed interest in and respect for my endeavors. I am thankful beyond expression for their love and support.

INTRODUCTION

Primal Scenes of Double Consciousness

In *The Souls of Black Folk* (1903), the great African American intellectual and political leader W. E. B. Du Bois described a state of identity particular to African Americans living within a culture that did not see them as equal. He termed this "peculiar" form of identity "double-consciousness, this sense of always looking at one's self through the eyes of others."[1] Du Bois suggests that identity forms in response to the other's gaze; his complete formulation locates the birth of the split subject within a sociopolitical matrix:

> [T]he Negro is a sort of seventh son, born with a veil, and gifted with second-sight in this American world,—a world which yields him no true self-consciousness, but only lets him see himself through the revelation of the other world. It is a peculiar sensation, this double-consciousness, this sense of always looking at one's self through the eyes of others, of measuring one's soul by the tape of a world that looks on in amused contempt and pity. One ever feels his two-ness,—an American, a Negro; two souls, two thoughts, two unreconciled strivings; two warring ideals in one dark body, whose dogged strength alone keeps it safe from being torn asunder.

Playing on the theme of a split self, the passage characterizes African American identity as second-sighted, doubled, twinned, and divided. The passage itself works on a double entendre: the figure of the veil connotes both the caul supposed to mark a baby born with second sight—the ability to see the future—and the barrier dividing the black world from the white.[2] This double meaning creates a telling paradox: "the Negro's" vision is both preternaturally sharpened and impeded by the American context; he has the gift of "second-sight" but lacks "true self-consciousness."[3] If the self is both split and doubled, then African American subjectivity is constituted by lack and surplus. The doublings and splits multiply throughout the passage: the social world breaks in two—one black, one white—separated by a "veil," the individual's self-image fractures through the double lens of seeing "one's self through the eyes of others," and national identity is split by the implicit contradiction between being Negro and being American. These several realms of division complicate any two-dimensional conception of Du Bois's famous color line, suggesting that racial difference splits society and the self along social, psychic, and national lines.

Although the term "double consciousness" is standard shorthand for a key motif of African American identity, its implications for theorizing racial constructions of subjectivity remain relatively undeveloped. This is not to say that "race" as a social construct has been ignored. Important work in African American and American studies since the 1980s has exposed the discursive processes that produce the sociolegal categories "race," "black," and "white." Key texts such as *"Race," Writing, and Difference* (1986), the seminal collection of essays edited by Henry Louis Gates Jr., have deconstructed race, making it an academic commonplace that race is a social construct.[4] But these discourses have paid far less attention to the processes by which subjects negotiate, resist, and internalize these ideological groupings; "race has been most thoroughly examined in terms of domination and agency rather than subjectivity."[5] On the other hand, psychoanalysis—the theory of subjectivity par excellence—has analyzed subject formation almost exclusively in terms of sexual difference; it is only beginning to consider race as a constitutive factor of identity.[6] Yet Du Bois's formulation anticipates both of these critical approaches in recognizing that ideological forces shape racial categories and that a split subjectivity forms in response to those forces, here figured as the organizing image of self offered by the other's gaze. For these reasons, I take it as a key concept for analyzing racialized constructions of subjectivity. For despite the deconstruction of "race" and the decentering of the subject, race continues to define salient political, cultural, and personal categories.

If underutilized as a theoretical concept, double consciousness—as a trope for the acquisition of racial identity—is a common theme of American literature about race. Texts of fiction and autobiography frequently represent the subject's acquisition of double consciousness as a singular event; characters "discover" racial difference in dramatic scenes involving photographs, mirrors, or acts of witnessing. Although these "stock scenes of racial discovery"[7] depict a visual event, characters assume a racial identity not so much by seeing skin color as by learning its cultural significance. In such scenes, the self is simultaneously defamiliarized and reconstituted within the cultural discourse on race.[8] *The Souls of Black Folk* contains such a stock scene that allegorizes Du Bois's apprehension of racial ideologies. Just before the passage on double consciousness, Du Bois narrates an event from childhood that marks the moment he discovered that his social status was different from and less than that of whites:

> It is in the early days of rollicking boyhood that the revelation first bursts upon one, all in a day, as it were. I remember well when the shadow swept across me. I was a little thing, away up in the hills of New England. . . . In a wee wooden schoolhouse, something put it into the boys' and girls' heads to buy gorgeous visiting cards—ten cents a package—and exchange. The exchange was merry, till one girl, a tall newcomer, refused my card,—refused it peremptorily, with a glance. Then it dawned upon me with a certain suddenness that I was different from the others; or like, mayhap, in heart and life and longing, but shut out from their world by a vast veil. (4)

In a flash, Du Bois falls from childhood innocence into awareness of the color line. As the veil drops between him and the white world, his previously whole self divides. If it seems unlikely that Du Bois would have internalized knowledge of racial difference in a moment, he nevertheless narrates this autobiographical incident as the inaugural event that ultimately leads to his vision of the African American experience explained in *Souls*.

Du Bois did not coin the term "double consciousness," though he was the first to use it in relation to African American identity. By the turn of the century the term carried at least two connotations—one deriving from European romanticism and American transcendentalism and the other from the fields of medicine and psychology.[9]

Dickson D. Bruce Jr. tracks the transcendentalist meaning to several possible nineteenth-century influences, including Emerson's 1843 essay "The Transcendentalist," in which the term describes the conflict between spiritual transcendence and worldly cares (Bruce, 300). According to Bruce, the transcendentalist sense of the term enabled Du Bois "to privilege [African American spirituality] in relation to the materialistic, commercial world of white America" and to place it "in connection with a more general body of Romantic ideas and imagery" (301). At the same time, by the 1890s medical literature commonly used the term "double consciousness" to characterize cases of double personality. As early as 1817, a medical journal used the term to describe the case of a woman reported to alternate between two distinct personalities, each of which had no knowledge or memory of the other (305). Psychologist William James, Du Bois's mentor at Harvard, studied several such cases and wrote about the phenomenon's theoretical implications in 1890, while Du Bois was at Harvard (303). Bruce argues that the medical connotations of double consciousness were "useful to Du Bois, given his desire to develop a positive sense of racial distinctiveness out of a distinctively African heritage" (305). Thus, Du Bois's use of "double consciousness" seems to partake of both the transcendentalist and psychological meanings.[10] The dual connotations of the term are yet another aspect of the concept's doubleness. Although critics have analyzed Du Bois's concept in relation to its several sources in order to parse his formulation of African American identity (How much is African, American, or both? Is it an essentialist or constructivist vision?) and his political project for resolving its various splits (To what extent did he support assimilation? Or did he advocate the preservation of cultural specificity?), I would concur with Bruce that Du Bois "was using a term that set up a variety of connotations for the educated reader . . . to give . . . a reference point on the basis of which to understand the tragedy of racism . . . and also to appreciate his own program for a new definition of what it meant to be black in America" (307).[11] The very impossibility of reducing the trope of double consciousness to a simple formula of racial or national identity indicates the generative possibilities of its ambivalence.

James Weldon Johnson signifies on Du Bois's ambivalent concept of African American identity in his novel *The Autobiography of an Ex-Colored Man* (1912).[12] Like Du Bois, the unnamed narrator discovers he is black in the course of a school day. On this particular day, his teacher separates the children by race; the narrator is shocked to discover that he is put with the black children. This scene differs from Du Bois's in that the narrator literally does not know that he is, by social definition, black; he looks white and has already internalized racial prejudice against blacks. When he returns home from school, the narrator rushes to a mirror and tries to discern the trace of blackness in his features. He discovers not that dark skin carries with it cultural disadvantages—this he already knows—but that his white skin does not guarantee racial privilege. In this sense, the narrator's skin color highlights the arbitrariness of the designation "colored." The event is formative:

> Since I have grown older I have often gone back and tried to analyze the change that came into my life after that fateful day in school. There did come a radical change, and, young as I was, I felt fully conscious of it, though I did not fully comprehend it. Like my first spanking, it is one of the few incidents in my life that I can remember clearly. (9)

Johnson goes on to "theorize" the significance of this formative event in terms that echo Du Bois's descriptions of separate and unequal worlds of blacks and whites, divided by a veil that keeps whites from knowing blacks and that requires blacks to veil their "true" selves. That memorable day

> wrought the miracle of my transition from one world into another; for I did indeed pass into another world. From that time I looked out through other eyes, my thoughts were colored, my words dictated, my actions limited by one dominating, all-pervading idea which constantly increased in force and weight until I finally realized in it a great, tangible fact.
>
> And this is the dwarfing, warping, distorting influence which operates upon each and every colored man in the United States. He is forced to take his outlook on all things, not from the viewpoint of a citizen, or a man, or even a human being, but from the viewpoint of a *colored* man. . . . And it is this, too, which makes the colored people of this country, in reality, a mystery to the whites. . . . This gives to every colored man, in proportion to his intellectuality, a sort of dual personality; there is one phase of him which is disclosed only in the freemasonry of his own race. (9)

The multiple forms of doubling both echo and extend Du Bois's formulation. The narrator experiences self-division in relation to the dominant culture, but his duality is doubled again in his ability to accommodate himself interchangeably to either the black world or the white. Struggling to choose between them, the narrator decides, in the text's terms, between a purposeful life of racial uplift as a black man or a sterile life of material comfort as white. Ultimately, the narrator engages in the *duplicity* of passing for white, but the text implicitly censures his decision to abandon the noble struggle for civil rights. Johnson's cultured and educated narrator, who passes for white but whose choice inspires neither sympathy nor envy, dispels stereotypes and racial essentialism—all the while refuting the rhetoric of "the Anglo-Saxon's superiority." In this way, Johnson double-crosses his white audience as well: the faux autobiography promises whites a peek behind the veil, admittance to the "freemasonry" of African American culture, only to reveal that the exhibit has escaped.[13]

Johnson's terms echo Du Bois in this representation of a crisis that precipitates double consciousness, but the trope occurs in at least one earlier work. In Frederick Douglass's *Narrative of the Life of Frederick Douglass* (1845) several critical scenes mark shifts in Douglass's self-perception. As I demonstrate in chapter 2, the scene in which he witnesses his aunt being whipped by his master instantiates Douglass's subjectivity as a slave. The scene of his fight with the slavebreaker Covey allows Douglass to shed that identity in his own mind, if not in the eyes of the law. These two events, along with learning to read and earning wages, effect the transformations stated in the *Narrative*'s most famous chiasmus: "You have seen how a man is made a slave; you shall see how a slave was made a man."[14] The stock scene of racial discovery is, then, a striking convention of the African American literary tradition.

In representing racial acculturation through dramatic crises of double consciousness, the stock scenes of racial discovery both parallel and complicate the psychoanalytic claim that subjectivity forms in response to visual traumas. For Freud, gender identity arises from the primal scene and other anatomical sightings.[15] The primal scene precipitates castration fear and so forces the boy-child through the Oedipus complex, compelling him to renounce his mother as object of desire and to identify with his father. In other words, the Oedipus complex—as represented through the crisis of the primal scene—causes the child to internalize the proper gender identity as dictated by the social order. Lacan also posits a visual event as critical for subject formation. He locates the birth of self-perception in the mirror stage.[16] From his mirror image the child gets an organizing vision of himself as subject and an awareness that he appears as an object to others. This primary alienation underlying subjectivity—seeing the self as object—bears similarity to the self-alienation of double consciousness. Psychoanalytic theory maintains that the child must pass successfully through the oedipal and mirror phases (though not in that order) to achieve social integration as a gendered subject. These specular moments thus constitute dramatic representations of critical phases in the formation of subjectivity.

Like much American literature on race, psychoanalytic discourses compress the complex and invisible processes of subject formation into visual crises. From this commonality between African American and psychoanalytic discourses—both describe visual traumas that trigger identity formation—I establish a framework of reciprocal analysis. In this book, I juxtapose American literature and theory on race with psychoanalytic theory to explore how race and gender intersect in subject formation. Intending to privilege neither discourse, I do not simply use psychoanalytic theory to read African American literature. Rather, I examine how literature on race disrupts psychoanalysis's conventional models of gender identification, forcing a reconsideration and reconfiguration of many foundational psychoanalytic texts. By considering the politics of race in psychic development, I aim to address psychoanalysis's historic inattention to race; to extend psychoanalysis beyond the scope of its modernist, European origins; and to ground analysis of subjectivity in a material and social context. In turn, psychoanalysis provides a critical vocabulary for theorizing racialization, as it intersects with sex and gender, for both black and white Americans.

This conjunction of race and psychoanalysis might discomfit some, given psychoanalysis's record on race and cultural difference. A modernist discourse of subjectivity, classic psychoanalysis ignored race as a constitutive factor of identity, perpetuated colonialist ideologies of the savage primitive, and touted as universal its paradigms, which were, in fact, drawn from European culture. Early psychoanalysis not only declined to address racial difference as a constitutive factor of subjectivity but also veiled its own implicit racialist assumptions. For one of psychoanalysis's key insights—that gender is constructed—depends on the category of the essential and unchanging "primitive" for articulation. In Freud's works, notably *Totem and Taboo*, the "primitive" exists in a timeless, unevolved state associated with infancy, femininity, homosexuality, and neurosis.[17] With the primitive forever marking this starting point of human evolution, Freud can trace the psychosocial development of the white, European, male subject. Comparing colonialism's figure of the "Dark Continent" of Africa to the impenetrable mysteries of feminine subjectivity, Freud constructs a "metonymic chain . . . which links infantile sexuality, female sexuality, and racial otherness."[18] Although the image of the black primitive pervaded the white imagination of Europe and America at the start of the twentieth century, psychoanalysis did not recognize its force in the white unconscious. As Jean Walton demonstrates, even key early psychoanalysts, such as Joan Riviere, Melanie Klein, and Marie Bonaparte, who strived to advance theories of feminine subjectivity, treated their own and their analysands' fantasies of racial difference "as though they were irrelevant."[19] It is not, then, that race is absent from early psychoanalysis, but rather that it is put to stealthy use without being considered a legitimate subject of analysis.[20]

Beginning in the 1970s, feminists reinterpreted Freud through Lacan's linguistic framework in order to demonstrate the constructedness of gender and decenter the subject, but feminist psychoanalysis continued to ignore race as a constitutive factor of identity. Walton deftly explains: "If feminist theory has been at all invigorated by psychoanalytic discourse, it is in part because Freud's writings, despite their susceptibility to be read biologistically, posit sexual difference as the ambivalent outcome of psychosocial processes, rather than a pregiven trait. But psychoanalysis does not offer the same useful model for thinking about racial difference."[21] Even quite recently, feminist psychoanalysts have continued to privilege sex and gender over race, arguing that racial differentiation is secondary to, rather than constitutive of, subjectivity.[22]

For these several reasons, many theorists of African American literature and culture have considered psychoanalysis irrelevant to analyzing race or, worse, complicit in perpetuating the dominance of Western paradigms of knowledge.[23] Barbara Christian's well-known essay "The Race for Theory" (1988) exemplifies this skepticism toward poststructuralist theory in general, invoking terms of cultural imperialism to describe its rise in the academy: "[T]here has been a takeover in the literary world by Western philosophers from the old literary élite, the neutral humanists."[24] Christian's skepticism persists, specifically in relation to psychoanalysis, in *Female Subjects in Black and White* (1997), a collection subtitled "Race, Psychoanalysis, and Feminism" and edited by Christian along with Elizabeth Abel and Helene Moglen. In the introduction, the editors admit that "[a]lthough two of us had originally hoped that a revised psychoanalytic discourse could provide a common set of terms for coordinating race, gender, and subjectivity, the three of us came to envisage this collection as a series of dialogues, rather than reconciliations, between feminist psychoanalysis and African American representations of female subjectivity."[25] Christian resisted the "common language" of a "revised psychoanalytic discourse" out of a concern that "the academy acknowledged only methodologies that fell within the Western intellectual tradition."[26] Christian clarifies that her opposition to psychoanalytic and other poststructuralist theories is not that they have nothing to add, but that their deployment perpetuates the power and visibility of one cultural tradition to the exclusion of another. Toni Morrison has also warned against using the deconstruction of "race" to justify the exclusion of African American culture and experience.[27] Although Morrison acknowledges that the "narrative into which life seems to cast itself surfaces most forcefully in certain kinds of psychoanalysis," she also reminds us that "if all of the ramifications that the term ["race"] demands are taken seriously, the bases of Western civilization will require re-thinking."[28] It would be wrong, however, to suggest that black feminist critics do not engage with poststructuralist or feminist theory because, as Carol Boyce Davies reminds us, "gender/race discourses in the academy as initiated by Black women have had substantial impact on recent theorizings of postmodernism and of feminism without being identified."[29] Certainly the decentered subject is one pivotal concept indebted to feminist race theorists as much as to the poststructuralists who usually garner credit.

Despite concerns that "theory" has not acknowledged its debts to race studies and continues to promote Western perspectives, many critics of race and ethnicity have forged an alliance—sometimes an uneasy one—between approaches that foreground African American cultural specificity and those that derive from other critical traditions. Henry Louis Gates Jr. carefully asserts this synthesis in "Criticism in the Jungle" (1984), a "state of the field" essay at the time it was published: "I have been concerned . . . with that complex relationship between what is useful to call 'the representative' in black letters and its modes of 'representation,' of mimesis. To explore this relation, moreover, I have attempted . . . to 'read' the black tradition closely, drawing rather eclectically upon the activity of reading as practiced by critics outside the black literary traditions."[30] Davies also describes a strategy of negotiation: "My position, then, is not to abandon or jettison theory or theorizing, but to offer radical interventions into their claims to complete knowledge and, further, to find ways to negotiate the various theoretical 'minefields' as we define ourselves."[31] Gates and Davies imply the tension that exists between deconstructing categories of "race," on the one hand, and attending to racial, ethnic, and cultural specificity, on the other. R. Radhakrishnan addresses this tension explicitly, making an appeal for conjoining ethnic specificity and poststructuralism:

> The constituency of "the ethnic" occupies quite literally a "pre-post"-erous space where it has to actualize, enfranchise, and empower its own "identity" and coextensively engage in the deconstruction of the very logic of "identity" and its binary and exclusionary politics. Failure to achieve this doubleness can only result in the formation of ethnicity as yet another "identical" and hegemonic structure. The difficult task is to achieve an axial connection between the historico-semantic specificity of "ethnicity" and the "post-historical" politics of racial indeterminacy.[32]

Radhakrishnan articulates the paradox of ethnic and race studies in the wake of theoretical developments that deconstructed "race" as an essential category: how to account for the lived experience of those persistent categories while also deconstructing the logic and politics that gave rise to them. In this book, I try to negotiate the tension between cultural specificity and poststructuralist theory, in part, by writing from and to discourses of African American literary and cultural theory and of psychoanalysis.

At the risk of repeating an argument I have made elsewhere, I want to emphasize that, in noting critical skepticism about the relevance of psychoanalysis to the politics of racial difference, I am not suggesting that we lack a large body of theoretically complex African American literary and cultural theory. Nor do I mean to say that even most critics in the field today are skeptical of poststructuralism. Rather, "I would argue that the politics of disciplinary traditions and the biased omissions of psychoanalytic theory have contributed toward a significant and persistent divergence between psychoanalytic and African American discourses."[33] Although I cannot here examine fully the conflict between psychoanalytic and African American critical discourses, nor can I resolve the differences between them, I do want to argue that examining racial subjectivity is crucial to the critique of racist sociopolitical systems. Frantz Fanon—psychiatrist, psychoanalyst, and anticolonial revolutionary—made this call first, of course. Explicitly revising Freud's individualism in favor of a socioeconomically inflected psychoanalysis, Fanon explains his methodology in *Black Skin, White Masks* as "psychological," but with

> an immediate recognition of social and economic realities. . . . Reacting against the constitutionalist tendency of the late nineteenth century, Freud insisted that the individual factor be taken into account through psychoanalysis. He substituted for a phylogenetic theory the ontogenetic perspective. It will be seen that the black man's alienation is not an individual question. Beside phylogeny and ontogeny stands sociogeny.[34]

As Françoise Vergès writes, for Fanon "[i]ndividual alienation and political alienation are related; both are the product of social, political, and cultural conditions that must be transformed."[35] Stuart Hall also underscores Fanon's prescient recognition that we must bring

> the post-structuralist and psychoanalytic engines of contemporary theory [to bear] on the primordial—and primordially resistant—structures of racism and the historic colonial relation . . . . [A]n account of racism which has no purchase on the inner landscape and the unconscious mechanisms of its effects is, at best, only half the story.[36]

An account of racism that ignores subjectivity is only half the story because, though race is an ideological construct (like sex), it is instituted in the subject on the level of the unconscious. Simply understanding that social categories of race and sex are constructed does not free us from their psychic constraints. As Judith Butler reminds us, lest we misinterpret the performativity of gender as granting total freedom of self-determination, "[w]hat has been understood as the performativity of gender—far from the exercise of an unconstrained voluntarism—will prove to be impossible apart from notions of such political constraints registered psychically."[37] Extending Butler's caveat to race, we remember that how we perform race and gender identities depends on the constraints of the sociosymbolic order. To put it another way, individuals internalize ideologies of race and gender by way of the psychic processes of symbolic accommodation. The symbolic, in turn, is interrelated with ideologies of race and gender.

Because of "the absolute imbrication of ideology and subjectivity," we cannot loosen the constraints of racial ideologies without considering their relation to the symbolic order.[38] How, then, to change the constraints determining the performance of identity, the "prohibitions and taboos" of the symbolic order?

The intransigence of the Lacanian symbolic has been a sticking point for feminist/queer psychoanalytic theorists. Lacanian theory claims sexual differentiation is coterminous with the acquisition of language; the individual becomes a speaking subject by accepting a gendered position as male or female within the symbolic order. This gendered position is determined by our kinship structure, specifically the incest taboo, which is instituted in the subject through the Oedipus complex. In other words, Lacan conflates the subject's entry into language with accommodation to the Name-of-the-Father. In this way, the subject is always already fully determined by the symbolic order s/he would hope to change. What possibilities are there for changing structures of sex if the subject is always already formed by them?

Kaja Silverman offers one way out of the Lacanian bind of the symbolic inevitability of patriarchy and heteronormativity by separating symbolic law into two laws: those of language and those of kinship. Whereas the lack produced by the "Law of Language" is the unavoidable and universal condition of signification (language originates out of the absence of the thing signified and so "castrates" the subject by founding meaning and identity on lack), the "Law of Kinship" is articulated in culturally and historically specific ways. Therefore, the Name-of-the-Father, which describes Western culture's form of kinship, is contingent rather than universal.[39] To clarify, although all kinship systems are organized around the incest taboo, which necessitates exogamy and establishes affiliation between and among families, Western culture's particular expression of the incest taboo ensures the exchange of women among men. Traditionally, the women "exchanged" have been legally and socially subsumed within the social identities of the men participating in the exchange. Lacan calls our particular kinship structure the Name-of-the-Father in acknowledgment of this patriarchal structure. Although Lévi-Strauss and Lacan assume that the exchange of women is a universal expression of the incest taboo,[40] Silverman follows Gayle Rubin in arguing that it is, in fact, a variable and contingent arrangement.[41]

Silverman concludes that our ideologies of sex and gender interpret the (universal) Law of Language through the (contingent) Law of

Kinship by "conceptualiz[ing] the lack installed through language as the absence of the male sexual organ" (37). In other words, subjective lack—what is lost with the subject's entry into language—is represented as castration, and desire—that which is fantasized to restore wholeness—is signified by the phallus. Although the phallus is simply one possible signifier of desire and its absence one possible metaphor for subjective lack, "the phallus often emerges within the Lacanian text as a universal signifier of desire rather than as the variable metaphor of an irreducible lack" (38). Silverman concludes that "the kinship structure through which a particular symbolic order articulates the incest prohibition would also seem capable of determining the ideological signifiers through which lack is represented" (37). If we understand our kinship structures—based on exogamy or the exchange of women among men, which is rendered in psychoanalysis as the incest taboo—as contingent, then the heteronormative and patriarchal matrix whereby men have and women are the phallus no longer seems inevitable. This is not to say that the symbolic can be altered simply by changing kinship structures.[42] But separating kinship from signification makes variation possible within what has seemed to be a closed system.

Though Silverman usefully unhinges the effects of kinship structure from those of language in subject formation, her formulation assumes that sexualization is the "inaugural difference" that founds subject formation and structures ideology (23). In this sense, she represents the traditional psychoanalytic view that sexual differentiation alone constitutes the subject; racial identity somehow develops later. But, as I aim to show in the chapters that follow, racial differentiation is equally constitutive. In fact, Silverman's insight about the contingency of kinship clears space for reconceptualizing how race enters the symbolic through kinship structures. Specifically, I want to recognize another key principle of Western culture's kinship structure, one that goes unremarked by Lévi-Strauss and Lacan (as well as Silverman): the miscegenation taboo.[43] Traditionally, Western culture not only requires exogamy—that men exchange women or marry outside a given (familial) group, but also endogamy—that men exchange women or marry within a given (racial) group. Thus, the incest and miscegenation taboos work in tandem.[44] However, the miscegenation taboo operates differentially by racial group. In the American context and certain others with colonial legacies, the miscegenation taboo has dictated that women, white and black, be circulated by and among white men, while black men be denied access to white women. Thus, to paraphrase Silverman, the circulation of women (white and black) can be seen to represent the most rudimentary articulation of the Name-of-the-White-Father—the most basic mechanism for defining white men, in contradistinction to women and black men, as the producers and representatives of the social field (36). The symbolic order thus institutes intersecting regimes of racial and sexual difference.

Several consequences follow from this claim that the symbolic organizes a regime of racial difference that founds subjectivity. First, our symbolic compels individuals to assume raced subject positions as white or nonwhite—though racial difference has been figured most forcefully in American law and custom as a black/white binary. In positing a (racial) symbolic organized in relation to the privileged signifier whiteness, I follow Kalpana Seshadri-Crooks's conclusion that whiteness operates as a master signifier (without a signified) that establishes a structure of relations, a signifying chain that, through a process of inclusions and exclusions, constitutes a pattern for organizing human difference. This chain provides subjects with certain symbolic positions such as "black," "white," "Asian," and so forth, in relation to the master signifier.[45]

Second, just as the incest taboo determines the phallus as signifier of lack, so also does the miscegenation taboo inflect the terms through which symbolic lack is signified. Like the phallus, whiteness signifies desire; the absence of whiteness signifies subjective lack. Consequently, whiteness, too, covers the lack of being with a fantasy of sufficiency and wholeness.[46] Third, the "racial symbolic" also operates through the Laws of Language and Kinship; the miscegenation taboo determines the subject's relation to paternal law and the Name-of-the-Father. Fourth, the symbolic order of racial difference and its attendant fantasy of white sufficiency are reflected in America's ideology of white supremacy, which operates through "state apparatuses" or discourses of law, science, custom, and violence that legislate and maintain racial groupings. There is, then, a mutually determining relationship between a symbolic order of racial difference and an ideology of white supremacy.

The regime of racial difference subscribes to the binary logic of an essential, natural, and ineluctable difference between whiteness and nonwhiteness. It therefore produces and depends on a fantasy of racial purity. A set of laws, cultural practices, and scientific discourses has been marshaled to maintain the fantasy of racial purity that rationalizes white supremacy. Many of these laws regulate kinship in order to designate racially discrete groups where none exist. For example, juridical laws have required that individuals of "mixed blood" always be classified as black, a regulation known as the "one-drop rule."[47] In addition to the one-drop rule, antebellum laws organizing racial categories included antimiscegenation laws, antimanumission laws, and the decree that children of slave women shall follow the condition of the mother.[48] In the wake of Reconstruction, threatened racial divisions were reconsolidated through Jim Crow segregation. From the 1880s to about 1910, new laws mandating that the races be separated socially, politically, and economically made segregation systematic. Segregation required a clear-cut, binary distinction between black and white, and so by 1915 the one-drop rule came to be accepted throughout the nation. Extralegal practices such as lynching, rape, and other terrorist tactics by such groups as the Ku Klux Klan helped enforce segregation law. Before and after abolition, scientific discourses of anthropology, medicine, eugenics, and psychiatry corroborated the myth of biological racial difference and its correlative, white supremacy. Although most of these laws have been revoked since the 1950s, the ideology of racial purity persists through such mechanisms as the U.S. Census, which, until the year 2000, required individuals to choose only one racial category to identify themselves. Such laws constructing racial categories regulate sex and organize kinship (through the miscegenation taboo) so as to determine legitimacy, descent, and inheritance; in other words, to organize racial subjects' relation to paternal law.[49]

These laws and practices did not, of course, curtail interracial sex, but they organized its outcome. In fact, the fiction of racial purity—and the symbolic regime of racial difference itself—is belied by the laws themselves, which must recognize the failure of racial separation in order to regulate its effects. While effectively minimizing sex between white women and black men, they actually facilitated mixing between white men and black women by ensuring that children of such unions could not inherit the social, legal, or symbolic rights that ordinarily derived from the father. In this way, white men could father children with black women without assuming legal paternity. Moreover, the violent and coercive components of the race system enabled white men to obtain sexual access to black women and white women. Symbolic ideas of sex and gender further rationalized the system. It is well known that white supremacy and its supports—from lynching to school segregation—were justified in the name of protecting White Womanhood from the supposed sexual predations of black men. Correlatively, black women were deemed licentious, a label that rationalized white men's practices of rape and sexual coercion. If the miscegenation taboo operates so as to facilitate certain combinations of race mixing, then it contradicts the fantasy of racial purity. Ultimately, the symbolic regime of racial difference is structured on an internal contradiction that unravels its own logic. This internal contradiction offers the possibility for critique and, perhaps, for dismantling the system.

How are individuals accommodated to this racial symbolic, interpellated by ideologies of race? Conventionally, psychoanalytic theory holds that the individual is interpellated into the symbolic order through the Oedipus complex. The Oedipus complex delivers the threat of castration so as to propel the individual into a masculine or feminine subject position. However, the oedipal scenario—and, by implication, the nuclear family—is insufficient (though not irrelevant) in considering a racial symbolic. Although regulatory practices of our race ideology operate in familial terms, socialization does not happen exclusively, or even primarily, within the family proper. Any psychoanalytic critique of race must, then, consider the *politics* of the family. We must look beyond the oedipal scenario, the family, and the period of infantile development to examine racialization and to move psychoanalytic inquiry into the sociopolitical sphere.[50]

Frantz Fanon's critique of colonial race relations, *Black Skin, White Masks,* models just such a method for extending psychoanalysis beyond the familial frame. He breaks psychoanalytic discourses of identity out of the oedipal frame, writing a socially contextualized paradigm that accounts for the ways that power, economics, gender, and nationalism construct racial identity. Even more important, Fanon levels a devastating critique of colonial power relations and their psychic consequences. Fanon's is not the first psychoanalytic study of a colonial dynamic, but it is the first to use the approach for political critique. Before Fanon, psychoanalytic studies of colonized peoples, such as O. Mannoni's study of French Madagascar, *Prospero and Caliban,* depended on and reinforced imperialist stereotypes about "primitives" in order to justify colonialism.[51] Rather than seeing colonialism as the cause of psychic responses in the Malagasy, Mannoni claims that colonization simply brings to light their inherently savage and inferior characteristics. By contrast, Fanon—a Martinican-born,

French-trained psychiatrist and psychoanalyst—examines the psychic effects of colonialism's power structure. Though not situated in the racial context of the United States, Frantz Fanon's study of colonial race relations inaugurates a politicized psychoanalytic discourse of race.[52] In chapter 1, I examine primal scenes of double consciousness in Fanon's seminal *Black Skin, White Masks* to establish an analytic model for my subsequent readings of texts in the American frame.

Although Fanon is the cornerstone of my inquiry into the intersections of raced identity and social power, *Black Skin, White Masks* contains a significant gender bias—as one might expect from a work first published in 1952. Focusing on masculine identity, Fanon discusses women primarily as mediators of a competitive relationship between white men and black men. This masculine focus does not omit women, but rather indicates their instrumental position in the colonial structures that produce racial identities. In an extension of Luce Irigaray's and Gayle Rubin's conceptions of a sex-gender economy that organizes a "traffic in women" according to the incest taboo, I explore the idea that a homosocial, heterosexual colonial economy circulates women as objects of exchange according to a miscegenation taboo that determines a racial hierarchy between groups of men. Fanon's description of raced masculinity itself has further implications for feminist analysis. His claim that racial identity is produced by an objectifying white gaze parallels feminist assertions that femininity is constructed by a male gaze. By arguing that a dominant gaze constructs both raced and gendered subject-positions, I point toward the ruptures in—rather than the hegemony of—scopic regimes. Questions of racial difference thus pry open the seemingly closed system of representation and gender where women, exclusively, are equated with lack.

Fanon's *Black Skin, White Masks* provides a theoretical model for adapting psychoanalysis to study political, economic, and gendered forces of racialization. Frederick Douglass's *Narrative of the Life of Frederick Douglass, An American Slave, Written by Himself* serves as a model representation of African American masculine subjectivity. Long considered the paradigmatic representation of African American identity, Douglass's *Narrative* commandeers American myths of self-reliance and heroic rebellion to represent Douglass as the emblematic African American man. In chapter 2, I argue that Douglass's specimen story resembles psychoanalysis's paradigm of masculine subject formation, the Oedipus complex. While enslaved, Douglass experiences competing identifications of race and gender that prefigure

Freud's formulation of *both* masculine and feminine subject positions. Douglass must resolve these competing identifications so as to authorize his voice and his claim to American citizenship. Comparing Douglass's *Narrative* to Freud's accounts of the Oedipus complex, I argue that Douglass claims American citizenship by rewriting his relationship to the Name-of-the-Father and to cultural myths of masculinity. Although Douglass cannot entirely subvert categories of race and gender, he alters his relation to the Law according to the political and historical conditions of his day. His success at manipulating contradictory identifications of gender and race helps us rethink the terms and stability of symbolic Law. Furthermore, I use Douglass's representation of competing identifications to re-read Freud's paradigm of heterosexual masculinity, specifically in relation to his case study of "the Wolf Man."

If Douglass narrates his accomplishment of normative and sufficient masculinity, Nella Larsen's modernist novel *Quicksand* offers no comparable success story for her feminine subject. Helga Crane fails to accommodate any of the various, but equally restrictive, subject positions available to her as a mixed-race woman in the 1920s. In chapter 3, I argue that Larsen deploys the figure of the tragic mulatto, who belongs in neither the white world nor the black, to explore the symbolic constraints on race/sex performativity. Further, as the daughter of an African American father and a white mother, Helga embodies the violation of the miscegenation taboo. I explore how Helga, as an embodiment of that broken taboo, undermines the ideological fiction of racial difference and the fantasy of racial purity.

I further explore the implications of the miscegenation taboo through a reading of William Faulkner's *Absalom, Absalom!* in chapter 4. Here I shift from a focus on the ways that African American men and women accommodate and resist racial ideologies to the ways that the dominant white culture is instituted and maintained through ideologies of gender, race, class, and nation. I also explore class as a constitutive factor of subjectivity that reciprocally defines the categories of race and gender. Thomas Sutpen, the white protagonist of Faulkner's *Absalom, Absalom!* displaces his anxiety about his low class position onto blacks, associating economic "lack" with blackness. Exploiting slave labor, Sutpen obsessively amasses wealth, property, and (white) heirs to compensate for his sense of class inferiority. But the slave system itself, particularly the miscegenation taboo that grants white men sexual access to black women, actually facilitates the contamination of his family line with "black blood," so as to sabotage his shored-up white masculine identity. The slave system and its supporting ideologies of racial purity are ultimately unraveled by their own internal contradictions.

In chapter 5, I explore questions of feminine agency, specifically in relation to the tension between group and individual identity. Although the circumstances of their lives are vastly different, *Beloved*'s Sethe, like *Quicksand*'s Helga, has violated norms of femininity within her African American community. Yet the whole community is symbolically bound by that violation, Sethe's murder of her child. As a floating signifier of slavery's effects, the ghost Beloved represents Sethe's killed daughter, the self-division Sethe experiences in relation to her memories of her unspeakable slave past, the sixty million who died in the middle passage, the collective experience of slavery for African Americans, and slavery's legacy to the nation. By thus representing the historic trauma of slavery through the vicissitudes of a mother-daughter relationship, *Beloved* forges a link between feminine subjectivity and communal identity. Moreover, *Beloved* explicitly links the pathology of individual trauma and the problem of inherently belated historic knowledge of slavery. This linkage suggests not only that there is a structural similarity between individual trauma and history, but that the subjective perspective is crucial to understanding the history of slavery. Sethe and Beloved's struggle between intersubjective merging and individuation also recalls the process of subject formation described by the psychoanalytic discourse of object relations. According to object relations, subjectivity forms in relation to the mother rather than in submission to paternal law and produces a self-in-relation rather than a split subject. I argue that Beloved poses an alternative to the phallus as a signifier of desire, thus forging a link between the claims of both Lacanian- and object relations–based psychoanalytic feminisms.

Examining the "stock scenes" of double consciousness in American literary works on race alongside the primal scenes of psychoanalytic theory, this book asks psychoanalysis to account for race as a constitutive factor of identity; to explore intersections of race, gender, and sexuality; to analyze how American ideologies of race and citizenship, in conjunction with a racial symbolic, work to produce racialized subjects; and to argue for the relevance of the unconscious to the politics of race. These are, no doubt, goals I can hope only to approach, not complete. I must also acknowledge some of the project's obvious limitations of scope and imagination. My analysis of "race" is limited to constructions of blackness and whiteness because "prevailing discourses of race and racial segregation in late nineteenth- and early twentieth-century American culture deployed this bifurcation more pervasively than other models of racial diversity."[53] Moreover, I focus primarily on the construction of African American identity; I devote less attention to discussing representations of white subject formation. This is not to say that only blacks—or members of other minority groups—are raced subjects or that white subjectivity is necessarily more coherent than others. It has simply been my interest and commitment to analyze the aporias of psychoanalysis and the violence of the racial symbolic from this direction.[54] Even within this focus on representations of African American racialization, I cannot account for all such narratives dating from the mid-nineteenth through the twentieth century. The limited number of examined texts cannot fully represent differences of gender, class, sexuality, and nationality that might complicate representations of racialization. Finally, I do not consider texts that deviate significantly from the paradigm of double consciousness. I have chosen to focus on now-canonical texts on race as exemplary "cases" that represent a pervasive mode of *narrativizing* racialization, but I do not claim that my conclusions correspond to the lived experiences of all African Americans.

CHAPTER 1

Who Is That Masked Woman? Gender and Frantz Fanon

Recent literary and discourse theory is shot through with references to Frantz Fanon's first book, *Black Skin, White Masks,* a psychoanalytic study of race relations in colonial Martinique.[1] Since the 1990s, this work has become a touchstone—as evidenced by allusive titles such as "White Skins, Black Masks: Minstrelsy and White Working Class Formation before the Civil War" (David Roediger), "Blackface, White Noise: The Jewish Jazz Singer Finds His Voice" (Michael Rogin), "White Skin, Brown Masks: The Double Mimesis, or With Lawrence in Arabia" (Kaja Silverman), to name but a few. These references to *Black Skin, White Masks* manipulate the terms of its chiasmatic title to connote various permutations of psychic racial "cross-dressing," such as minstrelsy, mimicry, and cultural appropriation. They suggest that the resurgence of interest in Fanon coincides, not incidentally, with the development of performative theories of identity. In addition, Henry Louis Gates Jr. points out that Fanon's recent critical recuperation "has something to do with the convergence of the problematic of colonialism with that of subject-formation."[2] Homi Bhabha has done much to amplify Fanon's claim that colonial power and native resistance operate through psychic mechanisms of desire, language, masquerade, and fetish.[3] Although psychoanalysis is traditionally an individualistic discourse, Fanon demonstrates how to use it for social analysis without evacuating agency or politics. The work thus serves as a cornerstone for my inquiry into the intersections of racial subjectivity and social power.

Fanon's recent reinstatement as "a global theorist," to cite Gates, marks at least a tacit convergence of the questions inhering in psychoanalysis and postcolonialism (457). Fanon transposes psychoanalysis—a theory of subject formation based on sexual difference—to a register where it would account for race as one of the fundamental differences that constitutes subjectivity. He asks how sexuality and language, the primary constituents of the symbolic, are inflected by race, as well as how they construct categories of race. He opens the spatiotemporal window of subject formation beyond the family and infancy, since he does not confine crucial moments in the formation of racial identity to the oedipal dynamic, the psychoanalytic scene of sexual differentiation and language acquisition. By transporting psychoanalysis from its European origins to the colonial sphere, Fanon releases the theory from the limits of its class, race, and historic specificities. Though he focuses on the dimension of racial subjectivity, his analysis of the individual is always rooted in the larger socioeconomic, material framework of colonialism. *Black Skin, White Masks* effects, then, a paradigm shift that reconfigures psychoanalysis to account for racial identity and that enables a psychoanalytic critique of racism.

Writing out of the context of the French Caribbean, Fanon asserts that black identity is shaped by the oppressive sociopolitical structure of colonial culture:[4]

> [T]he effective disalienation of the black man entails an immediate recognition of social and economic realities. If there is an inferiority complex, it is the outcome of a double process:
>
> —primarily, economic;
>
> —subsequently, the internalization—or, better, the epidermalization—of this inferiority. (10–11)

By making explicit the cultural construction of racial subjectivity, Fanon de-essentializes both race and psychoanalytic models of subject formation; psychoanalysis becomes a tool with which to evaluate relations of power and cultural hegemony.[5] The "black man," he writes, is loaded with an "arsenal of complexes that has been developed by the colonial environment" (30). Even if it were desirable, psychic assimilation would be impossible for the colonized black, for the French Caribbean black man will never be accepted by the French, no matter how closely he follows their precepts: "the educated Negro suddenly discovers he is rejected by a civilization which he has nonetheless assimilated" (93).[6] Neurosis and alienation are the normal states of the black man in the colonies or in equally racist France. And Fanon's "colonized as constructed by colonialist ideology is the very figure of the divided subject posited by psychoanalytic theory to refute humanism's myth of the unified self."[7]

Though *Black Skin, White Masks* is a foundational text for reconfiguring psychoanalysis to account for race, Fanon, like Freud, takes the male subject as norm. For the exemplary colonized subject, Fanon uses the term "the black man." This masculine universal clearly refers not to humankind generally, but to actual men—since Fanon describes these colonized subjects as studying in Paris, lusting after white women, and competing with white men for intellectual recognition. The French-educated Martinican who appropriates the superiority of the colonizing culture by ostentatiously wielding proper French is, by assumption, male: "When he marries, his wife will be aware that she is marrying a joke" (25). That Fanon's "universal" subject describes the colonized male in particular indicates that racial identities intersect with sexual difference. Fanon does not ignore sexual difference altogether, but he explores sexuality's role in constructing race only through rigid categories of gender.

In *Black Skin, White Masks,* women are considered as subjects almost exclusively in terms of their sexual relationships with men; feminine desire is thus defined as an overly literal and limited (hetero)-sexuality. But though feminine subjectivity clearly deserves broader description, the dimensions of its confinement within *Black Skin, White Masks* indicate the architecture of raced masculinity and femininity in the colonial contexts. So while it is not surprising that Fanon, writing in the early 1950s, takes the masculine as the norm, it is necessary not only to posit alternative representations of femininity, but to consider how his account of normative raced masculinity depends on excluding femininities. By examining the role of gender in *Black Skin, White Masks,* I aim to broaden Fanon's outline of black women's subjectivity and to work toward delineating the interdependence of race and gender. Although they may emanate from a common construction of otherness in psychoanalytic discourses,[8] racial difference and sexual difference intersect and interact in contextually variable ways that preclude separate or determinist description.[9] Relying heavily on feminist psychoanalytic theory as a model for revising the discourse of psychoanalysis from within, I hope to review Fanon's construction of gender while illuminating the contributions of his psychoanalytic framework of racial identity.

Fanon's almost mythical significance for postcolonial theorists and, more recently, for others gesturing toward multicultural contexts nearly forestalls a gender critique of *Black Skin, White Masks*. In an article tracing Fanon's recuperation as a "global theorist," Gates notes that Fanon is mobilized as an "ethnographic construct" and is used as "both totem and text" to model a "unified theory of oppression" ("Critical Fanonism," 459, 457, 470). Figuring Fanon as transcultural and transhistorical means that "in the course of an appeal for the specificity of the Other, we discover that [Fanon as the] global theorist of alterity is emptied of his own specificity" (459). These invocations don't lead to critical analyses of his work, but make the colonial paradigm the "last bastion for the project, and dream, of global theory" (469–70). According to Gates, pressing Fanon into the service of a "global theory" of colonialism produces either a "sentimental romance of alterity," complete with a utopian vision of a fully achieved independence from the colonial relation, or a conception of the colonial relation as a closed, inescapable system. For Gates, these incompatible positions structure the central conflict within colonial discourse theory: the tension between utopian narratives of liberation and deterministic models of subject formation and discourse formation. To unlock this binary, Gates proposes a more grounded approach that would "historicize" Fanon through biographical critique. Gates would weigh, for example, reports that Fanon did not identify with and even found distasteful the common people of the cultures he championed theoretically and politically.

This recourse to the "factual" authority of biography may demythologize the man but does not disprove his theory or resolve the dilemmas of colonial discourse analysis. Fanon's alienation from the local and the "low" is in fact the subject of *Black Skin, White Masks*; the dialectic between solidarity with and alienation from the colonized population is integral to his analysis of the colonially educated black man's psychology. Rather than historicize Fanon, I want to challenge postcolonialism's uses of him and encourage a deeper engagement with issues of gender—not to constitute a better "unified theory of oppression," but to question the dominant practice of "separate but equal" psychoanalytic discourses of race and gender.

Visual Difference: Is the Gaze White?

"What does the black man want?" (8), the question that launches Fanon's inquiry into the psychology of colonialism, wrests the psychoanalytic territory of otherness from femininity. As Homi Bhabha notes, "With a question that echoes Freud's *what does woman want?* Fanon turns to confront the colonized world."[10] In contrast to Freud's question, which has become emblematic of woman's inability to determine her own meaning within patriarchal signification, Fanon's recovers a certain power of self-definition.[11] Freud addresses his question to men, not women, and elicits masculine desire for women, rather than women's desire. But Fanon is both subject and object, enunciator and addressee of this question of desire. Relating psychic desire to politics, he clears a space for his articulation of black subjectivity. Bhabha writes that "in privileging the psychic dimension, [Fanon] changes not only what we understand by a *political* demand but transforms the very means by which we recognize and identify its *human agency*."[12] But for whom exactly does he recover this power of self-definition? Ironically, in transposing Freud's question of the other from gender to race, Fanon excludes black women. Whereas Freud opposes white women to white men, Fanon opposes black men to white men. This intertextual shift from Freud to Fanon exemplifies black women's double exclusion.

Although gender seems to be erased from Fanon's formulation, his account of the psychic processes that construct race shares much with Freud's schema of sexual difference—especially an emphasis on the role of sight in producing difference. Fanon proposes to answer this question of what the black man *wants* with a description of what the black man *sees*—or rather how he sees himself being seen by whites: "I stumbled, and the movements, and the attitudes, the glances of the other fixed me there, in the sense in which a chemical solution is fixed by a dye" (109).[13] As Bhabha notes, "To this loaded question . . . Fanon responds with an agonizing performance of self-images," an observation that highlights the instability of racial identity, which depends on masquerade, projection, and representation.[14] But if race is determined by sight, it is experienced profoundly in the body. The white man's gaze produces a psychic splitting that shatters the black man's experience of bodily integrity:

> The black man has no ontological resistance in the eyes of the white man. . . . In the white world the man of color encounters difficulties

> in the development of his bodily schema. Consciousness of the body is solely a negating activity. It is a third-person consciousness. (109–10)

Superimposed on the black man's experiential self is a racial stereotype that creates a disorienting gap between the self-image and the white ideal. This racial mirror phase precipitates the formation of racial identity by forcing a "recognition" of lack.[15] Significantly, Fanon sets the scene for this moment of racial birth and concomitant internalization of lack with a dramatic dialogue that plays up the specularity of the event: "Mama, see the Negro! I'm frightened!" (112).[16]

Fanon's emphasis on the visual field as instigating racial difference—for both white spectator and black object of the gaze—is remarkably similar to Freudian accounts of gendered subject formation. In Freud, pivotal moments of seeing trigger a "recognition" of sexual difference: sightings of female genitals "convince" the child of women's castration and primal scenes—in which the boy-child witnesses intercourse between his parents—also "prove" women's lack.[17] These Freudian crises in subject formation, along with Lacan's mirror stage (which precedes sexual differentiation), constitute specular, dramatic, and epiphanic enactments of critical phases in the formation of gendered subjectivity. These crises are dramatic spectacles in two senses. For the burgeoning subject, the crisis is triggered by a moment of visual perception, which is represented dramatically in psychoanalytic discourse by anecdotal "scenes" and case histories. Such moments of perception actually stand in for the longer process by which the child learns social constructions of sexual difference. For example, Freud posits that, in a critical early-childhood episode, a male patient saw girls' genitals yet did not initially interpret anatomical difference as evidence of women's inferiority or "castration."[18] Only after "his development, his sexual excitation, his sexual researches" did the patient reinterpret his memories of such sightings as proof of women's lack.[19] Though Freud asserts the "fact" of women's castration,[20] the boy-child comes to see women this way only through a gradual process of internalizing ideologies of sexual difference.

Whereas Freudian and Lacanian psychoanalysis usually concerns itself with tracing the subject formation of the one who sees—the boy-child—Fanon speaks as the one who is seen. As a speaking object, Fanon represents not only the violence done to him by white fears, desires, and hatred, but also the lack these emotions reveal in the white viewer. Bhabha describes how this dynamic of visual violence works to (de)construct colonialism: "The black presence ruins the representative narrative of Western personhood. . . . The white man's eyes break up the black man's body and in that act of epistemic violence its own frame of reference is transgressed, *its field of vision disturbed.*"[21] Compare Bhabha's remark with Jacqueline Rose's remark that a "confusion at the level of sexuality brings with it *a disturbance of the visual field.*"[22] The mechanism whereby the gaze does violence to *racial* identity experienced on the level of the body echoes accounts of the link between the visual field and *gender* or *sexual* identity. Rose seems to comment directly on Fanon's experience of corporeal disintegration under the white gaze:

> The relationship between viewer and scene is always one of fracture, partial identification, pleasure and distrust. As if Freud found the aptest analogy for the problem of our identity as human subjects in failures of vision or in the violence which can be done to an image as it offers itself to view.[23]

Vision is instrumental in producing both racial and sexual difference.

But the violence done to the spectator is not the same as that done to the spectacle within the scopic regimes of race and gender. Sexual difference may operate in a visual field, but men and women are accorded different positions in that differentiation. The image of woman comes to symbolize lack, psychoanalytic feminist film theory has shown.[24] The masculine gaze displaces the anxiety of lack onto women by objectifying their images, silencing their voices, rendering their sexuality spectacular—in sum excluding them from occupying a place as subject within scopic systems of signification.

Like the objectified woman, the black man signals difference or castration and threatens lack. In Fanon's example, the black man, not the white woman, is seen by the frightened boy-child.[25] Moreover, whereas for Freud the penis or its absence serves as the visual cue of difference or castration, for Fanon skin color is the most notable cultural sign of racial difference.[26] In the Freudian/Lacanian scenario, sexual difference is signified by the literal and corporeal penis, which corresponds, if inexactly, to the intangible signifier of sociosymbolic power, the phallus.[27] But since the colonial relation allocates social power according to skin color rather than penis possession, the phallus is a less appropriate marker of social power—the penis even less so—and castration seems a less encompassing description of lack. To say that the phallus corresponds to whiteness is not to unhinge the phallus from the penis, but to complicate the association.[28] Racial and gender privilege are so intertwined that Fanon invokes castration to describe racial disempowerment: "What else could it be for me but an amputation, an excision, a hemorrhage that spattered my whole body with black blood?" (112).

That both women and blacks are identified as the bodily and sexual within the scopic regimes of gender and race (though Fanon's examples are primarily of black men and feminist film theory's primarily of white women) suggests a shared experience of the body and its relation to the image. But feminist film theorists explain women's melding of body and image through the Freudian narrative of sexual differentiation and so describe that melding as a gender-specific phenomenon. Citing Freud's description of the crucial moment in the process of sexual differentiation when the child sees the mother's genitals, Mary Ann Doane notes that girl-children instantly recognize the mother's "castration," while boy-children disavow it, acknowledging it only after a subsequent threat of castration. The girl-child's more immediate perception, along with the women's maternal role as the child's first object of desire, sutures the female body to the image, while for the man there is a spatiotemporal gap between body and image. Thus, "for the female spectator [of film] there is a certain over-presence of the image—she *is* the image."[29] For Fanon, however, blacks, too, are overdetermined as bodies and images, reduced to biology and the stereotype. As a film spectator, Fanon involuntarily merges with the screen image: "I cannot go to a film without seeing myself. . . . The people in the theater are watching me, examining me, waiting for me. A Negro groom is going to appear. My heart makes my head swim" (140). His coherent bodily schema breaks into the "thousand details, anecdotes, stories" (111). Although Doane argues that the opposition between feminine proximity to and masculine distance from the image "locates the possibilities of spectatorship within the problematic of sexual difference,"[30] Fanon's text suggests that spectatorship is also determined within a problematic of racial difference.[31]

Without denying the violence done by this system of racial objectification, I would suggest that Fanon may experience the system as additionally destructive to his masculine identity since he is made the recipient of the dismembering gaze that is normatively the male prerogative. The black man is thus placed in the "feminine" position. It is telling, then, that among the several recounted instances in which he is treated as a racial spectacle, Fanon offers resistance only when a white woman—in a reversal of gender roles—declares, "Look how handsome that Negro is!" (114). "Kiss the handsome Negro's ass, Madame!" he replies (114). By speaking of himself in the third person, Fanon derisively mimics the white woman's refusal to address him as a subject. He asserts his subjectivity even as he acknowledges his place as object of the gaze.

Race and the Homosocial

If feminine subjectivity—black and white—is absent from much of *Black Skin, White Masks,* women are nonetheless crucial to its formulation of raced masculine subject-formation. Though for Fanon colonial identity forms out of the mirroring relation between white men and black men, this process is played out through the bodies of women. In other words, women (both black and white) mediate between black and white men, enabling the construction of different masculine subject positions according to race. Fanon writes of "the Negro who wants to go to bed with a white woman" that "there is clearly a wish to be white. A lust for revenge, in any case" (14). The black man's ostensibly heterosexual interracial desire becomes an act of both identification with and resistance to the white man. Manifestly interracial, heterosexual desire in this case masks interracial homosocial fear and desire. White men's competition with black men for social authority is also played out on sexual terrain; white men articulate a fear of racial difference through concern with black ***men's*** influence over the bodies of white women: "Our women are at the mercy of the Negroes" (157). Sexual practices are a locus for the expression and exercise of power (both oppressive and resistive) between men.

Classic texts in anthropology (on kinship patterns), psychoanalysis (on the Oedipus complex), and Marxism (on women's role in reproduction of the labor force) point to the ways that culture is structured by the circulation of women among men according to historically and culturally specific patterns. Feminist critiques of these texts have highlighted the ways that such "trafficking in women," to use Gayle Rubin's term, establishes and institutionalizes the oppression of women.[32] Referring to the work of Freud and Lévi-Strauss, among others, Luce Irigaray writes, "The passage into the social order, into the symbolic order, into order as such, is assured by the fact that men, or groups of men, circulate women among themselves, according to a rule known as the incest taboo."[33] In addition to a sex-gender economy that organizes men into social groups through the distribution of women, there is an economy regulating the distribution of women so as to construct and perpetuate *racial* groupings. In the colonial context, the operative "law" determining the circulation of women among white and black men is the miscegenation taboo, which ordains that white men have access to black women, but that black men be denied access to white women. Both incest and miscegenation taboos enforce culturally dictated categories of permitted and prohibited sexual relations. But the race-sex economy of colonialism also produces a hierarchical relation between the groups of men it delineates.

The traffic in women not only describes an economy of heterosexuality, but marks a conjunction of the sexual economy with the material economy. Irigaray articulates the correspondence between women and wealth, gender and goods, by way of Marxist commodity theory:

> The exchange of women as goods accompanies and stimulates exchanges of other "wealth" among groups of men. The economy—in both the narrow and broad sense . . . requires that women lend themselves to alienation in consumption, and to exchanges in which they do not participate. (172)

Women's economic function as commodities circles back to the symbolic realm, however; the value of women lies not in their use, but in their possession. Woman thus becomes an abstraction, a symbol; she "has value only in that she can be exchanged" (176). And such symbolic abstraction reintroduces desire: "Man endows the commodities he produces with a narcissism that blurs the seriousness of utility, of use. Desire, as soon as there is exchange, 'perverts' need" (177). On a symbolic level men's desire for women is a product of and, in a sense, subordinate to a homosocial matrix. Women are "*fetish-objects,*" Irigaray contends, "inasmuch as, in exchanges, they are the manifestation and the circulation of a power of the Phallus, establishing relationships of men with each other" (183).

If women function as commodities mediating social and symbolic relationships among men, then colonialism may be contested largely through the ability of black men and white men to control the exchange of "their" women. For example, white men succeed in colonizing black men to the extent that they are not subject to black men's dictates regarding "their" (black men's) women (i.e., black women).[34]

This relation between colonial power and the circulation of women reveals Fanon's scathing condemnation of black women's desire in the second chapter of *Black Skin, White Masks,* "The Woman of Color and the White Man," as illustrative of his own desire to circumscribe black women's sexuality and economic autonomy in order to ensure the patriarchal authority of black men.[35]

Fanon and the Woman of Color

"The Woman of Color and the White Man," and its correlative chapter, "The Man of Color and the White Woman," provide a gendered comparison of the desire of some colonized blacks to inhabit whiteness through a sociosexual relationship with a white partner. Doane links this psychosexual desire to mimicry:

> The black's confrontation with whiteness is automatically pathological and most frequently takes the form of a certain mimicry. This mimicry is characteristic of both sexes and Fanon devotes a separate chapter to each, making his analysis circulate around a literary text in each instance.[36]

Apparently common to both men and women, this mimetic dynamic seems to operate somewhat differently for each sex:

> In analyzing *Je suis Martiniquaise* and *Nini,* we have seen how the Negress behaves with the white man. Through a novel by René Maran—which seems to be autobiographical—let us try to understand what happens when the man is black and the woman white. (64)[37]

That Fanon here takes note of gender difference in the construction and practice of sexuality seems remarkable since this section is the only one in *Black Skin, White Masks* that does *not* posit the black man as the universal example of black subjectivity. Elsewhere in the text, Fanon perfunctorily addresses his exclusion of black women: "Those who grant our conclusions on the psychosexuality of the white woman may ask what we have to say about the woman of color. I know nothing about her" (179–80). Even the chapter on black women's specificity begins with the masculine universal:

> Man is in motion toward the world and toward his like. . . . [A] movement of love, a gift of self, the ultimate stage of what by

> common accord is called ethical orientation. . . . [T]rue, authentic love . . . entails the mobilization of psychic drives basically freed of unconscious conflict. (41)

Framing desire as a matter of truth and ethics not only contradicts the psychoanalytic definition of desire as unconscious and thus amoral, but also sets an impossible test for black women—a test they are predestined to fail since, "[i]n this chapter devoted to the relations between the woman of color and the European," it is yet to be seen only "*to what extent* authentic love will remain unascertainable before one has purged oneself of that feeling of inferiority . . . or overcompensation" (42; my emphasis). Fanon's reference, in the next sentence, to Mayotte Capécia's autobiography makes clear that it is specifically a woman who needs to purge: "For after all we have a right to be perturbed when we read in *Je suis Martiniquaise*: 'I should have liked to be married, but to a white man'" (42).

Doane also notes this shift between the universal masculine pronoun and references to a specific woman in the chapter's opening. She writes that "[t]he constant slippage of pronouns here—from 'she' to the generic 'he' indicating the black man in general—signals the extent to which Fanon sees the black woman's desire as representative of a black pathology which he despises."[38] I would argue, however, that the slippage indicates not that Fanon means Capécia to be representative of all blacks, but that he makes a concerted—if tortuous—effort to confine this pathology to black *women*. Fanon excludes Capécia from his narrative point of view ("we" are "perturbed" because of her), aligns the reader with his own masculine subject position, and renders the black woman—rather than the white man—the demonized other. He condemns Capécia for her perceived submission to racist ideology:

> One day a woman named Mayotte Capécia, obeying a motivation whose elements are difficult to detect, sat down to write 202 pages—her life—in which the most ridiculous ideas proliferated at random. . . . For me, all circumlocution is impossible: *Je suis Martiniquaise* is cut-rate merchandise, a sermon in praise of corruption. (42)

And he resorts to name-calling: "May she add no more to the mass of her imbecilities. Go in peace, mudslinging storyteller" (53n12).

Typically, contemporary readers dismiss Fanon's condemnation as so obviously sexist that it does not merit analysis. But the *terms* of Fanon's censure reveal much about the economy of gender, class, and sexuality that binds black women. Fanon belittles Capécia's life story in terms of economic worth ("cut-rate merchandise") and sexual morality ("a sermon in praise of corruption")—the conventional charges brought against women's writing and other assertions of feminine autonomy. Indeed, Capécia's autobiography reveals that she exercises an "unfeminine" agency in the literary, sexual, and economic arenas.

During Capécia's adolescence, her mother dies and her father installs a young mistress—Capécia's own age—in the household while committing Capécia to Cinderella-like drudgery. Capécia achieves social and economic independence from her father by working as a laundress. And though she romanticizes her relationship with the white French soldier whose mistress she eventually becomes, the liaison is the only means apparent to her for improving her material and social conditions. While Fanon denounces Capécia as unfaithful to her race, she frames her domestic arrangement as the best of her circumscribed options, preferable to marrying a Martinican black man, since she fears any black man is likely to be unfaithful to her, as her father was to his young mistress.

Although Capécia sometimes—but not always—lapses into valorizing whiteness in her aspirations to privilege, her sociosexual behavior is largely influenced by the economic and sexual politics of a racist, patriarchal society.[39] She states that her occupation as a laundress is one of the few available to single black women in Martinique, aside from prostitution. But citing Capécia's professed pleasure at succeeding with an implicitly white clientele, Fanon claims that her choice of employment merely reflects a desire "to bleach" herself white like her laundry (45). By restricting his analysis of the gendered imperatives that women respond to in their economic and sexual investments, Fanon overlooks the ways that colonial society perpetuates racial inequality through structures of sexual difference. He sees women's economic and sexual choices as emanating from some psychic dimension of the erotic that is disconnected from material reality. Ironically, such a decontextualized analysis of black femininity recreates the structure of the colonialist discourse Fanon so successfully deconstructs in much of *Black Skin, White Masks*.

Fanon's castigation of Capécia (he compares her to the eugenicist Gobineau) contrasts markedly with his sympathy for her male counterpart, Jean Veneuse, the protagonist of Maran's novel *Un homme pareil aux autres* and the subject of Fanon's chapter "The Man of Color and the White Woman." Like Capécia, Veneuse valorizes European culture, feels racial inferiority, and wants a white spouse. And yet Fanon absolves Veneuse of responsibility for preferring whiteness and for colluding with the colonial enterprise as a French administrator in Africa; Fanon likens Veneuse's situation as an educated black man in racist France to that of "the lamb to be slaughtered" (66). While Capécia is reduced to the racial type, the "Negress" who "has only one possibility and one concern: to turn white" (54), Veneuse is an unraced and ungendered individual who "represents not an example of black-white relations, but a certain mode of behavior in a neurotic who by coincidence is black" (79). By conferring on Veneuse the "status" of a race-neutral neurosis, Fanon locates racial identity outside Veneuse's essential self.[40] Race serves only coincidentally as a conduit for Veneuse's neurotic anxiety.

To explain Fanon's intolerance of Capécia and his sympathy for Veneuse, Doane suggests that "[t]he white mask is most perceptible as a mask in the case of the woman of color who seems more at home in the realm of mimicry."[41] But why is the white mask more perceptible on the woman of color, and why does mimicry become, in effect, her domestic space?[42] The difference between Capécia and Veneuse lies not in their valuation of whiteness but in their *claim* to it. In Fanon's terms, Capécia—as a working-class black woman—can aspire to an unattainable whiteness only by aligning herself with a white man, whereas Veneuse has successfully internalized a white, European identity through intellect, acculturation, and class privilege. Veneuse's racial self-alienation is forced on him by whites who insist that he is different despite his "white" identity: "Jean Veneuse is not a Negro and does not wish to be a Negro. And yet, without his knowledge a gulf has been created" (71). Thus black women's attempts to inhabit a whiteness that Fanon consistently defines in masculine terms becomes mimicry, a feminine masquerade both of race and of gender.

Hierarchies of Difference

An elegiac analysis of *Black Skin, White Masks* by Homi Bhabha, Fanon's foremost postcolonial explicator and the staunchest advocate of his psychoanalytic approach, exemplifies the critical tendency to gloss over Fanon's elision of gender. Bhabha's essay, "Remembering Fanon," strives to preserve Fanon's near-mythical stature while acknowledging his theoretical limits. Gates notes a deftly managed ambivalence in Bhabha's essay:

> [I]t is an oddly touching performance of a coaxing devotion: he regrets aloud those moments in Fanon that cannot be reconciled to the post-structuralist critique of identity because he wants Fanon to be even better than he is. . . . Bhabha's rather passionate essay . . . can easily be read as an index to all that Bhabha wants us to forget. ("Critical Fanonism," 460, 462)

One of Bhabha's acknowledged "regrets" is, in fact, Fanon's treatment of sexual difference. That Bhabha expresses (represses?) his concern in the article's only footnote only doubles the pressure to "forget" this problematic aspect of Fanon's work. Claiming to "note the importance of the problem" of gender in Fanon, Bhabha raises objections only to minimize their significance—if not to dismiss their relevance altogether. I quote the subtly oscillating note in its entirety because it is symptomatic of the difficulty of theorizing race with gender:

> Fanon's use of the word "man" usually connotes a phenomenological quality of humanness, inclusive of man and woman and, for that very reason, ignores the question of gender difference. The problem stems from Fanon's desire to site the question of sexual difference within the problematic of cultural difference—to give them a shared origin—which is suggestive, but often simplifies the question of sexuality. His portrayals of white women often collude with their cultural stereotypes and reduce the "desire" of sexuality to the desire for sex, leaving unexplored the elusive function of the "object" of desire. In chapter 6 of *Black Skin, White Masks,* he attempts a somewhat more complex reading of masochism, but in making the Negro the "*predestined* depository of this aggression" (my emphasis) he again preempts a fuller psychoanalytic discussion of the production of psychic aggressivity in identification and its relation to cultural difference, by citing the cultural stereotype as the predestined aim of the sexual drive. Of the woman of color he has very little to say. "I know nothing about her," he writes in *Black Skin, White Masks.* This crucial issue requires an order of psychoanalytic argument that goes well beyond the scope of this article. I have therefore chosen to note the importance of the problem rather than to elide it in a facile charge of "sexism."[43]

Bhabha observes that Fanon universalizes the masculine and ignores gender difference, but argues that Fanon does so because he sees gender as subsidiary to "cultural difference" (by which I think Bhabha means, in part, race). Bhabha seems ambivalent toward this hierarchy of differences—race over gender. He first acknowledges that Fanon subsumes gender difference "within" cultural difference, and then claims they are treated equally, that they occupy "shared" terrain. Finally, Bhabha dismisses this hierarchizing of differences with the vague label "suggestive." The only drawback of this approach, Bhabha reassures, is that it "simplifies the question of sexuality."[44]

Bhabha concedes that, for white women at least, Fanon flattens the complex concepts of sexual difference, desire, and sexuality to a literalized, one-dimensional "desire for sex." But to say that Fanon's gross reductionism merely "leaves unexplored the elusive function of the 'object' of desire" is a dramatic understatement. And Bhabha's ostensibly ameliorative observation that Fanon, in a later chapter, "attempts a somewhat more complex reading of masochism" leaves disturbingly intact *Black Skins, White Mask*'s equation of (white) women's sexuality with masochism. To explain the absence of black women from *Black Skin, White Masks,* Bhabha posits Fanon's own disingenuous claim to ignorance about "them." Bhabha thus implies that black women could simply be added to the schema later. More accurately, their exclusion is actually integral to the present formulation, a Morrisonian "ghost in the machine"[45] or an Irigarayan "blindspot." Fanon's formulation of a colonial relation between black men and white men inadvertently reveals a homosocial economy that commodifies women according to race. Bhabha's confession of Fanon's omission is also perplexing, because despite Fanon's claim to know nothing about the woman of color, it is not true that he has very little to say about "her" since Fanon devotes the chapter "The Woman of Color and the White Man" to black women's psychosexuality.

Although a critique of sexual difference may be too complex and too critical of Fanon for Bhabha's largely elaborative and somewhat celebratory piece, avowing interest in the effects of sexual difference while dismissing the issue as irrelevant to his discussion allows Bhabha to defer the problem and, like Fanon, to develop the discourse of race and psychoanalysis without considering sexual difference and women's subjectivity. Bhabha's caveat against turning a critique of gender into a "facile charge of sexism" is only the note's final determination to circumvent the problem. Gender comes to mean the special case of women rather than something fundamental to the construction of racial identity and to the construction of both femininity and masculinity.

By juxtaposing Fanon's account of racial subject formation with psychoanalytic models of gender differentiation, I have delimited some of the ways that race and gender are mutually constitutive and reciprocally informing. Thus, Fanon's account of "third-person consciousness," of being racially interpellated by an objectifying white gaze, complicates feminist film theory definitions of femininity as the object constructed by the dominant gaze. Questions of racial difference pry open a system of representation that seems closed when women, exclusively, are equated with lack. By insisting that multiple subject positions are produced through a dominant gaze, I want to point toward the ruptures in—rather than the hegemony of—scopic regimes of othering. But even as Fanon's text may infuse questions of race into feminist psychoanalytic discourse, his description of colonial psychodynamics as a relationship between white men and black men—a relationship that is, at times, mediated through women's bodies—removes feminine subjectivity from the center of his analysis. Yet this omission confirms women's role as objects of exchange in the homosocial, heterosexual colonial economy. Along with the specificity of Fanon's representative "black man," this economy reveals that racial identity is always differentiated by gender and suggests some of the specific constraints faced by black women. One important effect of conjoining postcolonial psychoanalysis and feminist psychoanalysis may well be to clear a space for black women as subjects in both discourses.

For the purposes of this study, my reading of Fanon's *Black Skin, White Masks* sets up several key analytic paradigms. Most important, Fanon models politicized psychoanalytic critique by dissecting how racist regimes compel submission on the level of subjectivity. At the same time, he posits the possibility for resistance to such interpellating regimes by representing the desire and gaze of the colonized subject as well as the effects of colonialism on white identity. Analyzing the vicissitudes of racialization, Fanon links the seemingly private realm of the unconscious to the political realm of colonialism—with its economic and sexual exploitation and cultural devaluation. Fanon's emphasis on the importance of the gaze in politicized processes of racialization sets the stage for the next chapter's comparison of primal scenes in Freud's texts on the Oedipus complex and Frederick Douglass's *Narrative*. But though I take Fanon as a theoretical model, this chapter also reads against the grain of *Black Skin, White Masks* in order to deduce the concept of the miscegenation taboo from Fanon's attention to the competition between white men and black men over women's bodies. This begins my exploration of the intersections of race and gender in subject formation, which I further develop in the following chapters. In chapter 2, specifically, I explore the miscegenation taboo's relationship to paternal law in order to consider how race inflects paradigms of masculine subjectivity. Finally, in this first chapter, I used Fanon's insights about visual difference to suggest directions for revising feminist film theory so as to account for intersections of race and gender in scopic regimes of othering. In chapter 2, I similarly use Douglass's text to reevaluate Freud's assumptions about the relation between sight and normative masculine identification. Chapter 1 thus exemplifies the triple thrust of my project: to engage in a politicized, psychoanalytic investigation of racialization; to explore how race and gender/sex intersect in subject formation; and to revise psychoanalysis by considering race as a constitutive factor of subjectivity.

CHAPTER 2

Myths of Masculinity: Frederick Douglass and the Oedipus Complex

In the Introduction, I argued that the stock scenes of racial discovery both parallel and complicate the psychoanalytic claim that subjectivity forms in response to visual traumas. The formative visual traumas of psychoanalytic discourse include Freud's primal scene, which generates the castration anxiety that precipitates a boy's Oedipus complex and instantiates sexual differentiation, and Lacan's mirror stage, which instantiates the infant's subjectivity or difference from the other. Both scenes induce subject-formation through a splitting. In discovering that he is not one with the world around him, especially the mother, the infant of the mirror stage sees that he is positioned within the external world: "the child's recognition of its own image means that it has adopted the perspective of exteriority on itself."[1] In "recognizing" the threat of castration, the boy-child internalizes paternal authority—the Name-of-the-Father—represses his desire for the mother, and assumes a masculine subject position. The assertion of paternal authority disrupts the mother-child dyad, thereby placing the boy within social systems of exchange and signification. The splitting, lack, or alienation that underlies these processes of subject-formation resembles the self-difference of double consciousness wherein the subject discovers his position within a racialized social structure—that is, sees himself from without as (white) others see him. Both discourses employ the trope of a single and specular event that compresses the processes of acculturation to an instantaneous recognition of difference. This common trope presents a juncture between the discourses of psychoanalysis and African American literature that allows us to critique psychoanalysis's general inattention to race. In addition, both discourses presume that the representative subject is male.[2] This chapter, thus, inquires into the relationship between double consciousness and psychoanalytic theories of the subject by comparing two paradigms of masculine identity: Frederick Douglass's autobiography, *Narrative of the Life of Frederick Douglass, An American Slave, Written by Himself* (1845), and Freud's Oedipus complex. Specifically, I address how the specular scenes of each account represent the consolidation of masculine identity against the image of a woman's castrated body. Comparing Douglass and Freud helps us explore how race inflects the masculine subject's relation to the paternal metaphor. It also advances our inquiry into how ideologies of race and nation shape identity in tandem with the symbolic order.

Because Douglass's account of one African American man's entry into the symbolic order occupies a crucial position within African American history and literature, the *Narrative* functions as a paradigmatic text of identity. No pre-emancipation text by an African American has enjoyed as much currency as Frederick Douglass's 1845 autobiography.[3] Long considered the paradigm of African American identity under slavery, Douglass's *Narrative* served as a forceful testament for the abolition movement and as a foundational text for African American literary and historical consciousness. Douglass commandeered defining American myths of self-reliance and heroic rebellion to describe his escape from slavery, thereby extending symbolic citizenship to African Americans.[4] His narrative identity modeled "a coherent self which subsequent generations could use as a point of origin of written Afro-American discourse and subjectivity."[5] Deemed the "prototypical, premier example of the form," Douglass's text eclipsed its fellow slave narratives and obscured the existence of other genres of slave writings.[6] Douglass's *Narrative* possesses, then, a singular capacity to evoke a sense of African American identity and slave experience; its representation of subjectivity produces a transformative—even transferential—effect.

Critics have generally attributed the *Narrative*'s resonance to its "literariness," that is its rendering of slave experience through, most notably, a unified narrative voice and a sophisticated set of metaphors.[7] But claims of transcendent literary value do not explain the *Narrative*'s mythical stature, its multivalenced celebrity, its "widespread explanatory power and appeal."[8] A second wave of Douglass criticism has recently begun to deconstruct the text's coherent and "representative" literary identity, arguing that Douglass claims universal subjecthood by idealizing his masculinity. Valerie Smith notes that his terms of self-reliance and achievement evoke and affirm a specifically masculine American myth.[9] Deborah E. McDowell chronicles the widespread, erroneous belief that Douglass wrote the first slave narrative—a misconception that, she argues, bolsters the text's importance in a tradition that grants authority to what is original, and consistently identifies originality as male.[10] George P. Cunningham suggests that comparisons between Douglass and "Founding Fathers" such as Jefferson and Franklin create a "genealogical model" that fixes a masculine African American literary identity.[11] What critics have often touted as the *Narrative*'s universal value is, in part, an effective adaptation of certain modes of representation, which makes intelligible this literary identity by eclipsing black women.[12]

Readers' sense of the *Narrative*'s truthfulness suggests that the text commands ideological belief, which "occurs at the moment when an image which the subject consciously knows to be culturally fabricated nevertheless succeeds in being recognized" as transparent reality.[13] Much of the text's allure undoubtedly stems from its articulation of black identity within normative terms of masculinity as a corrective to the ways that slavery and racism have precluded conventional masculinity for African American men.[14] But why, in particular, does Douglass's combination of metaphor and masculinity compel ideological belief? In addition to mastering conventions of autobiography and providing eyewitness accounts of the horrors of slavery, Douglass molds his metaphors of masculinity from the basic components of slave society. His acquisition of freedom and subjectivity, which fosters (in his terms) a transition from slave to man, involves problems of parental lineage, linguistic authority, and physical autonomy.[15] These problems mark the slave's generic, disempowered relation to the fundamental components of American national identity. They also resonate uncannily with the metaphorical terms of the Lacanian Symbolic: the Name-of-the-Father, the paternal Law, the Oedipus complex, the phallus. By describing his experience in slavery through metaphors corresponding to the tenets of American culture and the mechanisms of a historically specific symbolic order, Douglass manipulates the privileged terms of social hegemony. Kaja Silverman argues that our "'dominant fiction' or ideological 'reality' solicits our faith above all else in . . . the adequacy of the male subject"; Douglass's autobiography creates such an icon of masculine sufficiency.[16]

Freud's Oedipus complex and Douglass's *Narrative* are mythic *and* historically specific versions of the process by which male subjects submit to their symbolic systems. Both accounts engage a discourse of identity and difference; both are mythical case studies. By classifying the Oedipus complex as a myth, I mean that Freud's theory of the boy's incestuous desire for the mother and sexual rivalry with the father does not summarize masculine desire; rather, it is an allegorical account of the boy's position in his sociosymbolic structure. The Oedipus complex metaphorizes, specifically, sexual difference, which determines the child's relation to paternal law. Douglass's *Narrative* dramatizes a similar moment of sociopsychic alterity, but in this text racial and sexual differences violently affect ontogenesis. Since these differences combine to shape the subject's relation to the paternal metaphor, the *Narrative* demonstrates that classic psychoanalytic paradigms inadequately explain the relevance of race for subjectivity. Nevertheless, we cannot simply add race to psychoanalysis's conceptual frame. Vectors of racial identification operate constitutively in relation to those principles of sexuality and gender that we read in classic psychoanalysis. To illustrate this interdependence, I will interpret competing identifications in the scene in which Douglass witnesses his aunt being whipped by his master. Douglass claims that this event is formative for his identity; I consider this episode paradigmatic for the *Narrative* as a whole.

The *Narrative*'s oft-cited whipping scene, in which Douglass recounts the boyhood trauma of seeing his aunt whipped by his master while he is hiding in a closet, anticipates the content and structure of psychoanalysis's triangulated oedipal scenarios with their visual cues and primal scenes. The whipping scene's visual, sexual, and familial nature, along with the triangulation of its participants, align it with oedipal moments of subject-formation. Furthermore, like an oedipal trauma, this scene marks a moment of transition for Douglass into a new conception of self in relation to the social order. Douglass refers to this boundary crossing explicitly when he writes, "It was the blood-stained gate, the entrance into the hell of slavery, through which I was about to pass" (51). The whipping scene dramatizes an epiphanic apprehension of racial difference similar to psychoanalysis's visual crises, related in descriptions of castration fear and fetish, which instigate sexual difference.

Freud's account echoes Douglass's not because the Oedipus complex is universal, but because each is working out of comparable Western norms of masculinity. Douglass's account authenticates a normative identity in Western, bourgeois terms and so enters the public discourse on race. Wahneema Lubiano emphasizes the contingency of this self-fashioning; Douglass's *Narrative*, she writes, "is not simply a 'writing into being' but a 'writing into being *for*' or a 'writing into being *to*,' a politically cognizant act, an entrance into the graphic symbolic not simply as a textual making or a reminder of human 'being' but as a transaction in the domain of politics."[17] In recognizing the warp of Douglass's self-representation, I mean to ask: what is the cost of his investment in a stable and normative masculinity? This is not to overlook historical context or to criticize Douglass, whose self-construction in terms of an ideal American masculinity served the abolitionist purpose of justifying to a white readership freedom for African Americans. Thus it is necessary to locate any examination of the constructedness of race within specific historical and political coordinates and to recognize that race is a constructed category that, nevertheless, carries material effects and political weight.

Douglass's *Narrative* contains (at least) two critical scenes marking shifts in his self-perception. The scene in which Douglass witnesses his aunt being whipped instantiates Douglass's subjectivity as a slave; the scene in which he fights with the slavebreaker, Covey, allows Douglass to shed that slave identity in his own mind, if not in the eyes of the law. The effects of these events correspond to the transformations stated in Douglass's famous chiasmus: "You have seen how a man is made a slave; you shall see how a slave was made a man" (107). To these two transformative scenes of violence, we must add the scene of instruction in which Douglass witnesses Master Auld reprimand Mrs. Auld for teaching Douglass to read and thus unfitting him for slavery. "From that moment," Douglass writes, "I understood the pathway from slavery to freedom" (78).

Critics generally consider Douglass's 1845 *Narrative* more striking than his later autobiographies, *My Bondage and My Freedom* and *Life and Times of Frederick Douglass*; certainly it is read more frequently.[18] The publisher's note from the Penguin edition I am using attributes the choice to publish the 1845 version of Douglass's life to the *Narrative*'s ostensible originality, literariness, and heroic (masculine) representativeness—a privileging that critics such as Smith, McDowell, and Cunningham have critiqued:

> The choice of the 1845 version of Douglass's life as opposed to its subsequent revisions . . . was motivated not only by the *Narrative*'s status as an "original" in the abolitionist crusade but also by the work's brilliance as a literary work of art composed in the early wake of a "soul-killing" experience by an altogether remarkable spokesman. (30)

I attribute my decision to focus on the 1845 autobiography to its canonical status and to the way it, like psychoanalytic accounts of the Oedipus complex, condenses the gradual process of ontogenesis into a narrative flash. By comparison, *My Bondage* (1855) takes five chapters to relate the incidents of the *Narrative*'s first chapter. I will focus specifically on the *Narrative*'s whipping scene because it marks a crucial moment in Douglass's subjectivity, serving as a gateway to the text's themes of identity, literacy, and writing.

Is the Oedipus Complex Relative?

By comparing the Oedipus complex to Douglass's *Narrative,* I necessarily raise questions about the complex's universality and psychoanalysis's cultural specificity.[19] Without offering universal or transhistorical meaning, Freud's reading of Oedipus places ontogenesis in a culturally specific (Western, nuclear) family drama: the boy's sexual demand for his mother and sexual rivalry with his father. This triangle is but one configuration of kinship structures and symbolic systems that engender subjective desire. Can we extrapolate from Freud's culturally specific narrative other family systems?

Anthropologists have long debated the universality of the Oedipus complex. Bronislaw Malinowski launched this debate with his study of the matrilineal (and patriarchal) Trobriand Islanders of Northeastern New Guinea in *Sex and Repression in Savage Society* (1927). Malinowski found that Trobriand kinship patterns position the mother's brother as a boy's authority figure; correspondingly, the son "develops few ambivalent feelings toward the father."[20] Instead of rivalry with the father, the boy directs what we might call oedipal anxiety and aggression toward his maternal uncle, the kin member with the most cultural authority over him. Malinowski concludes that since the boy's matrix of sex/gender socialization differs from Freud's father-mother-child triad, we cannot simply "transfer" the Oedipus complex across cultures. The Oedipus complex is not universal, in other words. Nonetheless, Gananath Obeyesekere reinterprets Malinowski's evidence as indicative of an oedipal structure that genders and socializes the child even though its kinship structure differs from the Western nuclear family. He argues that Malinowski's account demonstrates that various configurations of kin members do determine the child's erotic and aggressive objects. These kinship structures compose an Oedipus complex in that they insert the child into its social order. The Oedipus complex thus signals not the specific story of a boy's erotic demand for his mother and sexual rivalry with his father, but a child's general internalization and projection of desire, authority, aggressivity, and identification: "Sexuality, nurturance, domination and so forth are not simply engendered in the child's body; they are primarily products of his social relations in the family."[21] The family structure engenders the subject's desire; the content of this desire, however, does not necessarily replicate Freud's standard model. In this respect, the Oedipus complex varies across cultures according to kinship patterns, but nonetheless serves as the mechanism of subject formation.[22]

Thus, Obeyesekere uses Freud's term, the Oedipus complex, to denote the process of familial socialization that varies with each culture's kinship structure. In doing so, he shifts the emphasis within Freud's framework from sexuality to power: "The centrality of the Oedipus complex lies in the structure of authority in the family, rather than in its sexual interrelations; consequently the Oedipus complex . . . varies with the type of family structure, especially in relation to the allocation of authority."[23] Obeyesekere reconceptualizes the Oedipus complex as a drama about kinship, in which the child encounters affective ties and social authority. In this respect, Malinowski clarified the importance of power and authority for the subject's identifications—dimensions that Freud's emphasis on "the erotic nature of the son's ties with the mother and the sexual jealousy he has for the father" largely underplays.[24] If authority and domination emerge from the shadow of sexuality as important (but not separate) components of the Oedipus complex, this paradigm is relevant to articulating dynamics of subject formation in a slave society.

Uncoupling links between authority and sexuality in family units not only gives the Oedipus complex more cultural specificity, but usefully severs this unit from biology. As Anne Parsons writes, "[H]uman societies do structure family patterns in different ways according to laws of kinship, or particular phrasings of the incest taboo, that by no means can be derived directly from the biological facts of mating and reproduction."[25] That the authority figure to whom the boy addresses his oedipal demand is not always physically present in the household suggests that cultural symbolism can substitute psychically for "actual" experiences. For example, a Trobriand boy may internalize images of his maternal uncle in ways that resemble Freud's oedipal structure, though the boy may have little actual contact with his uncle, who does not typically live in the same household. Additionally, that a child's identifications are often unconscious means that psychic conflicts can occur without people living in proximity. In this respect, we should not consider identification as a literal rendition of interpersonal relations: a child may identify with someone s/he has never met or who is no longer even alive.[26]

Obeyesekere's claim that kinship structure, whatever it may be, produces subjective desire is consistent, in a sense, with Lacan's interpretation of Freud's Oedipus complex. For Lacan, the Oedipus complex does not describe the universal *content* of unconscious desire, but rather the *structure* that produces it: a "symbolic constellation underlying the unconscious of the subject," which causes the desire that must always be newly discovered in each case.[27] For Lacan, Freud's Oedipus complex signifies a crucial metaphor for the West's symbolic order. This is why it is not necessarily the actual father who intervenes in the mother-child dyad to force the child to enter the order of signification, but rather the symbolic father of Name and Law.[28]

If the Oedipus complex inaugurates a subject's desire relative to a specific social order, then transposing it to Douglass's historically situated text does not reduce his desire to a question of incest and its prohibition. Nonetheless, since Douglass writes within and even aspires to the norms of the Euro-American social order from which psychoanalysis eventually arose, his account uncannily anticipates the Freudian/Lacanian oedipal paradigm. The similarities between Douglass and Freud/Lacan underscore that the social order not only regulates sexuality through mechanisms such as the incest taboo, but radically intervenes between the subject and its desire. Seen in this way, sexual desire for one's parents "can be historicized in ways that resist . . . formulaic universality."[29]

Family Values, or the Economy of Kinship in Slavery

Douglass begins the *Narrative* and introduces the oedipal whipping scene with a statement on his family origins. Though such a statement is typical of his autobiographical models, Douglass's beginning atypically represents his father's name and his mother's body as absent:

> My father was a white man. He was admitted to be such by all I ever heard speak of my parentage. The opinion was also whispered that my master was my father; but of the correctness of this opinion, I know nothing; the means of knowing was withheld from me. My mother and I were separated when I was but an infant. (48)[30]

For Cunningham, Douglass represents "his enslavement as the ontological dilemma of negation and absence."[31] This double absence of origin is the determining condition of slavery, or "natal alienation," from the legal decree that children of slave women do not inherit the name of their father but rather "follow the condition of the mother":

> The whisper that my master was my father may or may not be true, and, true or false, it is of but little consequence to my purpose whilst the fact remains, in all its glaring odiousness, that slaveholders have ordained, and by law established, that the children of slave women shall in all cases follow the condition of their mothers; and this is done too obviously to administer to their own lusts, and make a gratification of their wicked desires profitable as well as pleasurable; for by this cunning arrangement, the slaveholder, in cases not a few, sustains to his slaves the double relation of master and father. (49)

Douglass argues that slavery is wrong because it leads white Americans to violate their own laws of kinship: in cases of miscegenation, white fathers do not, for the most part, recognize their children. The juridical law of kinship, which states that children of slave women shall follow the condition of the mother, disenfranchises African Americans since the cultural terms of citizenship and property depend on paternal recognition.[32] Douglass's personal circumstances therefore highlight how the miscegenation taboo works on symbolic and ideological levels to construct racial difference and perpetuate slavery.

Slavery entails a symbolic and fiscal economy that exchanges African American men and women as property; this economy intersects with the "traffic in women" that consolidates male groups. The circulation of slaves—perhaps especially of male slaves—as nonsubjects also suspends actual and symbolic laws regulating paternity. This suspension affects especially African American males because laws of inheritance apply principally to men. As Hortense Spillers notes, "The notorious bastard . . . has no official female equivalent."[33] Thus Douglass's masculine identity allows him to desire the authority of white men and to locate the cause of slavery in a loss of inheritance rights; the lack of his father's name signifies Douglass's overall disempowerment.[34]

While the lack of paternal sanction has a material effect on Douglass, it also greatly excludes him from symbolic meaning. His illegitimate status deprives him of a discursive position within "paternal Law." For Lacan, the child fully enters the symbolic order and acquires language only by acceding to the symbolic order; the child must take up a masculine or feminine position in relation to the symbolic. This process of gendered internalization occurs through the oedipal crisis when the familial father enforces the incest prohibition by interrupting the narcissistic mother-child dyad. Though the "lack" produced by this disruption is constitutive of subjectivity for both the masculine and feminine, the patriarchal symbolic order accords men greater social and linguistic—that is, phallic—authority. Whether male or female, however, the slave has no claim or clear relation to the phallus. Thus Douglass's lack of established paternity compounds his distance from the Father's name, frustrating his claim to masculine identification and his authority to speak from within his oppressive social order. His illegitimate status recurs discursively, for while slavery excludes blacks from political representation as citizens, it also excludes them from symbolic representations as subjects: "The master as a figure in discourse reserves to himself the masculine authority to generate meaning."[35] In this way the Name-of-the-Father parses authority according to race and gender. Douglass must compensate for this lack to authorize his voice.

Douglass initially occupies no socially intelligible ground from which to speak: "To be a subject or 'I' at all, the subject must take up a sexualized position, identifying with the attributes socially designated as appropriate for men or women."[36] In the Lacanian schema, an individual who does not accede to the paternal metaphor—that is, who is locked within a closed circuit of the mother-child dyad, and who remains outside social, linguistic, and economic exchange, is psychotic. Douglass clearly is not psychotic, but he nonetheless suggests that slavery confines the individual to a self-referential unity that obstructs the exchange necessary for symbolization and self-consciousness. In his famous comment on slave songs, he writes, "I did not, when a slave, understand the deep meaning of those rude and apparently incoherent songs. I was myself within the circle; so that I neither saw nor heard as those without might see and hear" (57). "Within the circle" as within the presymbolic mother-child dyad, Douglass lacks awareness of his position within the social order. After discovering the value of literacy from his master's prohibition on learning to read, Douglass begins to gain perspective on his position as a slave. The scene of Master Auld's prohibition confers on Douglass "a new and special revelation, explaining dark and mysterious things[,] . . . to wit, the white man's power to enslave the black man" (78). Determined, thereafter, to learn to read, Douglass eventually peruses *The Columbian Orator,* finding therein arguments against slavery that "enabled [him] to utter [his] thoughts, and to meet the arguments brought forward to sustain slavery" (84). Seeing himself mirrored in these texts, Douglass gains an exterior perspective on his enslaved position within a larger social and moral structure that enables him to take future action as a subject. This revelation marks an awareness of the operations of racial power, the birth of double consciousness.

Under slavery, literacy assumes the role that language performs in the symbolic order: the ability to read paradoxically generates the sense of lack that positions the subject in relation to its social structure. Whereas Lacan uses the paternal metaphor to explain the child's initial capacity for linguistic symbolization, Douglass uses it to explain the subject's access to discourse, particularly written language.[37] As an African American slave, he is not authorized to speak or write as such, much less to denounce slavery. By representing his exclusion from signification, however, Douglass begins to articulate his subjectivity; he appropriates symbolic dictates and thus partly subverts them. Indeed, by describing himself *as a slave,* Douglass resists the assumption that slave identity is outside representation.

To authorize his slave subjectivity—an oxymoron in slavery's ideology—Douglass endeavors to appropriate normative masculinity. According to Jenny Franchot's superb analysis, Douglass authorizes his voice by fostering an ambivalent relation to the spectacle of his aunt's abuse: his "rhetorical exposure of the black woman's suffering body is crucial to his lifelong mission of disclosing the sins of the white fathers by turning slavery's hidden interiors into the publicized exterior of prose." More important, however, "Douglass's description of [Hester's] whipping serves finally to make visible his heroic attainment of control, irony, and distance in the narrative voice." Douglass vacillates between identifying as a slave to authenticate his narrative (and African American identity) and shedding that identity to authorize his voice as a man. He authenticates his voice as Representative American Negro Man by temporarily aligning himself with his aunt. Yet his mimetic mastery of writing also allows him partly to suspend his enslavement: inscribing the Name-of-the-Father displaces his humiliation as a slave onto an African American woman. Hester's "suffering provides him with his credentials as victim—critical to his self-authentication as fugitive slave-orator; her femininity enables him to transcend that identification."[38]

Douglass equates his journey to freedom with a transition from slave to man, an achievement contingent upon his literacy. Literacy, in turn, generates a textual subject that largely requires an absence of feminine agency and speech: Hester does not speak, she only screams. Douglass's intended wife appears only after he has narrated his escape from slavery; he omits that her money financed his escape. Douglass also omits from his 1845 text incidents that would illustrate emotional vulnerability. In *My Bondage,* Douglass's "first real introduction to the realities of slavery" is not the sight of Hester's tortured body, but rather his separation from his grandmother. After learning that he will no longer live with the woman who raised him, Douglass writes that he "fell upon the ground, and wet a boy's bitter tears, refusing to be comforted."[39] The image of a prostrate and "heartbroken" child, bereft of maternal love, replaces the 1845 account's image of a child silently witnessing his aunt's vulnerability. The 1855 text does narrate Hester's whipping some pages later, but the grandmother's loss is clearly formative:

> The reader may be surprised that I narrate so minutely an incident apparently so trivial, and which must have occurred when I was no more than seven years old; but as I wish to give a faithful history of my experience in slavery, I cannot withhold a circumstance which, at the time, affected me so deeply. Besides this was, in fact, my first introduction to the realities of slavery.[40]

In *Narrative,* however, Douglas's self-appointed relation to patriarchal authority allows him to articulate the unrepresentable subjectivity of male slaves. In this respect, a gap emerges between his *recognition* of the place that paternal law accords him and his *acceptance* of that place. Douglass indicates that beating the slave-breaker Covey widens this gap that literacy opened: "However long I might remain a slave in form, the day had passed forever when I could be a slave in fact" (113). This gap between an African American's sociosymbolic position and his actual subjectivity offers some agency and resistance before the Law, though obviously he remains limited by laws. This psychic gap also suggests a foray into the inner workings of double consciousness, in which one can submit to the law while rehearsing for later defiance.

Chiasmatic Identifications

Douglass's introductory discussion of paternity *articulates* how the symbolic order can regulate a slave society, but the whipping scene *dramatizes* the process by which Douglass learns his place in that order. This pairing, in the first chapter of Douglass's autobiography, of a description of the symbolic mechanism inscribing racial difference (the absence of the father's name) with a staging of its enactment (the whipping scene) corresponds to the relation in psychoanalysis between the paternal metaphor as a mechanism of symbolic control and the oedipal drama that clarifies the subject's submission to that metaphor. While psychoanalytic theory explains—by way of the Oedipus complex—how the subject apprehends sexual difference, Douglass's whipping scene demonstrates how an individual also learns racial difference.

Slavery fragments kinship structures and precludes the type of nuclear family that Freud describes in the oedipal triangle, but Douglass's triad of master-aunt-self nonetheless composes a "family" unit in slave society. The master is overdetermined as an oedipal Father; he is the agent of a racist social order prohibiting Douglass not only from satisfying sexual desire, but also from achieving basic autonomy, normative masculinity, self-determination, and access to language (literacy).[41] The master/father also possesses sexual access to the mother. That Douglass speculates that his father is his master, irrespective of historical accuracy, forges a "family romance" that reproduces the patriarchal authority of American slave society. Like the mother she replaces, Douglass's aunt is subject to the master/father's sexual demands. The whipping, Douglass implies, begins from the master's sexual jealousy: Hester would not stay away from a male slave with whom she was romantically linked.

> Consequently, the master took [Hester] into the kitchen, and stripped her from neck to waist, leaving her neck, shoulders, and back entirely naked. . . . After crossing her hands, he tied them with a strong rope, and led her to a stool under a large hook in the joist, put in for the purpose. . . . Her arms were stretched up at their full length, so that she stood upon the ends of her toes. He then said to her, "Now you d—d b—h, I'll learn you to disobey my orders!" and after rolling up his sleeves, he commenced to lay on the heavy cowskin, and soon, the warm, red blood (amid heart-rending shrieks from her, and horrid oaths from him) came dripping to the floor. (52)

These interrelations among master, aunt, and boy stage a scene that resembles Freud's account of the Oedipus complex. The whipping scene functions like a primal scene that triggers Douglass's "recognition" of racial difference from within the matrix of slavery's "family." The familial structure of Douglass's brutal scene ironically reinterprets proslavery rhetoric that likened the "peculiar institution" to the nuclear family. Douglass's nuclear "family" tells us something about the structures that legislate, but it also signals Douglass's desire to represent himself within the frame of this legislation.

The whipping scene is primarily a visual event; that Douglass *witnesses* the whipping renders it formative:

> I remember the first time I *witnessed* this horrible exhibition. I was quite a child, but I well remember it. I shall never forget it whilst I remember any thing. It was the first of such outrages, of which I was doomed to be a *witness* and a participant. It struck me with an awful force. . . . It was a most terrible *spectacle*. . . . I was so terrified and horror-stricken at the *sight,* that I hid myself in a closet, and dared not venture out till long after the bloody transaction was over. I expected it would be my turn next. It was all new to me. I had never *seen* anything like it before. (51, 52; my emphasis)

The scene makes Douglass recognize his enslaved state; until this moment, he had been "out of the way of the bloody scenes that often occurred on the plantation," but he now "expected it would be [his] turn next" (52).

The function of sight bore other meanings in the nineteenth century, but I want to read this scene against at least two pivotal moments of seeing in Freud's account of ontogenesis to help clarify the role of fantasy and ambivalence in all racial and sexual identification.[42] According to Freud, the first crisis is when a boy sees female genitals. This generally "convinces" him of women's castration. The second is the primal scene, in which a boy sees or imagines intercourse between his parents and again "discovers" women's castration and passivity. Douglass's whipping scene complicates this oedipal framework by placing racial difference crucially among the psychodynamics of sexual difference. To clarify this dynamic, we must revisit Freud's account of feminine and masculine castration.

According to Freud, castration anxiety usually assists the boy in "dissolving" his oedipal conflict and thus attaining masculine identification. The boy, however, does not at first believe castration is a threat; he begins to fear it *only after he comes to accept female castration*:

> For to begin with the boy does not believe in the threat [of castration] or obey it in the least. . . . The observation which finally breaks down his unbelief is the sight of the female genitals. . . . [N]ow his acceptance of the possibility of castration, his recognition that women were castrated, made an end of both possible ways [i.e., desire for each parent] of obtaining satisfaction from the Oedipus complex.[43]

We can infer from Freud that masculine identification hinges on a psychic understanding of female castration. The girl's assumption of a feminine identity also hinges on her "acceptance" of women's castration, though this recognition initiates, rather than resolves, the feminine version of the Oedipus complex.[44] For both genders, however, normative identification seems contingent on the belief that women are inferior to men; this belief derives from the apparent "fact" of their castration (that they don't have a penis).

This fact devolves on a visual event. In Freud's account, the sight of a woman's genitals precipitates castration anxiety in boys. Though this sight makes no immediate impression, the boy subsequently recalls this memory when his oedipal desire is impeded; he retroactively "realizes" that women are castrated:

> [W]hen a little boy first catches sight of a girl's genital region, he begins by showing irresolution and lack of interest; he sees nothing or disavows what he has seen. . . . It is not until later, when some threat of castration has obtained a hold upon him that the observation becomes important to him: if he then recollects or repeats it, it arouses a terrible storm of emotion in him and forces him to believe

> in the reality of the threat which he has hitherto laughed at. This . . . leads to two reactions, which may become fixed and . . . permanently determine the boy's relation to women: horror of the mutilated creature or triumphant contempt for her.[45]

By contrast, the girl is supposed to "recognize" her lack immediately; we recall these now notorious lines: "She makes her judgment and her decision in a flash. She has seen it and knows that she is without it and wants to have it. . . . [S]he begins to share the contempt felt by men for a sex which is the lesser in so important a respect."[46] In this scenario, assumptions about feminine inferiority are projected onto the female body, making gender difference a matter of sight and observation.

In the whipping scene, not only does the father figure represent the Law and the mother figure represent castration, but slavery and femininity seem to correspond, as do freedom and masculinity. The aunt's powerlessness before the master mirrors the mother's castration relative to paternal Law. Seeing his aunt stripped to the waist, bound and beaten by his master, Douglass can disavow neither her lack nor her passivity. Although this scene's sexual content involves Hester's gender, it also implicates her race and status as a slave. As in Freud's account, Douglass discovers "lack" in Hester's body. However, Douglass clarifies better than Freud that the interpretation of sexual difference as lack derives from social context and its tyrannies.[47]

Along what lines does Douglass identify? His perspective as both "witness and participant" suggests that spectatorship is both an active and a transformative experience; the ambiguity of "participant" nonetheless begs a question about his exact role. What conclusions does Douglass draw from this sight of feminine lack? Does he identify along racial lines and perceive himself as similarly castrated—that is, as occupying a normatively feminine position—or does he distance himself from the slave's fate by identifying with his master's power? Does he come to identify with his master or his aunt—that is, with his gender or his race? Douglass's gender implies identification with the master's authority; his race suggests identification with his aunt and her powerlessness. Like the boy who fears castration by his father, Douglass dreads that he will be whipped next; like the girl who internalizes a sense of inferiority, however, Douglass recognizes the slave's powerlessness as he passes through "the blood-stained gate" (51). Franchot puts this dilemma succinctly: "To achieve 'manhood' . . . is to forsake not only the mother but her race, whereas to achieve 'blackness' is to forsake the father and his virility."[48] How does Douglass resolve these cross identifications?

Douglass's account of his spectatorship suggests that he identifies with *and* distances himself from his aunt's position. Like Freud's boy, Douglass is "horror-stricken" by the sight of her lack. This phrase implies sympathy and anxiety—a paralyzing fear of "seeing" femininity that recurs most clearly in the myth of Medusa. To distance himself from subjugation in slavery and to avoid a sexual relation to the master/father by substituting for his aunt, Douglass appears to repress his identification with his aunt. All the same, slavery's racial structure runs counter to the "normative" oedipal dynamic, since it requires Douglass to identify with his "mother." Freud defines this psychic configuration as the "negative" Oedipus complex, or "feminine attitude," because the boy deems the father an object of desire, not a rival. Douglass's identification with the father is also blocked because, as a slave, he cannot claim the full benefits of masculine identity; this also endorses his "feminine attitude." Accordingly, the *Narrative*'s triangulated scene partly implies a homoerotic structure that requires enslaved African American men first to identify with, then to desire, and always to fear, white men.

It is tempting to associate Douglass's "negative" or "feminine" Oedipus complex with the extenuating circumstances of slavery's mixture of race, sex, gender, and power. Yet Freud also interprets this "inversion" in a white European patient known as the Wolf Man. At one point in his tortuous way through the oedipal maze, the Wolf Man takes his father as an object of desire, thus identifying with his mother. Though Freud attributes this "feminine attitude" to an earlier "seduction" by his older sister—traumatic not because of a premature introduction to things sexual but because his sister's active role violates the boy's gender position—Freud explains that the Wolf Man's desire for his father is possible because he has not yet grasped the "fact" of women's castration.[49] If the boy accepted women's castration, he would probably relinquish this "feminine" relation to avoid a similar fate. This argument clarifies that psychoanalysis tends to equate male homosexuality and femininity with passivity. Although popular conceptions of the Oedipus complex assume that the boy's central task is to renounce the mother as object of desire, in this case study, fear of castration seems necessary to make the boy renounce his *father* as a comparable object.

Rerouting the Wolf Man's sexuality back to the masculine, heterosexual track seems to depend, as it does for Douglass, on appreciating the "fact" and price of women's castration. The Wolf Man grasps this price by witnessing (or fantasizing) his parents having sex: this primal scene "was able to show him what sexual satisfaction from his father was like; and the result was terror, horror of the fulfillment of the wish, the repression of the impulse."[50] Freud claims that the Wolf Man initially "misinterprets" the scene as an act of violence performed by his father against his mother, but he later "realizes" that his mother's passive, receptive position is normal and that castration is "a necessary condition of intercourse with the father."[51] This shift from misinterpreting coitus as violence to "realizing" that women's receptivity signifies castration does not eliminate associations of violence from the sexual scene, but it does ground them in natural law. This means not that heterosexual sex is tantamount to violence against women, but rather that society interprets the missionary position as an enactment of the patriarchal gender hierarchy. The bottom position is associated with impotence and victimization. Before the boy sustains his masculine identification, he "sees" the father's superiority as cruel and coercive. After assuming masculinity, he reinterprets the mother's submission as biologically mandated. In other words, to assuage his terror of paternal domination, the Wolf Man renders the woman a natural receptacle for patriarchal force; after he discovers that she is castrated, the father's dominant posture appears psychically inevitable. In this way, the boy rescinds his identification with his mother to avoid *following her condition.*

This account of masculine identification tells us a great deal about Douglass's comparable dilemma. For instance, Douglass's account of his horror at the whipping resonates with Freud's description of the Wolf Man's initial horror at witnessing his parents having sex. However, these scenes of violence are not comparable; whereas the Wolf Man imagines violence that signifies patriarchy's oppression, Douglass witnesses the actual violence of slavery.[52] Douglass's *Narrative* stages the violence and coercion of the relationship between master and slave woman as an act of violence with a strong sexual undercurrent. Slavery may therefore partly realize what is implicit in other social and sexual arrangements. Like the Wolf Man, Douglass wards off the terror of the master/father's authority by confining vulnerability to the African American woman and by adopting a masculine identification. By revisiting the whipping scene as its author, Douglass controls the spectacle of the woman to confirm her status as a slave. While Freud's Wolf Man finally interprets the primal scene as proof of woman's castration, Douglass seems to attribute Aunt Hester's violation to her gender and her race.

Though the process by which Douglass actually learned the significance of being African American in slaveholding America might have occurred over time, the whipping scene compresses the process to a spectacular moment. This narrative compression of gradual ideological indoctrination into an instance of transformative witnessing matches Freud's attempt to illustrate and explain how the masculine subject learns to think of women as castrated by positing the past occurrence of actual and specific sightings of women's genitals in traumatic scenes. Since women are not actually castrated, the boy's coming to see them this way is more a matter of internalizing the symbolic significance of sexual difference than of recognizing biological reality. This is why the boy can be faced repeatedly with the "fact" of women's castration, yet refuse to realize its "truth": he has not yet learned the sociocultural determinations of gender and the corresponding distribution of social power and legitimacy. Freud has several ways of saying that boys reject the fact of women's inferiority even when it is plainly visible: they refuse to see, disavow what they see, or do not understand what they see. In fact, boy children do not yet attach social significance to the sight; they do not yet know its symbolic import. In lieu of an explanation of ideological or symbolic transmission, however, Freud postulates visual experiences to explain and make narratable the process by which boys (and girls) come to grasp the ideology of sexual difference. Reinterpretations of visual memories, for both Douglass and Freud, suggest the workings of the sociosymbolic to socialize subjects through the production of hierarchies of difference.

The slave woman is an embodiment of slavery in that her abused body is a standard motif of abolitionist literature. Although the *Narrative* states that men were also the victims of corporal abuse, with one exception Douglass describes horrific violence only against women. In addition to his account of Aunt Hester's humiliation, Douglass recounts that the "head, neck, and shoulders" of a young slave woman named Mary were "literally cut to pieces"; her head was "nearly covered with festering sores, caused by the lash of her cruel mistress" (80). Another "lame, young woman" was whipped "with a heavy cowskin upon her naked shoulders, causing the warm red blood to drip" (99). About the abuse he received, Douglass says only that he had been given "a number of severe whippings, all to no good purpose"—apparently, they did nothing to temper his defiance.

By depicting the bodies of abused slave women, Douglass conforms to a convention of abolitionist literature. Furthermore, Douglass clearly sympathizes with the tortured women and eschews self-indulgence by abbreviating descriptions of his own suffering. Yet he also defines agency as masculine by considering slave women as passive victims. Describing his fight with Master Covey, to whom he had been sent in part for disciplining, Douglass contrasts his defiance with the others' passivity. He describes in detail his own whipped body to justify his violent response, which attests to physical power and self-control.[53] Adding physical mastery to that of literacy, Douglass's pugilistic resistance "revive[s] within [him] a sense of [his] own manhood" and "inspire[s] him again with a determination to be free" (113). Christ-like, Douglass undergoes "a glorious resurrection, from the tomb of slavery, to the heaven of freedom" (113); his sisters remain hung from their crucifix-like joists. Since "'manhood' and 'freedom' function throughout Douglass's discourse as coincident terms," Franchot remarks, the black woman is left behind in bondage.[54] Douglass's notable chiasmus—"You have seen how a man was made a slave; you shall now see how a slave was made a man"—seems to consign the woman to the position of slave in the slave/man binary.

Douglass's repeated and aesthetically distanced accounts of slave women's, especially his Aunt Hester's, abuse in his three autobiographies have incurred charges that he is complicit with the master. For McDowell, he takes voyeuristic pleasure in recalling this abuse. For Franchot, he "simulates the slaveholder's sexual abuse" in representing it.[55] Douglass's compulsion to repeat this scene may indicate a partial identification with the master, but charges of abuse seem extreme. It might rather signal an attempt to control the loss of his aunt/mother as an object of desire or identification. As in Freud's account of the child who manipulates the presence and absence of an object because he cannot control his mother's appearances and disappearances, Douglass seems to manage his anxiety about slavery's abuse of women by exerting over it a textual control. I do not mean that Douglass was insensitive to the oppression of women, black or white. He opposed the abuse of enslaved women and supported women's suffrage. However, Douglass did break later with the suffragists when it seemed that black men would get the vote before black or white women. When forced to choose, he argued that black men needed such rights more than women did. He performed a similar triage in his *Narrative,* albeit unconsciously and indirectly.

If Douglass's account of the whipping scene helps us reinterpret Freud's case of the Wolf Man, his textual assertions that enslaved women are being beaten prompts us to reconsider another of Freud's writings, "'A Child Is Being Beaten,' A Contribution to the Study of the Origin of Sexual Perversions."[56] In this often confused and contradictory "contribution," Freud analyzes a pleasurable fantasy frequently reported by "people who seek analytic treatment for hysteria and obsessional neurosis," in which an authority figure beats a child (179). According to Freud, this fantasy has three stages. Freud locates the origin of the fantasy—for both men and women—in the child's sadistic wish to see a sibling-rival for the father's love beaten by him. This stage next transforms into a masochistic one: the child's desire for the father, when repressed through the oedipal process, becomes a guilt-laden, masochistic-erotic fantasy of being beaten by him (198). This childhood fantasy of being beaten by the father ultimately undergoes another transformation, but this third and final stage of the fantasy differs in men and women. In adult men it takes the form of a masochistic/erotic fantasy of being beaten by the mother or a mother substitute; in adult women it takes the form of an asexual and sadistic fantasy of watching an adult male beat a male child who, in one of those contradictory moments, Freud says is a substitute for the woman herself (it would seem, then, that the third phase is both masochistic and sadistic for women). The second, "incestuous" phase of the fantasy, the one in which the child fantasizes that s/he is being beaten by the father, remains unconscious and is only uncovered through the analytic process. The boy has repressed this stage not only because it is incestuous, but because it is homosexual. Freud asserts that the boy "evades his homosexuality" by turning the beater into his mother—a fantasy of which he is conscious. "[T]he remarkable thing about his later conscious fantasy," Freud writes, "is that it has for its content a feminine attitude without a homosexual object-choice" (199). That Freud, once again, defines masochism and sexual receptivity as inherently feminine indicates not only his personal bias but the culture's as well, since many of his patients ostensibly report that, in fantasizing they are beaten by a woman, they play "the part of a woman." The woman's final stage also entails a gender inversion. Freud asserts that the woman's dual role as spectator and as boy-victim (and perhaps as sadist) in the final phase of her fantasy is a masculine position. In both cases, then, there is an inversion of normative gender roles.

How does Freud's account of beating fantasies in cases of sadomasochistic perversion square with Douglass's account of the whipping scene and other actual beatings of women slaves? It is significant, of course, that Douglass witnesses actual beatings rather than fantasizing them. In slavery, a child *is* being beaten. I do not mean to minimize the atrocity of such beatings by comparing them to fantasies. Nonetheless, we are concerned, here, with the symbolic significance of Douglass's textual representations of them. What processes of desire and identification do they indicate? In Hester's case, the master's whipping springs from his desire for her. In this sense, the father figure does express his "love" through beating. So, if Douglass yearned for love or recognition from his father, as his opening complaint about his father's absence suggests, Hester's beating shows him what form that "love" would take. To receive his father's love, he would have to assume a position the culture defines as masochistic, feminine, and enslaved. Douglass must renounce any wish for his father's love in order to claim normative masculinity. But substituting a mother figure for the father/master, as Freud's male patients did, would not advance his purpose because he would remain in a passive and masochistic, hence "feminine," position. So he follows the path of Freud's female patients: in his accounts of beatings, he focuses on victims whose sex differs from his and he remains a spectator. In this way, he can repress desire for the father while maintaining a masculine position as voyeur/spectator. As with Freud's women patients, this voyeuristic position implicates Douglass structurally—regardless of his feelings—in a sadistic relation to the beaten women he is powerless to help. But because the slave women are also substitutes for Douglass himself (he might be next), he structurally occupies a masochistic position as well. Ultimately, it is an impossible position for Douglass as witness and as author bearing witness, one that implicates him in sadism, masochism, guilt, shame, and anger. This reading, perhaps, clarifies why Douglass describes his relation to the whipping scene as that of "witness" and "participant," all the while lamenting his inability to "commit to paper the feelings with which [he] beheld it" (51). The slave system implicates him in an economy of perversion he must work to escape.

If Douglass partly displaces his disempowerment as a slave by reducing slavery to his aunt's abused body and by engaging in a compensatory linguistic representation of her abuse, he seems to cope with subjective lack by insisting on female castration and by deploying linguistic authority to maintain this truth. That Hester is castrated for Douglass exemplifies a psychoanalytic model in which all subjects are constituted by lack, but male lack is usually repressed by mistaken assumptions that the father simply *is* the Law and that the penis *is* the phallus, et cetera.[57] Douglass hints at this assumption and its symbolic compensation when, in contrast to Hester's silent suffering, Douglass's abused body authorizes his speech: "My feet have been so cracked with the frost, that the pen with which I am writing might be laid in the gashes" (72).[58]

That Douglass's text seems to *need* women's castration and violation, in which women are reduced to literally mutilated bodies, helps clarify a shift in psychoanalytic theory from Freud to Lacan. Douglass's *Narrative* uses the image of a castrated woman to foster masculine fantasies of control over meaning. The link between a woman's damaged body and a man's ability to make meaning demonstrates Lacan's claim that what Freud sometimes explained as anatomical fact (female castration) is really a symbolic condition for signification. Freud's oedipal drama of castration, in which the boy identifies with his father on the condition that he see his mother as castrated, is, for Lacan, an allegory for the lack that signals the subject's entry into language.

Under conditions of slavery, in which only white men approximate paternal Law, whiteness has a privileged relationship to meaning. In such social formations, the symbolic order grants power to the phallus and to whiteness. That psychoanalysis privileges the phallus as signifier of desire highlights its presumption that the order of symbols is determined by gender and sexuality, and not by race.

Douglass's *Narrative* manipulates contradictory identifications of gender and race according to political and historical determinants. By comparing Douglass's *Narrative* to Freud's accounts of the Oedipus complex, I have suggested that Douglass claims American citizenship by rewriting his relationship to the Name-of-the-Father. I do not mean that Douglass has entirely subverted categories of race and gender, but that he has altered his relation to the Law. Mapping these identifications clarifies not only how race inflects the subject's relation to language and to sexuality, but also how Douglass and Freud circulated various myths of masculinity. My reading of the *Narrative* indicates that racial identifications constitute *and* frustrate gender identification. The coexistence of these identifications can help us rethink the terms and stability of symbolic Law.

CHAPTER 3

The Mulatto and the Miscegenation Taboo: Nella Larsen's Ambivalent Subject

If Douglass's *Narrative* represents his masterful resolution of the Oedipus complex—in part, by displacing racial lack onto the feminine—in order to accede to normative (sufficient) masculinity, Nella Larsen's *Quicksand* (1927) offers no comparable success story for her feminine subject. Episodic and repetitive rather than linear and progressive, the novel's narrative structure reflects Helga Crane's vacillating subjectivity as she repeatedly fails to accommodate the various, but equally restrictive, subject positions available to her as a mixed-race woman in the 1920s. As a "tragic mulatto," the literally and symbolically orphaned Helga anxiously seeks a sense of racial belonging, first as an uplift teacher, then as Harlem bourgeoise, next as an expatriate in Europe, and finally as a minister's wife among the rural "folk."[1] Content for a time in each milieu, she soon becomes frustrated with the local community's particular norms of race, sex, and class. "She could neither conform nor be happy in her unconformity," the novel announces early on (7). By the novel's end, Helga is plotting her next move, even though it is unlikely she will live to make it. Helga's persistent angst and impending death at the narrative's end indicate the cost of resisting ideological interpellation, of failing symbolic accommodation. Rather than representing a stable subjectivity formed through the crucible of the primal scene—or even several primal scenes—as Douglass's *Narrative* does, *Quicksand* reworks the tragic mulatto trope to represent a feminine, racialized, and modernist subjectivity as continually negotiated within and against the constraints set by a racial symbolic. Through this modernist version of the tragic mulatto, I want to explore the relationship between American ideologies of race and what I have termed the racial symbolic.

I propose to examine the sociosymbolic constraints on Helga's subject-formation through two interrelated factors that shape the novel: Helga's status as a mulatto and her psychic ambivalence. Helga's psychic ambivalence—reflected in her failure to settle on a racial identity or a geographic home—mirrors her indeterminate social status as a mulatto.[2] The novel's epigraph, from Langston Hughes's poem "Cross," suggests that we read the novel through that frame of inheritance: "Being neither white nor black," stuck between "a fine big house" and "a shack," the mulatto experiences an ontological and material homelessness.[3] Suspended in this spatial crossroads, the mulatto marks the chiasmus, or crossing, of supposed racial opposites that produces an ambivalent racial subject that is "neither/nor." Moreover, as the daughter of a white mother and an African American father, Helga represents the supreme violation of the miscegenation taboo, rather than the tacitly accepted form of miscegenation between white men and black women. Thus, Helga's psychic, social, and symbolic ambivalence—linked to her mulatto status—indicates how the racial symbolic works in relation to the miscegenation taboo.

As a figure of racial ambivalence, Helga functions to illuminate the social and political structures that regulate the binary race system. For early critics, however, Helga's mulatto status actually militated against a political analysis of the novel. This was because the literary figure of the mulatto was seen as categorically tragic—as if mulatto identity were inherently pathological. Consequently, early readers interpreted *Quicksand* through this convention and missed much of the novel's social critique. For example, Robert Bone dismissed Helga as "a neurotic young woman of mixed parentage, who is unable to make a satisfactory adjustment in either race."[4] Later critics tried to rescue Larsen's art and politics from this stereotype by celebrating Helga's psychic complexity. But this very tension between Helga as a psychologically complex, desiring subject and as the well-worn tragic mulatto trope exemplifies one of the crucial paradoxes of African American self-expression, that is, the challenge of articulating individual identity within a category inscribed through stereotype.[5] This tension between individual and trope is, then, indicative of the tension between subjectivity and a racial symbolic.

Because early critics dismissed Helga as a tragic mulatto, it is important to recover Larsen's critique of the uplift movement, the black bourgeoisie, white primitivism, and African American folk culture. In this spirit, Cheryl Wall refocuses attention from the personal to the political, writing that Helga's struggle is not primarily with her parentage; rather, "her real struggle is against imposed definitions of blackness and womanhood. Her 'difference' is ultimately her refusal to accept these definitions even in the face of her inability to define alternatives."[6]

Helga's "difference" and Larsen's social critique vary with each locale Helga inhabits. At Naxos, the Tuskegee-like southern school where she teaches, Helga rebels against the uplift "machine" that retools African American folk to assume productive, but subservient, positions in the lower rungs of society by systematically grinding down their individuality, artistry, and sexuality. In Harlem, Helga finds culture and community among the bourgeoisie, but comes to despise that class for its hypocrisy, snobbery, and sexual repression. Through Helga's rejection of Harlem and Naxos, Larsen "refused the [narrative] resolutions offered by [the] developing code of black middle class morality at the same time as she launched a severe critique against the earlier but still influential ideology of racial uplift."[7] Fleeing Harlem to her mother's family in Copenhagen, Helga intends to escape American segregation and racial categories altogether but finds she is expected to play the part of exotic primitive for Danish society. As Deborah McDowell notes, Helga is caught between black middle-class sexual repression and white primitivism; her psychic divisions thus represent not only her mixed racial heritage, but her contradictory "desire for sexual fulfillment and a longing for social respectability."[8] Upon returning to the United States, Helga marries the Reverend Mr. Pleasant Green, thereby finding social sanction for her sexual desire. But the patriarchal folk culture of rural Alabama to which she moves brings the squalor of poverty and a patriarchal division of labor that assigns women the life-sapping duties of domestic and reproductive work.[9] Thus, as Mary Helen Washington summarizes (about *Quicksand* and Larsen's other novel, *Passing*), Larsen's novels

> are about the chaos in the world of the black elite, the emptiness in the climb to bourgeois respectability. They are about the women in that world who are inhibited and stunted by cultural scripts that deny them any "awakenings" and punish them for their defiance.[10]

Though it is crucial to place Helga within her sociopolitical context, two more recent essays, by Claudia Tate and Barbara Johnson, have noted that something about Helga's self-destructive responses to the admittedly strangling codes of race, sex, and class exceeds a sociopolitical explanation. Her response seems decidedly psychological—even pathological. She craves security and respectability but repeatedly sabotages every opportunity by rejecting suitors, quitting jobs, and pulling up stakes. Even she does not understand her quicksilver moods. "[W]hy," she wonders after quitting her job at Naxos and storming out of Principal Anderson's office, "had she permitted herself to be jolted into a rage so fierce, so illogical, so disastrous, that now after it was spent she sat despondent, sunk in shameful contrition?" (22). Helga fears that a "ruthless force . . . within herself," "some peculiar lack in her," repeatedly undercuts her happiness (11, 81). Johnson asks how, then, "can one account for the self-defeating or self-exhausting nature of Helga Crane's choices?"[11] Because Helga's radical ambivalence seems to exceed sociopolitical causation, Tate and Johnson have emphasized the necessity of attending to the *intersections* of the individual and the social, the psychological and the material—in Tate's words, to examine the "interplay between *Quicksand*'s political and libidinal narratives."[12] They both draw on psychoanalysis for a conceptual vocabulary that can accommodate the novel's representation of desire and subjectivity. Their useful and often excellent readings of the novel attend closely to the intersections between the social and the psychic in many ways; ultimately, however, they retreat from the sociopolitical by psychoanalyzing the main character as damaged because of absent or nonempathic parent figures.

Tate and Johnson locate the cause of Helga's neurosis in her childhood family experiences, but they do not analyze the family structure in relation to the larger social order. Tate explains Helga's contradictory behavior as a consequence of "Helga's repressed desire and disavowed affection for the father," who abandoned the family during Helga's infancy.[13] Given Tate's perspicacious analysis of how desire functions in the text, it is surprising that she ultimately collapses

Helga's psychic turmoil into an absent-father complex, explaining that Helga's contradictory behavior boils down to an attempt to replace her lost father through a succession of men. Johnson also pinpoints the origin of Helga's neuroses in a psychic wound caused by early family experiences. She argues that Helga has internalized a negative self-image mirrored for her by her white relatives, who fear and hate her: "[S]he actually learns to empathize with their view of her as a problem *for them*."[14] Lacking a self, Johnson reasons, Helga finally enacts her white relatives' wishes that she would disappear through the self-erasure of her religious conversion and subsequent marriage to the Reverend Mr. Pleasant Green. Although the politics of race certainly condition Helga's white relatives' distaste for her and her black father's abandonment, in Tate's and Johnson's analyses race becomes incidental to Helga's subjective processes. Each reading offers a probable cause of Helga's emotional pain, but neither adequately explains the relationship between the text's representation of Helga's emotional life and its critique of race, gender, and class categories.

We can look beyond family dysfunction and individual pathology to analyze a larger racial symbolic through a Lacanian framework that "read[s] and rewrit[es] . . . Freud's oedipal model in linguistic and socio-cultural terms."[15] It is not the literal family, but rather the structure indicated by the symbolic function of the Name-of-the-Father that facilitates the individual's entry into the symbolic order. We need to ask how this function is raced. Moreover, although the family is a primary mechanism for socializing the individual, we have learned from Fanon that other sociopolitical forces work to racialize the individual throughout a lifetime. For both these reasons, we will not explain the relationship between Helga's psychic distress and racial identity by pinpointing an originary unconscious wound. It would be reductive to identify a singular psychic origin of Helga's neurosis, not least because the text generates so many convincing diagnoses. Helga does appear to exhibit low self-esteem from negative mirroring, abandonment issues and consequent melancholia, compensatory narcissism, a compulsion to repeat self-destructive behavior, repression and sublimation of sexuality, and an unresolved Oedipus complex—both positive and negative. The explanation is not to be found, then, in a singular family dysfunction or childhood trauma, but rather in the sociosymbolic order that constrains Helga's subject-formation. If Helga's seeming pathology makes sense in response to repressive regimes of race, gender, class, and sexuality, then her *failure* to accede to normative feminine blackness indicates how racial ideology and the symbolic order work together to produce raced citizen-subjects.

Ideology and the Racial Symbolic

I mean to examine how *Quicksand* represents racialization by way of the mulatto trope in order to explore the relationship between ideologies of race and the symbolic order. This project would seem to call for Marxism (as that approach most concerned with ideology) and psychoanalysis (as the predominant theory of subjectivity). And yet these theoretical frameworks have historically seemed strange bedfellows—Marxism privileging class as the determining identity category and lacking a notion of the unconscious in its theory of ideological interpellation, and psychoanalytic theory ignoring issues of class and race, as well as material and historic specificities. More specifically, psychoanalytic theory has posited the Oedipus complex, governed by paternal Law, as the mechanism responsible for shaping subjectivity, but has not clarified the relation of the symbolic order and paternal Law to juridical law and other ideological discourses or apparatuses. In the Marxist camp, Louis Althusser is usually credited with linking ideology to subjectivity through his theory of interpellation. Yet his description of interpellation never fully explains the psychic mechanism involved. Thus, "the symbolic order occupies a determinative role within Lacanian psychoanalysis as the mode of production does within a materialist paradigm, and neither of those categories can be persuasively shown to be an effect of the other."[16] Two theorists in particular, Kaja Silverman and Slavoj Žižek, have worked to bridge these gaps between materialist and psychoanalytic discourses. I rely on their explanations of the relationship between ideology and the symbolic order in my efforts to explore this connection in relation to race. They argue, in effect, that we cannot understand ideological interpellation without recourse to psychoanalysis's model of symbolic accommodation and, especially, to its emphasis on the role of fantasy.

Symbolic accommodation and ideological interpellation are both founded on misrecognition or *méconnaissance*. In "The Mirror Stage," Lacan provides one example of symbolic misrecognition. As the child develops, s/he loses a sense of unity with the mother (and the outside world). The resulting split between self and other inaugurates subjective lack. The child compensates for this lack by identifying with the seemingly masterful image of self offered by the mirror reflection. The self of the mirror image appears to the child as a more organized, competent, and unified agent than the immature infant (supposed to be between six and eighteen months) actually is. Therefore, this process "situates the agency of the ego, before its social determination, in a fictional direction, which will always remain irreducible for the individual."[17] This identification with an ideal self-image constitutes a misrecognition in that an image exterior to the individual constitutes its internal sense of self. The self is, in a sense, exterior to the self; it is a fantasy mediated by representation, alienated in the form of a double.

Althusser follows Lacan in arguing that subjectivity is founded on a kind of split, fissure, or lack. He also uses the term misrecognition or *méconnaissance* to characterize that split (161). His most famous example of ideological interpellation reveals other similarities to Lacan:[18]

> [*I*]*nterpellation*, or hailing, . . . can be imagined along the lines of the most commonplace everyday police (or other) hailing: "Hey, you there!"
>
> Assuming that the theoretical scene I have imagined takes place in the street, the hailed individual will turn round. By this mere one-hundred-and-eighty-degree physical conversion, he becomes a *subject*. Why? Because he has recognized that the hail was "really" addressed to him, and that "it was *really him* who was hailed" (and not someone else). (163)

As in the mirror stage, interpellation involves a process of identification with the organizing image of self offered by the Other. Žižek explains,

> In this perspective, the subject as such is constituted through a certain misrecognition: the process of ideological interpellation through which the subject "recognizes" itself as the addressee in the calling up of the ideological cause implies necessarily a certain short circuit, an illusion of the type "I was already there."[19]

In other words, the subject gains a place within the social order by "taking as the reality of the self what is in fact a discursive construction, or to state the case differently, claiming as an ontology what is only a point of address" (Silverman, 21). Lacan's imaginary and Althusser's ideology both mark a permanent split from the unmediated Real in favor of an irreducibly mediated social reality. Misrecognition, then, characterizes the subject. Symbolic accommodation and ideological interpellation work similarly in that each (1) involves the individual's identification with an image offered by the Other, (2) produces the individual's location within the social realm, and (3) depends on misrecognition.

Although Althusser's example of the police hailing is drawn from adult life, ideological interpellation does not come *after* symbolic accommodation; ideology does not work on already formed subjects. He writes, "[Y]ou and I are *always already* subjects, and as such constantly practice the rituals of ideological recognition, which guarantee for us that we are indeed concrete, individual, distinguishable and (naturally) irreplaceable subjects" (161–62). As evidence that individuals are "always already" interpellated by ideology, Althusser cites Freud's analysis of

> the ideological ritual that surrounds the expectation of a "birth," that "happy event." Everyone knows how much and in what way an unborn child is expected. Which amounts to saying, very prosaically, . . . it is certain in advance that it will bear its Father's Name, and will therefore have an identity and be irreplaceable. (164)

Here Althusser implicitly links ideological interpellation to psychoanalysis's symbolic accommodation, the process through which the individual accedes to paternal Law, symbolized by the Name-of-the-Father. Althusser's recourse to Freud's family drama to explain how we are always already subjects indicates that "[t]he Law which stands outside all ideologies of class, but which provides the underpinning of ideological belief, belongs to the symbolic order rather than the mode of production" (Silverman, 33). Thus, ideological interpellation and symbolic accommodation are not separable and "even the earliest and the most decisive of the subject's identifications may be ideologically determined" (22).

If symbolic accommodation and ideological interpellation are mutually determining, then the developmental sequence of subject formation posited by psychoanalysis comes into question. How can we account for Lacan's claim that the mirror stage constitutes an "I" that precedes and stands outside the social determinations of later oedipal identifications and the order of language? Jane Gallop's suggestion that the mirror stage—as a developmental process and a theoretical concept—occurs retroactively is instructive. Reversing Lacan's sequence, Gallop explains that the infant who enjoys a newfound sense of corporeal mastery can only retroactively perceive his/her bodily inadequacy: "The image of the body in bits and pieces is fabricated retroactively from the mirror stage. It is only the anticipated 'orthopedic' form of its totality that can define—retroactively—the body as insufficient."[20] From this, she generalizes that any sense of self-mastery necessarily raises the specter of regression to a former state of chaos.[21] Moreover, the child's unified self-image is not derived from observation, but from "an abstract idea that shapes the observation."[22] Lacan suggests as much: "[T]he total form of the body by which the subject anticipates in a mirage the maturation of his power is given to him only as *Gestalt,* that is to say, in an exteriority in which this form is certainly more constituent than constituted" (2). Which comes first, the abstraction or the observation? Gallop says we can't know. She reads this same uncertainty of priority onto the theory of the mirror stage itself, which is an abstraction used retroactively to make sense of the bits and pieces of subject formation. It is a fiction as much as the self. By questioning the linearity and rigidity of psychoanalysis's theory of subject formation, Gallop's reading anticipates recent work on identification suggesting that such processes operate in nonlinear fashion throughout a lifetime, rather than beginning with the mirror stage and ending with the oedipal phase. As Diana Fuss writes, "The astonishing capacity of identifications to reverse and disguise themselves, to multiply and contravene one another, to disappear and reappear years later renders identity profoundly unstable and perpetually open to radical change."[23]

If we cannot pinpoint an originary scene of subject formation, then we should read Freud and Lacan's accounts of the mirror stage and the Oedipus complex less according to a linear timetable of child development and more as dramatic representations of ongoing processes of subject formation. Like the mirror stage, primal scenes of sexual differentiation "come into play retroactively," so such scenes are not necessarily any more primary than those of racial differentiation. If there is no temporal primacy to either symbolic accommodation or ideological interpellation, what then is the relation between them? How does ideology penetrate identity? For although Althusser claims to explain the mechanism, he begs the question by saying repeatedly that the individual is always already subjected or always happens to recognize himself in the call of the Other. In fact, Althusser readily acknowledges that interpellation does not actually happen according to the dramatic sequence he presents:

> Naturally for the convenience and clarity of my little theoretical theatre I have had to present things in the form of a sequence, with a before and an after, and thus in the form of a temporal succession. There are individuals walking along. Somewhere (usually behind them) the hail rings out: "Hey, you there!" One individual (nine times out of ten it is the right one) turns round, believing/suspecting/knowing that it is for him, i.e., recognizing that "it is really he" who is meant by the hailing. But in reality these things happen without any succession. The existence of ideology and the hailing or interpellation of individuals as subjects are one and the same thing.[24]

Žižek and Silverman attribute Althusser's failure to account for the psychic mechanism of interpellation to the fact that he accounts for identification, but not for fantasy in subject-formation.[25] Lacan's notion of fantasy explains how the subject recognizes the interpellative call of the Other. In acceding to language (symbolization), the subject sacrifices wholeness (plenitude) to meaning within the symbolic order. This sacrifice produces lack (or symbolic castration), which, in turn, motivates desire for an object that, the subject fantasizes, will restore the wholeness lost to symbolization. In other words, the subject attempts to compensate for symbolic castration through the object of desire, the Other.[26] The fantasy is that the Other can restore wholeness.

Žižek and Silverman argue that the mechanism of fantasy and identification that constitutes subjectivity also constitutes ideological belief. Ideology is, then, subjectivity writ large for group identity. Using Žižek's terms, any ideological system subjects the Real to a process of symbolization. This process leaves something over, "an original 'trauma,' an impossible kernel which resists symbolization, totalization, symbolic integration" (6). This kernel or "surplus," which represents the "distance separating the Real from its symbolization," is analogous to subjective lack: it "functions as the object-cause of desire" (3). Ideology "masks [this] insupportable, real, impossible kernel (conceptualized by Ernesto Laclau and Chantal Mouffe as 'antagonism': a traumatic social division which cannot be symbolized)" (45). In other words, fantasy covers over the lack generated by the process of symbolization that produced the ideological system in question. In this way, fantasy produces social reality itself: "The function of ideology is not to offer us a point of escape from our reality but to offer us the social reality itself as an escape from some traumatic, real kernel" (45). The traumatic kernel is not accessible to conscious processes; it is outside social reality. Therefore, the illusion of ideology cannot be unmasked by pointing to it; it can only be approached via confrontation with the unconscious Real of our desire. Žižek illustrates this point using anti-Semitism as an example of ideological fantasy that masks the divisions of social reality:

> It is not enough to say that we must liberate ourselves of so-called "anti-Semitic prejudices" and learn to see Jews as they really are—in this way we will certainly remain victims of these so-called prejudices. We must confront ourselves with how the ideological figure of the "Jew" is invested with our unconscious desire, with how we have constructed this figure . . . to stitch up the consistency of our own ideological system. (48)

The fantasy that Jews are *the* problem masks the internal contradictions of the social reality scapegoating them.

Silverman also argues that the fantasy constitutive of subjectivity is inextricable from the fantasy of ideology. In a kind of social mirror stage, ideology provides the image not only with which the individual identifies, but also of the world in which the subject fits, the "*vraisemblance*" in Althusser's terms. Ideological hegemony "comes into play when all the members of a collectivity see themselves within the same reflecting surface" (24). Ideology is, then, the shared fantasy or collective belief in a society that governs the relations among the members of that society. Silverman calls this shared fantasy of ideological reality the "dominant fiction," a term she takes from Jacques Rancière and which he defines as "'the privileged mode of representation by which the image of the social consensus is offered to the members of a social formation and within which they are asked to identify themselves'" (quoted in Silverman, 30).

Although Žižek resists naming any particular ideological system that determines our social reality (and that masks a central antagonism through processes of fantasy), Silverman stakes a more specific claim.[27] She argues that "our dominant fiction" or primary ideological belief system "solicits our faith above all else in the unity of the family, and the adequacy of the male subject" (15–16):

> [O]ur present dominant fiction is above all else the representational system through which the subject is accommodated to the Name-of-the-Father. Its most central signifier of unity is the (paternal) family, and its primary signifier of privilege the phallus. "Male" and

> "female" constitute our dominant fiction's most fundamental binary opposition. Its many other ideological elements, such as signifiers like "town" and "nation," or the antithesis of power and the people, all exist in a metaphoric relation to these terms. (34–35)

"Our" (Western culture's, I presume) primary ideological system corresponds, then, to the Lacanian symbolic that institutes sexual difference. Ideology and the symbolic are mutually determining: the subject comes to believe in the dominant fiction of the sufficiency of the male subject by passing through the Oedipus complex, which is the "primary vehicle of insertion" into our society's ideological reality (2). The ideology of the family facilitates the subject's relation to the symbolic at the level of the imaginary, through identification and fantasy. But only if those identifications and fantasies line up with ideological belief is this subject exemplary, that is, accommodated to the Name-of-the-Father (41).

If Žižek and Silverman demonstrate the relationship between ideological interpellation and subjective accommodation, neither accounts for racialization in those processes. Žižek approaches the topic through his examples of anti-Semitism, but avoids sustained analysis in order not to privilege one ideological system over any other. Silverman focuses on sex and gender as the inaugural and dominant factors organizing ideology and the symbolic. In short, she argues that symbolic structures of kinship are instituted in the subject through the ideology of the family. However, as I noted earlier, she formulates kinship in relation to the incest taboo; she does not consider the miscegenation taboo. How, then, would the miscegenation taboo affect the ideology of the family that Silverman says is responsible for determining ideological reality?

The "Mulatto" Masks the Traumatic Kernel of Race

The miscegenation taboo functions as a hinge for the ideological-symbolic order of race.[28] The taboo both determines and is sustained through the ideology of the family. This ideology is reflected in the various miscegenation and racial classification laws that, historically, have racialized the family in order to delimit the color line. These laws conspired to deny practices of race mixing by ensuring that the issue of miscegenation could neither attain the standing of "white," nor enjoy the associated legal benefits. Although these laws and practices varied by state and over time, ultimately they worked to sustain binary categories of white and black, and so to preserve a social and psychic fantasy of racial difference. In part because race mixing occurred with regularity, race laws worked on an internal contradiction: they regulated the very practice that ideologies of racial purity refused to recognize. This contradiction marks a point of ideological vulnerability and cultural anxiety.

As a mixture of black and white, the mulatto embodies the violation of the miscegenation taboo meant to sustain the illusion of racial difference. S/he thereby testifies to the phantasmatic nature of "race." Furthermore, the mulatto undercuts the belief that racial difference is obvious, natural, and visible. But there is an additional dimension to how the figure of the mulatto threatens to expose the constructedness of the racial symbolic: the mulatto is, at once, a product *and* a refutation of that ideology. Because the miscegenation taboo does not really prohibit all interracial sex, but rather facilitates sex between white men and black women while prohibiting the inverse, the racial symbolic *produces* the mulatto. At the same time, race ideology *disavows* that mixing by denying white fathers' paternity and their children's claim to whiteness. The one-drop rule, the slave law decreeing that children follow the condition of the mother, and antimiscegenation laws released—and even prohibited—white men from paternal responsibility.[29] The race/sex symbolic nexus contains, then, a structuring paradox: its articulation of kinship grants white men access to all women, thereby ensuring the birth of mixed-race children who belie the fantasy of racial difference and must, therefore, be disavowed.

Embodying the violation of the miscegenation taboo and undermining the fiction of racial difference, the mixed-race individual represents the "traumatic kernel," the unspeakable remainder of the Real leftover from the process of racial symbolization. In other words, the symbolic work done to produce an ideology of "race," whereby people are seen as white or black, or even white and nonwhite, cannot accommodate the concept of a mixed-race individual. Such an individual belies the fiction of racial difference and so cannot be represented within the ideological system. The ideological figure of the "mulatto" works to cover over this traumatic kernel that resists symbolization. To clarify, we recall Žižek's explanation that ideological systems result from a process of symbolization. In this process, the Lacanian Real, the presymbolic realm to which we do not have conscious access, is submitted to the symbolic order. This process of symbolization leaves something over, "an original 'trauma,' an impossible kernel which resists symbolization, totalization, symbolic integration." This "left-over" is analogous to subjective "lack" in that it "functions as the object-cause of desire" (Žižek, 6, 3). Desire—of the subject or ideology—seeks to cover over lack through the fantasy that the desired object will restore the wholeness lost to symbolization. In this way, ideology masks the impossible kernel through a fantasy that produces the illusion of ideological consistency. Social reality consists of the fantasy that obscures the "impossible kernel," the thing that cannot be represented within the symbolic/ideological system. I would argue that the figure of the (tragic) mulatto covers over that original trauma, impossible kernel, or leftover from the process of symbolizing "race." The symbolic work that constructs the dominant fiction of a binary between white and black cannot account for the mixed-race person; s/he therefore "resists symbolization, totalization, symbolic integration" (6). Racial ideology masks this gap with the figure of the pathologized mulatto in order to preserve the fantasy of racial difference and white supremacy. Therefore, to understand our ideology of race (and to modify Žižek slightly), we must confront ourselves with how the ideological figure of the "mulatto" is invested with our unconscious desire.

The mulatto gives the lie to the fiction of racial purity while embodying the history of legal, social, and physical violence used to preserve it. "[S]tranded in cultural ambiguity," writes Hortense Spillers, the mulatto "conceals the very strategies of terministic violence and displacement that have enabled a problematic of alterity regarding the African American community in the United States."[30] Succinctly summarizing Spillers's brilliant essay on the "neither/nor" split of mulatto identity and symbolic meaning, Barbara Johnson writes,

> [T]he mulatto represents both a taboo and a synthesis, both the product of a sexual union that miscegenation laws tried to rule out of existence and an allegory for the racially divided society as a whole, both un-American and an image of America as such.[31]

The mulatto is evidence of both interracial rape and love that are disavowed in order to perpetuate racial difference and white supremacy. So threatening to America's racial ideology was the mulatto that scientific discourses of the nineteenth century insisted the mulatto was physically and mentally degenerate—even sterile—in order to "prove" that race mixing was unnatural (and racial difference natural). And the tragic mulatto trope, as represented in antiabolitionist and "plantation school" fiction, also corroborated the notion that the mulatto was not fit to survive. "[W]hite anxiety," writes Nancy Bentley, "came from knowing what law and the social order would not recognize: that blood relations bound Africans and Europeans and subverted the idea of a natural boundary between black and white."[32] Through law, science, representation, and custom, America's racial ideology denies legitimacy to the mulatto who confounds the dominant fiction of a racial binary.

The Tragic Trope

The mulatto is a recurring literary trope precisely because it bears so crucially on our racial symbolic. And yet the trope differs for the mulatto and the mulatta character. A number of critics have noted that the "tragic mulatto" is usually a woman, whereas the male mulatto character is often heroic. Bentley explains that this difference not only reflects the fact that mulattas were subject to sexual exploitation that men were spared, but also the different meaning accorded to men's and women's bodies in the conventions of the domestic novel: "[F]or women's bodies and black bodies the infliction of violence or abuse can be a means by which the individual achieves a transcendent grace of enriched dignity and identity. But for the body of the white male, this law does not hold." Hence, the specter of the abused body of the mulatto male or "white slave" was obscene and degrading. Therefore, mulatto men are more often represented as "the heroic agent of violence."[33] In recognition of the gendering of the "tragic mulatto," I will distinguish between figures of the mulatto and the mulatta from now on. Embodying the violation of the miscegenation taboo, the mulatta signifies black women's supposed licentious sexuality. Thus, as Siobhan Somerville notes, African American women writers of the late nineteenth century were "[a]cutely aware of the ways in which the supposed boundary between 'black' and 'white' bodies was built on discourses of sexual pathology" and use the mulatta figure to "reconfigure cultural constructions of black womanhood."[34]

Nineteenth-century African American women writers reconfigure images of black womanhood, in part, by representing their mulatta heroines as sexually chaste and morally upright, according to the ideologies of the Cult of True Womanhood and racial uplift. For example, the heroines of Frances E. W. Harper's *Iola Leroy, or Shadows Uplifted* and Pauline Hopkins's *Contending Forces* are threatened with, but ultimately spared, sexual exploitation at the hands of white men. Their sexual morality is sanctioned through marriage to African American men who serve as leaders of racial uplift.[35] In this way, the mulatta heroines—who have been raised as white—discover their "true" identities and embrace their "true" people. Although these novels testified to the suppressed history of miscegenation and its effects on family ties while also contradicting pseudoscientific and ideological belief in a natural distinction between the races, they also, paradoxically, reconfigure essentialist constructions of "race."[36] These novels join uplift ideology with the conventions of sentimental or domestic fiction to validate black identity and civil rights, but in so doing, their characters sacrifice a complex inner life for moral transparency and racial representativeness.

In contrast to the moral fiber and racial loyalty of Harper's and Hopkins's mulattas and the heroism of nineteenth-century mulattos, early twentieth-century mulatto/a characters possess more psychological complexity and moral ambiguity. Novels such as Larsen's *Passing* and *Quicksand* and James Weldon Johnson's *Autobiography of an Ex-Colored Man* cast the neither/nor bind of mulatto/a identity as a form of modernist alienation. The mulatto/a protagonists sometimes choose to pass rather than embrace African American identity; they do not devote their lives to uplift work or to representing their race. In these characters' ambivalent relationship to African American identity, they sustain more clearly than their nineteenth-century counterparts the message that race is cultural rather than biological. They thematize modernist alienation and Du Boisian double consciousness as the individual's ongoing attempts to negotiate ideologies of race, sex, and class—a process that Fuss calls the individual's "struggle to negotiate a constantly changing field of ambivalent identifications."[37]

Such alienation contrasts with the prevailing sociopolitical conventions of the uplift movement and the black bourgeoisie in the first decades of the twentieth century, which, like the dominant culture, adopted the "one-drop rule" of racial classification.[38] But the period in which Larsen wrote *Quicksand* was not only one of uplift and civil rights struggle, but also of African American culture coming into a sense of its own vitality through the Harlem Renaissance. If the uplift movement and the civil rights struggles emphasized the needs of the group, the discourse of rights and the Harlem Renaissance led to the validation of black individuality, artistic genius, and spirit. In this sense, the new novelistic representations of nonrepresentative, morally compromised African American characters might be seen as a political assertion of black rights to individuality. We might say that the tragic mulattos and mulattas of Johnson's and Larsen's novels are tragic *agents* rather than tragic victims; although they are ultimately constrained by the binary system of race ideology, they nevertheless make *choices* that have tragic consequences.

Taboo Subjects/Abject Identities

With no symbolic position available to the mixed-race subject, Helga must assume a symbolically designated position as black woman—even if her specific mulatta designation bears implications of race and sex. The content of the black woman's identity prescribed for Helga varies to some degree by culture and geography, but Helga refuses—or fails—to perform the role in any sustained way in each of the locales she inhabits.[39] In thus failing to be interpellated by racial ideology, in refusing to recognize herself as that named by the category "Negro," Helga resists the misrecognition that produces the raced subject. She refuses to "tak[e] as the reality of the self what is in fact a discursive construction" (Silverman, 21). She refuses the racial symbolic that compels individuals to assume a position as either black or white, to see themselves as essentially belonging to a natural category that is, in fact, constructed. By refusing accommodation to the racial symbolic, Helga actually obeys the Lacanian ethical imperative not "to giv[e] ground relative to one's desire," not to lose sight of what is lost in the process of symbolization/racialization.[40] Helga's failure to conform reveals, then, "the structural mechanism which is producing the effect of [raced] subject as ideological misrecognition" (Žižek, 2). Because all racial subjectivity, white and black, is founded on a similar ideological misrecognition, Helga's case is representative of racial subject-formation more generally. As the "tragic mulatta," she simply makes visible the split that founds normative racial subjectivity but is ordinarily covered over by ideological fantasy.

Helga resists conforming to the racial symbolic but experiences social and psychic distress as a consequence. Helga's resistance demonstrates the constructedness of race, but the negative consequences demonstrate the nonvoluntary nature of race (and gender) performativity. In *Bodies That Matter*, Judith Butler emphasizes the symbolic constraints on gender construction to counter celebratory conceptions of performativity as free choice:

> The "performative" dimension of construction is precisely the forced reiteration of norms. In this sense, then, it is not only that there are constraints to performativity; rather, constraint calls to be rethought as the very condition of performativity. Performativity is neither free play nor theatrical self-presentation; nor can it be simply equated with performance.[41]

As with gender, racial performativity is constrained "under and through the force of prohibition and taboo, with the threat of ostracism and even death controlling and compelling the shape of the production, but not . . . determining it fully in advance" (95). Conventional psychoanalysis holds that the prohibitions and taboos that constrain gender performativity are instituted in the oedipal scenario through the threat of punishment, figured as castration, "the fear of castration motivating the assumption of the masculine sex, the fear of not being castrated motivating the assumption of the feminine" (96). In the threat of castration that compels the assumption of "sex," Butler finds "at least two inarticulate figures of abject homosexuality, the feminized fag and the phallicized dyke" (96). In other words, "the feminized fag" and the "phallicized dyke" represent the punishable consequences of failing to accede to a normative gender subject-position in relation to the phallus. I would argue that, in the racial symbolic that compels the assumption of "race" (as either black or white), the mulatto is an "inarticulate figure of abject" heteroraciality.

With the neologism "heteroracial" and its implied converse "homoracial" echoing the terms heterosexual/homosexual, I invoke the oedipal matrix of identification and desire that constitutes subjectivity. As we know, the Oedipus complex introduces symbolic law to the individual, by force of threat, to compel identification with the same sex and desire for the opposite. Yet feminist and queer psychoanalytic theorists have emphasized that these vectors of desire and identification are never so discrete or fixed as we suppose. Identifications are ongoing, shifting, incomplete processes; they are "multiple and contestatory"; they inevitably fail to match the symbolic ideal; and they are hopelessly entangled with desire.[42]

The fundamental ambivalence of identification and desire is evident, for example, in "Group Psychology and the Ego," wherein Freud explains that children take on normative gender identity by identifying with the appropriate parent: "A little boy will exhibit a special interest in his father; he would like to grow like him and be like him, and take his place everywhere."[43] Such same-sex identification enables the development of desire for the opposite sex: "At the same time as this identification with his father, or a little later, the boy has begun to develop a true object-cathexis towards his mother" (105). Thus, "[t]hese two psychical mechanisms [desire and identification], which together form the cornerstone of Freud's theory of sexual identity formation, work in tandem to produce a sexually marked subject."[44] But though identification is fundamental to subject formation, it is a profoundly unstable process. In the same text, Freud also writes that the boy-child who learns masculinity by identifying *with* his father might turn that identification into a sexual desire *for* the father: "[T]he identification with the father has become the precursor of an object-tie with the father" (106). So there is ambivalence between *identification with* and *desire for* the object. Not only can an identification slide into a "bad" love-object choice, but a child can take a "bad" object of identification: Freud cites his patient Dora, who identified with her father when she should have taken him as an object-choice according to the "normal" Oedipus complex. In Dora's case, writes Freud, "*object-choice has regressed to identification*" (107, emphasis in the original). In both these cases of inverted or negative Oedipus complexes, identification has gone wrong according to normative gender laws: the boy desires his father, the girl identifies with hers. As with so many of Freud's explanations of identity formation, the subject as often as not *fails* to take the proper route.

Calling attention to the fragmentary, shifting, continuous, multiple, and intersecting processes of identification and desire has enabled theorists to deconstruct the heterosexual/homosexual, masculine/feminine binaries of sexual identity. As Fuss writes, "The critical displacement of the identification/desire opposition, evident even in Freud's own work, opens up a new way of thinking about the complexity of sexual identity formation outside the rigid thematics of cultural binaries."[45] Some of the scholars responding to this work have theorized how compulsory heterosexuality is constructed, realizing that cross-sex identification and same-sex desire exist within normative identity processes and postulating how we might intervene to change symbolic law. For example, the discussion of Freud's case of the Wolf Man in chapter 2 highlights the ways in which the oedipal process must work to repress the boy's desire for the father in order to produce a heterosexual subject. In *Gender Trouble,* Butler also analyzes how the oedipal production of gender identification and heterosexual desire requires the subject to repress or disavow desire for the parent of the same sex: "[G]ender identification is a kind of melancholia in which the sex of the prohibited object is internalized as a prohibition."[46] Identification and desire are, then, ambivalent from the start. I want to bring this sense of the ambivalence inherent to identification and desire to a consideration of Helga's racial ambivalence as a way of opening up the rigid thematics of *racial* binaries.

How does the oedipal production of identification and desire intersect with race? The symbolic requires the girl-child to identify with her mother (same sex) and desire her father and his substitutes (cross sex). The racial symbolic requires the subject to identify and desire along same-race (homoracial) lines. In Helga's case, certain oedipal gender identifications are at odds with racial identifications. If she identifies with her white mother according to gender norms, she is identifying across racial lines in violation of the racial symbolic. If she identifies with her black father on the basis of race, does that confuse her response to the demand that she desire him and his substitutes? Although many more permutations of Helga's doubled and crossed identifications and desires are possible, I want to emphasize what Fuss calls the "fundamental indissociability of identification and desire," which I figure as *ambivalence.*[47] I turn now to a more extended reading of *Quicksand* to examine how Helga's ambivalence marks ongoing processes of identification and desire as she tries to negotiate the symbolic orders of sex and race. I propose to read Helga's ambivalent dialectic of identification and desire through the frame of Freud's notion of the uncanny. The uncanny—also characterized by ambivalence—offers a model for deconstructing the binary oppositions upon which identity categories such as male/female and black/white depend and for exploring how the subject experiences movement between such identity binaries.

Uncanny Race

What does the concept of the uncanny—associated with phenomena of horror—have to do with the ambivalent structure of identification and desire? Though Freud's circuitous essay "The Uncanny" does not yield a direct answer, we can begin by noting that the uncanny comprises a *particular* form of terror: it is not just anything that "arouses dread and horror," but specifically "that class of the frightening which leads back to what is known of old and long familiar."[48] The uncanny concerns, then, the ambivalence between the strange and the familiar. Freud finds this identity between the strange and familiar in the dictionary definition of the German word for uncanny, *unheimlich,* or rather its opposite, *heimlich,* which means homely ("homey" in American English), intimate, tame, and familiar, but also concealed, secret, and kept from sight. If *heimlich* can mean on the one hand familiar and agreeable, while on the other hand secret and sinister, then "*heimlich* is a word the meaning of which develops in the direction of ambivalence, until it finally coincides with its opposite, *unheimlich*" (226). The movement between these poles of meaning, between the familiar and the secreted, produces the peculiar sensation of horror: the "uncanny is in reality nothing new or alien, but something which is familiar and old-established in the mind and which has become alienated from it only through the process of repression" (241). More specifically, "an uncanny experience occurs either when infantile complexes which have been repressed are once more revived by some impression, or when primitive beliefs which have been surmounted seem once more to be confirmed" (249). Uncanny reminders of repressed infantile complexes include doubles because they represent parts of the self the ego projects "outward as something foreign to itself" and experiences of déjà vu or "involuntary repetition," which signal the "compulsion to repeat" repressed instinctual impulses (226).

Freud takes as his central example of the uncanny E. T. A. Hoffmann's story "The Sandman" (1816), which, he argues, explores the revival of another repressed infantile complex: castration fear. His explanation of how that fear is revived, however, disavows the role played by femininity. By recovering the repressed feminine, we can see how the uncanny relates to the ambivalence of gender identification. Hoffmann's sinister tale concerns a young man, Nathaniel, who is slowly driven to suicide by the machinations (it's never clear if they are real or imagined) of an evil inventor who intends to steal his eyes for a female automaton he is bringing to lifelike completion. Freud attributes the story's uncanny effect to the way that the evil inventor Coppélius—the title's Sandman and the possible murderer of Nathaniel's father—and his double, the occulist Spalanzani, arouse in Nathaniel "the anxiety belonging to the castration complex of childhood" by threatening to blind him ("Uncanny," 233). However, in arguing that the arousal of castration fear is an affair between men

(Coppélius and his double are supposed, by Freud, to double for Nathaniel's father), Freud disavows the significance of the automaton, Olympia, the figure of woman. Significantly, Nathaniel makes the final break with sanity not so much because Coppélius threatens to steal his eyes, but because Nathaniel sees that Olympia has none. As Coppélius and Spalanzani wrestle for possession of Olympia,

> Nathaniel stood numb with horror. He had seen all too clearly that Olympia's deathly-white face possessed no eyes: where the eyes should have been, there were only pits of blackness—she was a lifeless doll! (120)

If, as Freud insists, the loss of eyes signifies castration, then what Nathaniel "sees" is women's castration. It is *this* sight that makes real to him the threat of castration. This scenario resembles another of Freud's famous paradigms: the boy-child's sighting of the female genitals that confirms for him women's castration and makes real the previously disavowed threat of castration. Moreover, as Jane Marie Todd writes, this "is also the structure of the *Unheimliche*: the reappearance of something that has been 'disavowed.' Female genitals are *unheimlich* for precisely this reason: they seem to confirm what the male has wished to deny—the reality of castration."[49] Hoffmann's story not only confirms that the dominant fiction interprets feminine difference as lack, but that woman's perceived castration renders her, like Olympia, nonhuman.

Feminine difference is uncanny—both familiar and strange—in its relation to the masculine norm. But it is uncanny for another reason as well. If masculine gender identification *depends* on interpreting feminine difference as castration, then the specter of woman as *un*castrated would possess a terrifying power to destabilize masculinity.[50] We can see how masculinity depends on feminine lack in Nathaniel's desire for Olympia. He repeatedly imagines that Olympia returns his looks of love: her eyes "grew ever warmer and more lively" until they "gazed back at him full of love and desire."[51] Bathing in the imagined glow of Olympia's gaze, Nathaniel throws over his less pliant girlfriend, Clara. Thus, when Nathaniel learns that Olympia's eyes were man-made and, consequently, that the organizing image of self offered by the feminine gaze was merely his own fantasy, he goes mad.[52] In other words, Nathaniel's inability to sustain the belief that woman is castrated, not simply his own fear of castration, triggers his insanity. And if woman is not castrated, then the opposition between masculinity and femininity cannot be sustained. Without that trumped-up sexual difference, masculinity "develops in the direction of ambivalence, until it finally coincides with its opposite": femininity ("Uncanny," 226). The sensation of uncanniness occurs when the binary oppositions sustaining coherent identifications deconstruct. In effect, the uncanny describes the ambivalent structure of gender identification.

A number of themes from Freud's essay and its feminist critique bear on my discussion of *Quicksand*: the structure of ambivalence, the compulsion to repeat, the return of the repressed, the significance of sight, and the underlying identity of home (*heimlich*) and secret (*unheimlich*). I want to argue that these aspects of the uncanny inhere not only in processes of gender identification, but also in ambivalent processes of racial identification. As I have noted, Helga repeatedly constitutes and then dissolves a raced identification in each locale she inhabits. Sensations of nausea, dread, and vertigo accompany these ambivalent, uncanny processes. In short, Helga's racial identifications replicate the structure of the uncanny in that an identification ceaselessly develops in the direction of ambivalence until it coincides with its opposite. Helga finds each locale congenial and homey at first. She identifies with and performs the local norms of gender, race, and class. But then a repressed identification resurfaces, disrupting the necessary illusion of a unified ego/racial identity that Helga had achieved temporarily. The racial identity category that had recently seemed safe and homey comes to seem sinister. As she begins to disidentify with the available role, she experiences a painful ambivalence, with symptoms of nausea, choking, dread, and vertigo. Significantly, this process of ambivalent racial identification is closely tied to external social causes, although Helga experiences the resulting instability of identity as "a lack somewhere" in herself (Larsen, 7). Each of these identifying breaks is catalyzed by a primal scene and precipitates her move to the next locale. There she inhabits a different position within the ambivalent trajectory between black and white and the symptoms of lack temporarily desist.

The novel's focus on home recalls the uncanny's oscillation between homey and unhomey. In the novel, as in Langston Hughes's poem, home is a metaphor for racial identity. Helga, like Hughes's mulatto poetic persona, is literally and symbolically homeless. Forever lodging in others' homes (a Naxos dormitory, a room at the Chicago YWCA, Anne Grey's house in Harlem, the Dahl's house in Copenhagen; even the Reverend Pleasant Green's house isn't entirely hers), Helga is stranded between the worlds of black and white, and even between various black worlds. She is, then, constantly in search of a home, some place that will feel "familiar and agreeable." In each locale, she achieves a temporary feeling of racial familiarity. Soon, however, a repressed identification resurfaces, giving a sinister aspect to what had seemed so natural before. Her compulsion to repeat this ambivalent slide from identification to disidentification parallels the semantic movement between heimlich and unheimlich; Helga's racial identity "develops in the direction of ambivalence, until it finally coincides with its opposite." Racial identity is inherently uncanny because consolidating a coherent identity as either black or white requires that aspects of the other term be repressed, disavowed, or projected as radically external to the self. If that repression, disavowal, or projection wavers, the externalized aspect of self resurfaces so as to produce an uncanny sensation. As the embodiment of racial blending, the mulatto brings to light what has been repressed in order to construct the fiction of racial difference. Thus, the figure of the mulatto is, itself, uncanny.

Ambivalence and Identification

Although Helga's pattern of identificatory ambivalence is apparent in the Naxos and Chicago scenes, the Harlem episode provides the first full cycle of identification/disidentification. Helga is, at first, smitten with Harlem's possibilities for black identity. She feels "joy at seeming at last to belong somewhere. For she considered that she had, as she put it, 'found herself'" (44). In comparison to Naxos's austerity, the culture and gaiety of Harlem agree with Helga's aesthetic and class sensibilities. She experiences

> a sense of freedom, a release from the feeling of smallness which had hedged her in, first during her sorry, unchildlike childhood among hostile white folk in Chicago, and later during her uncomfortable sojourn among snobbish black folk in Naxos. (46)

She identifies with this African American community largely because it seems to offer a broader definition of blackness and larger possibilities for experience than does Naxos or Chicago.

But Helga soon discovers Harlem's limits in its class-consciousness and racial essentialism. Helga's friend Anne Grey, with whom she lives, exemplifies Harlem's hypocrisy. Anne "fed her obsession" with the race problem; she "frequented all the meetings of protest, subscribed to all the complaining magazines, and read all the lurid newspapers spewed out by the Negro yellow press. She talked, wept, and ground her teeth dramatically" (48). But though she claims to value "all things Negro, she yet disliked the songs, the dances, and the softly blurred speech of the race" (48). She hates white people, and yet "she aped their clothes, their manners, and their gracious ways of living" (48). Helga views Anne's political protestations as merely a performance of racial authenticity, noting that "she reveled in this orgy of protest" (48). Although Helga sees through Anne rather quickly, she does not immediately recognize the process of disidentification from Harlem that has begun. Like Freud's paradigmatic boy, she disavows what she has seen.

As the process continues, Helga begins to feel dissatisfied but cannot identify a cause. She fears her own ambivalence:

> As the days multiplied, her need of something, something vaguely familiar, but which she could not put a name to and hold for definite examination, became almost intolerable. She went through moments of overwhelming anguish. She felt shut in, trapped. . . . She became a little frightened, and then shocked to discover that, for some unknown reason, it was of herself she was afraid. (47)

Helga's ambivalence elicits fear because it signals the impending breakdown of the coherent racial identity she has achieved in Harlem. If she cannot sustain the performance of a normative (feminine and bourgeois) racial identity in Harlem, Helga risks losing community and home and becoming a figure of abjection. Moreover, her dissatisfaction threatens to lead to subjective dissolution. Butler explains the danger inherent in failing to accommodate the symbolic through regulated performance:

> "[P]erformance" is not a singular "act" or event, but a ritualized production, a ritual reiterated under and through constraint, under and through the force of prohibition and taboo, with the threat of ostracism and even death controlling and compelling the shape of the production. (95)

The constraints on Helga's performance of racial identity in Harlem are clearest in the injunction of Mrs. Hayes-Rore (her temporary employer, who brought her to Harlem) that she conceal the fact that her mother was white:

> The woman felt that the story, dealing as it did with race intermingling and possibly adultery, was beyond definite discussion. For among black people, as among white people, it is tacitly understood that these things are not mentioned—and therefore they do not exist. (39)

Helga's origin story of miscegenation threatens to disrupt the racial binary upon which both black middle-class and white racial ideologies of the time rest. But the psychic effort required to maintain the mask of racial authenticity becomes more obvious as Anne's cavils against whites "stirred memories, probed hidden wounds" (49). In uncanny fashion, Helga's intimate, familial relation to whiteness—repressed until now—begins to return.

As Helga continues the process of disidentification, her fear and loathing shifts from herself to those around her:

> Abruptly it flashed upon her that the harrowing irritation of the past weeks was a smoldering hatred. . . . It was as if she were shut up, boxed up, with hundreds of her race, closed up with that something in the racial character which had always been, to her, inexplicable, alien. Why, she demanded in fierce rebellion, should she be yoked to these despised black folk? (54–55)

Refusing to identify with "these despised black folk," Helga displays an ambivalent relationship to assuming the mark of "castration." Helga's crisis resembles that of Butler's "body marked as feminine" that

> occupies or inhabits its mark at a critical distance, with radical unease or with a phantasmatic or tenuous pleasure or with some mixture of anxiety and desire. If she is marked as castrated, she must nevertheless *assume* that mark, where "assumption" contains both the wish for an identification as well as its impossibility. For if she must assume, accomplish, accede to her castration, there is at the start some *failure* of socialization here, some excessive occurrence of that body outside and beyond its mark, in relation to that mark. . . . Indeed, there is a body which has failed to perform its castration in accord with the symbolic law, some locus of resistance, some way in which the desire to have the phallus has not been renounced and continues to persist. (*Bodies,* 104)

If Helga in "some way" desires to disavow racial castration or identification, she cannot achieve an alternative subject position. She remains ambivalent and, almost immediately, the hostility she had turned outward turns back on her: "Self-loathing came upon her. 'They're my own people, my own people,' she kept repeating over and over to herself. It was no good, The feeling would not be routed. . . . Panic seized her" (Larsen, 55). As her seamless identification with the Harlemites fails, the workings of ideological interpellation are revealed to her. In a version of double consciousness, she simultaneously identifies as African American and wishes to refuse the symbolic meaning of that subject position. Facing the specter of the Real, seeing the seams of the symbolic order, Helga feels panic and claustrophobia.

Although identity performance is compelled by the symbolic, the symbolic is nonetheless tied to the material realm. One can sometimes afford to flout normative identity categories if one has enough money. Helga receives a small legacy from her maternal uncle, which provides her with the option of leaving Harlem. As soon as she realizes this, she makes a final psychic break with the Harlemites.

This break constitutes what we might call the primal scene of the novel's Harlem section. It takes place on a night that is "gay, grotesque, and a little weird" in an illicit chamber, a secret underground nightclub to which her party "descended through a furtive, narrow passage, into a vast subterranean room." From the dark street and the darker passageway, Helga is born into light and noise: "A glare of light struck her eyes, a blare of jazz split her ears" (58). Amid the chaos of light, "savage" noise, and "swirling" movement in this quintessential Harlem jazz club scene, the specter of racial abjection emerges that haunts Helga's imagination. She sees across the room Audrey Denney, a light-skinned African American woman described as "gravely smiling," of "deathlike pallor," and "sorrowful." As Helga's underworld alter ego, Audrey is sitting with Helga's own Dr. Anderson, the principal from Naxos. In explaining to Helga who the woman is, Anne Grey excoriates Audrey Denney as a race traitor for socializing with whites, especially white men. She declares that Audrey "ought to be ostracized" (60). But Helga finds Anne's racial orthodoxy—inflected here by gender and sexuality—"revolting"; it gives her a "sickish feeling" and a "flash of anger" touches her (61). Helga's visceral reaction marks the ambivalent slide of her racial identification. But though she chafes at the constraints of the bourgeoisie's codes of race, sex, gender, and class, Helga does not dare risk social ostracism herself; she laments that she lacks Audrey Denney's "courage . . . to ignore racial barriers" (62).

Helga continues to watch Audrey as she dances with Anderson; she again notes Audrey's sorrow, but this time also her sensuality: "She danced with grace and abandon, gravely, yet with obvious pleasure, her legs, her hips, her back, all swaying gently, swung by that wild music from the heart of the jungle" (62). The loaded terms here—"hips," "swaying," "wild," "jungle"—clarify that Audrey is an appealing spectacle not so much for her "alabaster" skin tone, her approximation of whiteness, as for her power of racial and sexual self-definition. She *will* go about with white men if she chooses, but this is not to disavow her connection to blackness. She is not afraid to be seen as a sensual black woman who enjoys moving her body to jazz. Anne Grey and her ilk would not be caught in such a compromising position for fear of embodying the dominant culture's image of a licentious black savage. That Audrey pays a price for refusing to conform (her refusal to reiterate the norms, in Butler's terms), a price of social death, is suggested by the repetition of terms describing her as sorrowful and almost cadaverous. She is other-worldly not only because she experiences a sort of social death, but because she is Helga's uncanny double; she pursues sexual desire by consorting with Anderson and by miscegenating with whites.

The spectacle of Audrey Denney clarifies for Helga the cause of her earlier symptoms of anxiety and malaise, that is, the Harlem bourgeoisie's constricted definition of blackness, which constitutes for Helga a sort of racial castration—though this awareness again elicits symptoms of panic and claustrophobia. Helga cannot take her eyes from the scene of Audrey dancing with Anderson:

> She forgot the garish crowded room. She forgot her friends. She saw only two figures, closely clinging. She felt her heart throbbing. She felt the room receding. She went out the door. She climbed endless stairs. At last, panting, confused, but thankful to have es[c]aped, she found herself again out in the dark night alone, a small crumpled thing in a fragile, flying black and gold dress. (62)

This scopic scene reconciles Helga to her broken identification with the group. In the next scene she is sailing for Copenhagen.

Helga seeks a new model of identification in Copenhagen with her mother's family where, she fantasizes, "she would be appreciated, and understood" (57) because "there were no Negroes, no problems, no prejudice" (55). Helga imagines she will not have to be authentically, essentially black according to the terms of uplift, the bourgeoisie, or white America. But because a racial symbolic does exist in Denmark—whether there are "Negroes" or not—Helga becomes dissatisfied with Copenhagen. However, she again questions whether her feelings are caused by some lack within herself:

> Frankly, the question came to this: what was the matter with her? Was there, without her knowing it, some peculiar lack in her? Absurd. But she began to have a feeling of discouragement and hopelessness. Why couldn't she be happy, content, somewhere? Other people managed, somehow, to be. To put it plainly, didn't she know how? Was she incapable of it? (81)

She recognizes her failure, again, to accommodate to the racial symbolic, although she is not yet able to analyze consciously the social causes of her dissatisfaction. Without a preferable alternative, she remains ambivalent; she still abhors the role she would have to play in the United States and Harlem: "Never could [Helga] recall the *shame* and often the absolute horrors of the black man's existence in America without the quickening of her heart's beating and a sensation of disturbing *nausea*. . . . The sense of *dread* of it was almost a tangible thing in her throat" (82, my emphasis). But the slide toward reidentification has begun. Almost as soon as Helga reminds herself why life as an African American is untenable, her identification as African American forcefully resurfaces through a primal scene that triggers double consciousness.

Helga attends a "vaudeville" performance by visiting African Americans that is clearly a minstrel show. The Danish audience loves it, but

> Helga Crane was not amused. Instead she was filled with a fierce hatred for the cavorting Negroes on the stage. She felt shamed, betrayed, as if these pale pink and white people among whom she lived had suddenly been invited to look upon something in her which she had hidden away and wanted to forget. (83)

This passage recalls Freud's model of the uncanny as something hidden or repressed that is brought to light. Helga begins to realize that the Danes have been using her for their amusement, just as they view the minstrel performers. Unlike white America, they don't despise her for being black: "[T]hey had admired it, rated it as a precious thing, a thing to be enhanced, preserved" (83). Nevertheless, a gap has reopened in Helga's identity between herself as black and the Danes as "pale pink and white."

The ambivalent slide between conflictual identifications continues; Helga is drawn back to the vaudeville circus repeatedly as a "silently speculative spectator. For she knew that into her plan for her life had thrust itself a suspensive conflict in which were fused doubts, rebellion, expediency, and urgent longings" (83). Helga's "plan"—to marry the Danish painter Axel Olsen and live a rich life in Denmark away from American racial categories—is disturbed by the return of Helga's identification with African American culture. This identification derives not from some essence conveyed in her "black blood," but from the realization that her life in Denmark, her relationships with her white relatives and with Olsen, are premised on their consumption of her (and her performance) as an exotic spectacle like the minstrel performers. When Olsen indicates his disrespect by propositioning her to become his mistress rather than his wife, she detaches further from him and her life in Copenhagen. He finally proposes, but, "where before she would have been pleased and proud . . . she was now . . . aware of a curious feeling of repugnance" (85). In ruefully admitting that Helga's canny refusal to be his mistress has compelled his marriage proposal, Olsen finally unveils completely his view of her as licentious primitive: "'You have the warm impulsive nature of the women of Africa, but, my lovely, you have, I fear, the soul of a prostitute" (87). Although Helga had previously wanted the social respectability and financial security that Olsen offered, now that it comes with the demand that she submit to the sexualized and racialized identity as exotic primitive, she is not willing to pay the price. That as exotic/erotic primitive Helga had been an object of economic exchange—used by the Dahls (her relatives) for social climbing, for Olsen's fame and titillation, for Copenhagen's social spectacle—is materialized in Olsen's portrait of her as a "sensual creature" for which viewers made "many tempting offers" (89).

Only after this episode of nuptial negotiation, which makes clear the economic basis of marriage for women and its racial component for Helga, does Helga's desire to return to Harlem become conscious. These moments when she sees herself being made into a subject of race (or class or gender) are moments of double consciousness: she sees herself being seen. Olsen's portrait illustrates this psychic process: she can literally watch people looking at "her" through the lens of their racial suppositions, that is, through Olsen's vision of her as a "sensual" beast with the "soul of a prostitute." In Du Bois's words, the portrait yields her "no true self-consciousness, but only lets [her] see [her]self through the revelation of the other world. It is a peculiar sensation, this double consciousness, this sense of always looking at one's self through the eyes of others."[53] The portrait is a simulacrum: it is a representation or copy of a sensual primitive Helga that is actually the community's fantasy of Helga. But the text also registers the effect of sexual difference on Du Bois's masculine model in addressing women's economic/sexual commodification. The painting materializes Helga's status as a sexualized commodity fetish in Denmark.

The crowning incident that reveals Helga's heretofore unconscious desire for and identification with African Americans is a performance of Dvořák's "New World Symphony," which "samples" the spiritual "Swing Low, Sweet Chariot." Significantly, African American music, that privileged mode of African American cultural expression, reveals to her the feeling "that had lurked formless and undesignated these many weeks in the back of her troubled mind. Incompleteness" (92). Believing that being among African Americans once again will deliver that yearned-for completeness, Helga resolves to leave Denmark. And yet, on the very day of her departure, Helga "began to regret that she was leaving. Why couldn't she have two lives, or why couldn't she be satisfied in one place?" (93). That sense of completeness will remain elusive.

Her double consciousness is only exacerbated upon her return to Harlem. She feels anew that she is completely of black people and also that she cannot live in America:

> *These* were her people. . . . How absurd she had been to think that another country, other people could liberate her from the ties which bound her forever to these mysterious, these terrible, these fascinating, these lovable, dark hordes. Ties that were of the spirit. Ties not only superficially entangled with mere outline of features or color of skin. Deeper. Much deeper than either of these. (95)

Significantly, standard markers of racial essence—features, skin color—are held to be "superficial." Helga's kinship with African Americans is based not on biology or even sensibility, but on an ineffable common "spirit" (echoing Du Bois's "souls") born of the shared experience of being black in America. Despite this felt kinship, Helga rejects the "cramped" and "cruel" existence of life in America for blacks and intends to leave again. But she knows now that after leaving, she will want to return again: "This knowledge this certainty of the division of her life into two parts in two lands, into physical freedom in

Europe and spiritual freedom in America, was unfortunate, inconvenient, expensive" (96).

A final scene of witnessing marks Helga's last oscillation of desire and identification. The precipitating events involve Dr. Anderson, the former principal of Naxos, now married to Helga's friend Anne Grey. Anderson kisses Helga at a drunken party; she then resolves to offer herself sexually to Dr. Anderson, a man she has repeatedly told herself she hates, but is rebuffed. Mortified by the fact that she had finally risked social opprobrium to pursue her sexual desires only to learn that Dr. Anderson would not risk the same, Helga feels choked by humiliating "self-knowledge" (110). Wandering the streets of Harlem, she stumbles into a storefront church. It is music, first, that pulls her in—a hymn she recalls from long ago. At first, Helga serves as the spectacle of sex for "the hundred pairs of eyes upon her" (110), which belong to the worshiping women who see her as a "scarlet 'oman" and pore los' Jezebel" (112). But Helga looks back, watching their "frenzied" religious "performance" with "an indistinct horror of an unknown world" (113). "But the horror held her" until what seemed strange and alien becomes familiar and safe: "a curious influence penetrated her; she felt an echo of the weird orgy resound in her own heart" (113). Substituting sexual for religious eroticism (Larsen describes the religious rites as "Bacchic" and orgiastic), Helga falls, spellbound, into the "savage" arms of the church women. To still the "vertigo" (115) of her constant and sudden fluctuations of desire and in the hopes of finding "stability" and "permanent happiness," she gives herself over to religion and marriage to the Reverend Mr. Pleasant Green (117).

Upon moving with Green to rural Alabama, Helga soon experiences nausea again, this time as a consequence of pregnancy rather than from psychic ambivalence (123). She realizes that her decision to marry, while bearing more permanent consequences than her previous choices, does not guarantee satisfaction. In her final ambivalence, Helga resolves to leave Green and then resolves not to leave her children: "She meant to leave him. . . . Of the children Helga tried not to think. She wanted not to leave them—if that were possible. . . . No. She couldn't desert them" (134, 135). With no way to resolve the conflict between these mutually exclusive resolutions, Helga puts off action until she has no choice left; she is pregnant with her fifth child and apparently doomed to die from the strain of another childbirth. Helga's desirous reversals drive the narrative until this final suspension of action, which, paradoxically, ends the novel. In *Quicksand*, a succession of primal scenes precipitate double consciousness within successive social locations, but they mark ambivalent oscillations among contingent racializations rather than linear progress toward a unified and stable racial identity.

What do we do with the knowledge that Helga as the traumatic mulatta reveals the "secret" behind U.S. race ideology: that racial purity is a fiction and white supremacy a cruel fantasy? If the "only way to break the power of our ideological dream is to confront the Real of our desire which announces itself in this dream," then "[w]e must confront ourselves with how the ideological figure of the [mulatto] is invested with our unconscious desire, with how we have constructed this figure to escape a certain deadlock of our desire" (Žižek, 48). We must recognize how the tragic mulatta and the fantasy of racial purity allow us to stitch up our ideological system of nationalistic white exceptionalism. The next chapter pursues this question of how the fantasy of racial purity functions to shore up sufficient, white, American masculinity. Through a reading of William Faulkner's *Absalom, Absalom!*, I explore how a specifically American white masculinity, tied to economic myths of self-making, depends on the opposed figure of the abject black for definition. As the placeholder of lack, blackness functions to cover over the subjective split that founds all symbolic identity and threatens to reveal whiteness and masculinity as, in effect, "castrated." The chapter, then, explores the implications of the miscegenation taboo and the racial symbolic for white masculinity.

Chapter 4

Blackness and Class Difference in William Faulkner

Published in the same year, 1936, William Faulkner's *Absalom, Absalom!* and Margaret Mitchell's *Gone with the Wind* paint the Old South in such different hues that their very incommensurability invites comparison. Whereas Mitchell's historical romance enjoyed unparalleled and enduring popular success, Faulkner's anti-romance yielded lukewarm reviews and unspectacular sales. But *Absalom, Absalom!* soon gained critical respect as part of the myth-busting Southern Renaissance of literary realism in the post–World War I era, while Mitchell's novel was dismissed by scholars as a nostalgic resurrection of the myths of southern chivalry. Notwithstanding the fact that, more recently, critics have acknowledged that *Gone with the Wind* departs from antebellum southern ideology by lambasting the cult of True Womanhood and advocating a post-slavery industrial economy, the novel nevertheless dresses up slavery in the old-time, demure discourse of benign paternalism.[1] Though I would not suggest that Faulkner's fatalistic and Mitchell's optimistic accounts of southern history share an aesthetic sensibility or target the same structures for social criticism, I would note one point of convergence between the novels—though it is a similarity perhaps more of detail and setting than of theme or form. Scarlett's forbears derive from similar origins as their generational counterparts in *Absalom, Absalom!* Sutpen's first wife and Scarlett's maternal grandparents are Haitian Creoles of French origin. Even the name of Sutpen's cast-aside wife, Eulalia, is echoed by Scarlett's aunt Eulalie. And like Sutpen himself, Scarlett's father is a self-made man who acquires his plantation wealth through design and manly connivance rather than inheritance—a fact that makes them both interlopers to the closed and "family-conscious" Southern planter society. So these novels, nearly antithetical in their stances toward the slave system, similarly breed a trope of Haitian origins with the myth of American class mobility. Although I will consider only Faulkner's text in depth, I want to begin with this convergence of colonialism and capitalism in producing the southern planter class.

Recent essays on American colonialism and the rise of an American regional consciousness suggest a purposefulness in this conjunction of the Caribbean with American capitalism. In his influential essay "Caliban," Roberto Fernandez Retamar explores the development of a Latin American identity by tracing the linguistic and cultural genealogy of the related terms *Caribbean, cannibal,* and *Caliban* to their origin with Columbus's arrival in the New World. The region now called the Caribbean got its name from the Caribs, the most warlike of the indigenous tribes in the region. Columbus's inexact and fragmentary accounts of the Caribs and other indigenous tribes, as recorded in his navigational logbooks, led to the coinage of the term *cannibal* to mean anthropophagic human. That accounts from the New World impressed Europe is evidenced by Shakespeare's last play, *The Tempest* (1612), in which the character Caliban gets his name from an anagram for cannibal. The European imagination thus populated the Caribbean with fantastic visions of barbarous people akin to Prospero's "savage and deformed slave."[2] "Caribbean" and its related terms become "keywords" in the "construction and invention of 'America.'"[3]

Retamar notes the symbolic conjunction of *Africa* and the *Caribbean* in European culture's application of "the term *cannibal* not to the extinct aborigine of our [Caribbean-American] isles but, above all, to the African black who appeared in those shameful Tarzan films."[4] But Retamar acknowledges only obliquely the actual joining of these geographic locales through the Atlantic slave trade. Hortense Spillers speaks more directly to this geographical merging: "Apparently everywhere one might look on this massive scene of heterogeneous historical attitudes, it seems that 'Caliban' designates a copulative potential by way of the Atlantic system of slavery."[5] She further cites *Absalom, Absalom!* as a text that singularly illustrates the imbrication of apparently local U.S. events in this larger history of New World colonialism:

> The historic triangular trade interlarded a third of the known world in a fabric of commercial intimacy so tightly interwoven that the politics of the New World cannot always be so easily disentangled as locally discrete moments. Nowhere is this narrative of involvement more pointedly essayed than in Faulkner's *Absalom, Absalom!*[6]

What neither Retamar nor Spillers notes is that the strongest and most persistent fantasy of the Afro-Caribbean cannibal resides in Haiti. To this day, American popular culture virtually equates Haiti with voodoo and persists, despite a dearth of evidence, in associating voodoo with human sacrifice. In addition, Haiti occupied a special place in the imagination of the slaveholding South. The site of the only successful slave revolt and the first black-ruled country in the Americas, Haiti represented the terrifying possibility of slave rebellion.[7] Considering Haiti's tight association with voodoo and rebellion, we begin to see that, for nineteenth-century slaveholding America, Haiti embodied the cannibal/Caribbean/Caliban nexus.

Nineteenth- and even early twentieth-century American tracts defending slavery or post-emancipation forms of institutionalized racial inequality frequently point to the independent black state of Haiti as proof of blacks' inherent savagery and incapacity for self-government. Arguing for the U.S. annexation of Santo Domingo and Haiti (the two republics occupying one island), Samuel G. Howe writes in 1871:

> [T]he negroes of Hayti, as in other West India islands, where they are left entirely to themselves, tend to revert toward barbarism; as neglected fruit to the crab. Witness the savagedom in some parts of the interior of Hayti. Witness the perpetuation of the pagan worship of Obi. Witness the sacrifice of infants, and the eating of their flesh, which not the fear of executions has been able to put down.[8]

In *The American Negro: His Past and His Future* (1900), P. B. Barringer of the University of Virginia argues that freed blacks, no longer under the civilizing influence of slavery, revert to hereditary savagery: "Fifty centuries of savagery in the blood can not be held down by two centuries of forced good behavior if the controlling influences which held down this savagery are withdrawn as they have been in this case."[9] For evidence, he turns to the report of one Sir Spencer St. John, whom he quotes:

> Official peculation, judicial murder, and utter corruption of every kind underlie the forms and titles of civilized government; the religion, nominally Christian, is largely Voudoux, or serpent-worship, in which actual and horrible cannibalism is even now a most important element. Instead of progressing, the negro Republican has gone back to the lowest type of African barbarism.[10]

These exaggerated accounts suggest how the perceived threat posed by Haiti's black autonomy to Southern slavery is churned into the fantasy of Haiti as an anarchic zone of black magic and black barbary. After the slave revolt began in 1791, the once model colony known as "the pearl" of the greater Antilles came to represent—for the slaveholding South—an infectious agent of black freedom. After the Civil War, Haiti represented the just necessity of barring African Americans from political participation.

Even though Faulkner is implicitly critical of the American slaveholding society that feared and abhorred Haiti's black independence, he nevertheless deploys the frightening and exotic connotations of voodoo and revolt to mystify Sutpen's character. Much like *The Tempest*'s magical isle, Haiti functions in *Absalom* as a liminal space, outside historical time and society, where an enterprising man can establish a kingdom. Having been overthrown as lord of an Italian kingdom, *The Tempest*'s Prospero arrives at his off-the-map island, works his magic—which proves stronger than the local spells of the witch Sycorax—in order to subdue the natives and establish himself as ruler. Thomas Sutpen similarly arrives in Haiti without material resources or position, miraculously and single-handedly subdues a slave uprising that is galvanized by voodoo ritual, and wins the keys to the kingdom, as it were, from the plantation owner. Although Sutpen, like Prospero, eventually abdicates his possession, his passage through Haiti and especially his acquisition of slaves there facilitates his capitalist conquest upon returning to U.S. soil. But if Sutpen's debt to Caribbean colonialism signals the real economic interdependence of the American South and the Caribbean colonies, Faulkner's depiction of Haitian plantation slavery in the 1820s—as Richard Godden notes—postdates Haiti's independence, which had been achieved by 1804. This anachronism suggests that Haiti's symbolic importance to Faulkner's "history" outweighs the pressures of historical accuracy.[11]

Faulkner uses Haiti's image as "a little island set in a smiling and fury-lurked and incredible indigo sea, which was the halfway point between what we call the jungle and what we call civilization" to cloak Sutpen in mystery and power, as well as in blood and corruption.[12] If the paramount sign of cultural dominance is the imposition of the colonizer's language, then Sutpen's accommodation to the language of the Haitian slaves—which "a good part of the county did not know was a civilized language"—signals his cultural contamination by the very people he subjugated (67). Sutpen, in turn, infects the American land with "his crew of imported slaves which his adopted citizens still looked on as being a great deal more deadly than any beast he could have started and slain in that country" (42–43). If Sutpen has some of the cannibal about him, it is due not only to his association with Afro-Caribbean culture, but to his implication in a colonialism that, in effect, devoured human flesh. Having exterminated the indigenous Caribbean peoples, the European colonizers imported slaves from Africa to work the plantations. The death rate of Caribbean slaves was so high that the slave population could be maintained only through a continuous importation of fresh cargo (this in contrast to the United States, where the 1807 ban on the Atlantic slave trade required that the slave population reproduce itself biologically). So even as Faulkner capitalizes on America's fantasies of a savage Haiti to demonize his character, he implicates Sutpen and, ultimately, America's birth in a cruel and doomed project.

Sutpen's link to Haiti ties American capitalist enterprise to the international economy of colonial slavery so as to illuminate the politics buried within the national myths of the self-made man and the southern myth of the "birth of a nation." This is not to say that the South's plantation economy was structured like the bourgeois, industrial economy of the North—a point Eugene Genovese makes in his *The Political Economy of Slavery.* But even Genovese concedes that this "specific kind of slaveholding class . . . was and could only be a product of the modern, bourgeois world and its trans-Atlantic culture, the ethos and sensibilities of which it necessarily had to absorb even as it struggled to repudiate much of them." But though the slave system was embedded within the capitalist world, this mode of production and its numerically small planter class nevertheless "gave the South a social system and a civilization with a distinct class structure, political community, economy, ideology, and set of psychological patterns." This southern ideology consisted of "an aristocratic, antibourgeois spirit with values and mores emphasizing family and status, a strong code of honor, and aspirations to luxury, ease, and accomplishment," rather than profit as a value unto itself.[14] Faulkner also explores the planter ideology that shaped southern society through his representation of Sutpen's psychic investment in the values of family and status, the ends to which Sutpen's acquisition of wealth through slavery is only the means. *Absalom* explores, then, the relations among masculine subjectivity, national identity, and the economy of slavery.

Masculinity and National Ideology

To theorize the relation between masculine identity and national ideology, I return to Kaja Silverman's *Male Subjectivity at the Margins.* By marrying Althusser's theory of ideological interpellation to psychoanalytic theories of subjectivity, Silverman explores "the relation between a society's mode of production and its symbolic order."[15] She explains that the subject comes to see this relation as natural and real through ideological belief, or the "dominant fiction" (2). In turn, the subject comes to believe in the dominant fiction—the set of cultural images that is perceived as reality—by passing through the Oedipus complex. The Oedipus complex is, then, the "primary vehicle of insertion" into our society's ideological "reality." Ideology does not interpellate an already constructed subject, but rather commands belief on the level of the unconscious and through the earliest processes of subject formation. America's dominant fiction, argues Silverman, is closely tied to the terms of normative masculinity; its "privileged term is the phallus" and it "solicits our faith above all else in the unity of the family and the adequacy of the male subject" (2, 15–16). In other words, the subject's relation to the symbolic system and the mode of production is lived through ideological belief in a dominant fiction of masculine sufficiency and the patriarchal family. Ideologies of class, race, ethnicity, and nation "compel belief by articulating themselves in relation" to the privileged terms of the family and the phallus (41–42). The dominant fiction might thus be said "to negotiate between the symbolic order and the mode of production—to be that which permits two very different forms of determination to be lived simultaneously" (42). Because it "forms the stable core around which a nation's and a period's 'reality' coheres," the dominant fiction authorizes ideologies of nation as well as gender (41). The "collectivities of community, town, and nation," writes Silverman, "have all traditionally defined themselves through reference to [the] image [of the family]" (42).

By drawing on Silverman's discussion of masculine subjectivity, I revisit aspects of the symbolic order—such as the traffic in women, the Name-of-the-Father, the miscegenation taboo, and the equation between penis and phallus—already discussed in earlier chapters. I find it useful, however, to re-present these concepts in relation to normative, rather than minority, masculinity in order to explore how the dominant culture perpetuates itself. I want to shift from a focus on the ways that African American men and women accommodate and resist the dominant culture to the ways the dominant culture is instituted and maintained through ideologies of gender, race, class, and nation. Silverman's notion of classic masculinity as that which denies the fundamental "castration" of subjectivity makes clear that lack does not reside solely in the racial or gendered other—even if these others experience a greater degree of social devaluation. By understanding the mechanism of denial, it is possible to see how nationalist ideologies construct race and class with reference to the terms of normative masculinity.

To see how normative masculinity, defined as sufficient and "uncastrated," comes to play this pivotal role in setting the terms of the dominant fiction, Silverman starts with the symbolic. As I discussed in the introduction, she makes a perspicacious distinction between symbolic Law as it relates to the structure of language and as it relates to the structure of kinship—a distinction not maintained in Lacanian discourse itself, which conflates the subject's entry into language with accommodation to the Name-of-the-Father. Whereas Lacan's subjective "lack" belongs to the order of language (language originates out of the absence of the thing signified and so "castrates" the subject by founding meaning and identity on lack), the "Name-of-the-Father" more properly refers to kinship structure. Thus, "the symbolic order is organized around *two* laws . . . around what might be called the 'Law of Language,' and the 'Law of Kinship Structure'" (35).

Silverman parses the Law of Kinship so as to separate cultural expression from natural order. Structures of kinship depend on incest taboos, which necessitate exogamy and, consequently, establish affiliation between and among families. In Lévi-Strauss's words, the incest prohibition "expresses the transition from the natural fact of consanguinity to the cultural fact of alliance" (Silverman, 35). Western culture's particular expression of the incest taboo ensures the exchange of women among men of different families; traditionally, the women "exchanged" have been legally and socially subsumed within the social identities of the men participating in the exchange (father, brother, husband). "The circulation of women can thus be seen to represent the most rudimentary articulation of the Name-of-the-Father—the most basic mechanism for defining men, in contradistinction to women, as the producers and representatives of the social field" (36). The presumption that the exchange of women is essential to culture helps universalize and naturalize the phallic terms of the symbolic order. The Law of Kinship and the Law of Language intersect at the point where the "lack installed through language" is conceptualized as "the absence of the male sexual organ" (37). In other words, the dominant position of men within our kinship structure is reflected in the phallus's privileged place as the sole "unconscious representative of what is lost to the subject with the entry into language" (38).

But if, as Lacan says, neither men nor women have the phallus because everyone is constituted by lack upon entering the system of language, then this alignment of phallus with penis veils lack in the male. This veiling is facilitated by the organizing principle of kinship known as the Name-of-the-Father, which equates the father with the Law of Kinship and so exempts the male from the "castration" instituted by the Law of Language. In other words, the structure of language does not inherently accord lack to women and plenitude to men, but comes to participate in ideologies of sexual difference through the equation of phallus with desire and penis with phallus: "[W]hen the Name-of-the-Father organizes the rules determining marriage, reproduction, lineality, abode, and inheritance, the Law of Kinship Structure exists in a contradictory relationship to the Law of Language" (42). The dominant fiction hides this disparity between an all-powerful and a "castrated" masculinity by equating the symbolic signifier of plenitude, the phallus, with the biological male organ—by conflating the actual and symbolic father. Thus, as Silverman concludes, "conventional masculinity can best be understood as a denial of castration, and hence as a refusal to acknowledge the defining limits of subjectivity" (46).

The equation between penis and phallus is a misrecognition or *méconnaissance* sustained by collective belief in the dominant fiction. To explain how male subjectivity is formed around this misrecognition, Silverman turns to Freud's writing on the psychical consequences of the anatomical distinctions between the sexes and, specifically, to his claim that sexual differentiation is often marked by a "failure to recognize":

> The subject classically refuses to recognize an unwanted feature of the *self* by projecting it onto the other. . . . He or she refuses to recognize an unpleasurable or anxiety-inducing aspect of the *other* by disavowing it, a process which sometimes requires the support of a fetish. (45)

Freud associates the latter process, disavowal, with the male's need to protect himself against the terrifying sight of female castration. A fetish, which acts as a substitute for the woman's "missing" penis, allows the boy to disavow female castration and so to fend off the threat to his own penis implied by the sight of the woman's genitals.[16] Freud's explanation of fetishism presumes that women are, in fact, castrated. But if women's castration is not a given, then the male must have undergone a psychic process, prior to the disavowal, that transmuted anatomical difference into female castration. Silverman argues that the male comes to see the woman as castrated through a process of *projection.* The male projects onto women his own subjective lack, the "generalized castration . . . of the sacrifice exacted by language" that is "subsequently compounded" by other social and historical factors (Silverman, 46).[17]

Freud's discussion of Chinese foot-binding in "Fetishism"—one example among several meant to illustrate that fetishes help the male subject defend *against* the knowledge of female castration—inadvertently reveals that fetishes can also lend *support* to the illusion of female castration. Freud explains that the Chinese custom of foot-binding consists of "mutilating the female foot and then revering it like a fetish after it has been mutilated." By fetishizing the woman's mutilated foot, Freud surmises, "the Chinese male wants to thank the woman for having submitted to being castrated."[18] Aside from the startling implication that such fetishes serve women, Freud's commentary suggests that, in this case, female castration is *desirable* rather than horrific. As a sign of castration rather than a phallic sufficiency, the fetish of the mutilated foot contradicts Freud's premise that fetishism defends *against* the knowledge of female castration. So rather than exemplifying how fetish works to *disavow* female castration, the purposeful foot-binding literally effects the castration of women upon which male subjectivity depends. In other words, "the castration which is synonymous with sexual difference is not endemic to the female body, but is emblazoned across it by the male subject through projection" (Silverman, 46). The physical mutilation facilitates the process through which the male psychically deposits his own lack at the site of femininity and "makes [women] tolerable as sexual objects."[19] Classic male subjectivity thus "emerges . . . as a fetish for covering over the castration upon which male subjectivity is grounded" (Silverman, 47).

The image of a sufficient and uncastrated masculinity must be continually fortified because it "represents the most vulnerable component of the dominant fiction." The "male subject's identification with power and privilege is threatened" by association with less privileged social positions including those of class and race (47). Because the dominant fiction consists not only of the family and the phallus, but of other ideological elements, wrinkles in the social fabric can destabilize the practices determined by the Law of Kinship as well as the "coherence of the larger social formation" (48). The question is, what cultural work gets done to marshal and maintain the fictions of masculinity and the patriarchal family, especially in the face of challenges from socially disenfranchised categories of class and race that potentially undermine masculine ideals?

Family Jewels and the Slave Economy

To map the mechanism through which the dominant culture replicates itself, Silverman examines a historical moment at which the dominant fiction *fails* to command belief. The period after World War II marks a break in popular culture's representation of traditional masculinity. At this time, "the equation of the male sexual organ with the phallus could no longer be sustained," she argues, and "the disjuncture of these two terms . . . led to a collective loss of belief in the whole of the dominant fiction" (2). This moment of "ideological fatigue" is instructive because it demonstrates that "masculinity [is] a crucial site for renegotiating our *vraisemblance*"—for reshaping the set of images that constitutes ideological reality (2).

Whereas Silverman is interested in the implications for gender and the family of this post–World War II failure of belief in phallic sufficiency, I want to look at a different moment of "historical trauma" in America. Faulkner's *Absalom, Absalom!* represents the ideological crisis of belief in the fiction of white male supremacy that underlay the South's plantation slavery economy—a crisis that culminated most visibly in the Civil War. In Faulkner's story, the terms of masculinity and the family clearly depend on an unsustainable ideology of race and the doomed economic mode of slavery. By tracing the relation among the miscegenation taboo of the kinship structure, the mode of production of slavery, and the dominant fiction of white masculinity, I want to explore *class* status as one of the factors of subjectivity that reciprocally defines the categories of race and gender. *Absalom, Absalom!* makes an exemplary text because it explores, quite explicitly, how a kinship system structured according to the Name-of-the-Father, in tandem with the dominant fiction of masculinity and the family, are marshaled against, but ultimately unraveled by their unacknowledged dependence on the economic system of plantation slavery and its attendant ideologies of race and class.[20]

In a quintessentially American success story, Thomas Sutpen, who is born a poor white southerner, attempts to transcend his economically humble origins by acquiring a personal empire financed by plantation slavery.[21] Sutpen's entrepreneurial zeal is fueled, however, by a craven need to regain a sense of masculine mastery and sufficiency lost at the moment he discovered his inferior class position. To bolster the illusion that, as a normative male, he stands in for the Father and has the phallus, he displaces his own lack of economic status onto blackness and strives to found a racially pure and thus socially unimpeachable dynasty. Sutpen obsessively and fatally amasses not only wealth, property, and slaves, but also legitimate (white) heirs to compensate for his sense of class inferiority in relation to other white men. "Castration fear," or sociopolitical disfranchisement, is figured as a fear of racial contamination; male lack is projected onto an other race rather than the other gender (although the narrative does suggest that racial contamination originates by way of feminine deceit and produces effeminate progeny). But the planter class sustains an intimate and dependent relation to the class-race system from which it pretends separation. This means that kinship taboos and oedipal dynamics cannot maintain the strict racial binary stipulated by the South's dominant fiction.[22] When the taboos against miscegenation (and incest) necessary to uphold the Name-of-the-Father in the white-rule, antebellum South are poised to fail, Sutpen's dynasty is threatened with "contamination" by black blood. In his effort to enforce his family's submission to the miscegenation taboo, Sutpen finally destroys the very kin meant to ensure his patriarchal self-image.

If Sutpen's "design" requires an absolute distinction between the races, then repeated allusions to Sutpen's own blackness work to erase the color line he is intent on drawing. As James A. Snead notes, "The most striking breakdown of racial division comes in the figure of Sutpen himself, about whom Faulkner cleverly leaves open the question of origins."[23] Ironically, the course Sutpen follows to distinguish himself from the signification of blackness brings him within intimate proximity to and economic dependence on blacks. In his thirst for wealth, legitimacy, and distinction from blackness, Sutpen becomes an overseer on a Haitian coffee plantation that exploits black slave labor.[24] Just when he seems to have secured his fortune by marrying the Haitian plantation heiress in reward for having suppressed a slave uprising, he discovers that his wife is part black. Although he forfeits his claim to the plantation in order to "put aside" his wife and their son, he takes with him from Haiti the dozen "savage" slaves who are integral to "tearing" his plantation out of the Mississippi wilderness. The more his own success and psychic life depend on exerting mastery over blacks, the more inextricable is blackness from his own self.[25] Sutpen's likeness to his "wild Negroes" outrages his second wife who, upon discovering a scene of recreational hand-to-hand combat, finds herself "seeing not the two black beasts she had expected to see but instead a white one and a black one, both naked to the waist and gouging at one another's eyes as if their skins should not only have been the same color but should have been covered with fur too" (31). The fight—a "spectacle" of racial blending—yields to the image of "two Sutpen faces . . . once on Judith and once on the negro girl beside her" looking down on the fight from a loft; this reference to Sutpen's own miscegenation underscores the doubleness of Sutpen's racial identity (33).

When Sutpen's mulatto son from his first marriage, passing for white, intends to marry Sutpen's white daughter from his second marriage, the black blood Sutpen had tried to purge by disowning the first wife and son resurges. This proposed marriage raises the specter of both incest and miscegenation—a double violation of kinship structures and the dominant fiction of the American South.[26] As Eric Sundquist writes, it is the "debacle of miscegenation, which . . . brings Sutpen's design, like that of the South itself, to collapse."[27] Thus, *Absalom* links the terms of kinship and family—paternity, patriarchy, and patrilineage—not only to taboos against incest, but to taboos against miscegenation. In sum, the dominant fiction of a racial binary underwrites white male privilege; both depend on a kinship system structured through the miscegenation taboo.

Miscegenation threatens the ideology of racial difference that supports the economic system of slavery (and, after emancipation, the system of segregation). A 1905 tract titled *The Color Line: A Brief in Behalf of the Unborn*—albeit postbellum—waxes apocalyptic on the capacity of miscegenation to destroy the South's way of life:

> The moment the bar of absolute separation is thrown down in the South, that moment the bloom of her spirit is blighted forever, the promise of her destiny is annulled, the proud fabric of her future slips into dust and ashes. No other conceivable disaster that might befall the South could, for an instant, compare with such miscegenation within her borders. Flood and fire, fever and famine and the sword—even ignorance, indolence, and carpet-baggery—she may endure and conquer while her blood remains pure; but once taint the well-spring of her life, and all is lost—even honour itself.[28]

Although William Benjamin Smith here preaches the perils of miscegenation in general, we can see that Southern norms blamed primarily miscegenation between white women and black men for endangering racial distinctions in his explanation of "the instinct of the family, with its imperious and uncompromising demand for absolute female chastity":

> It is not here, in any controlling measure, a question of individual morality. We make no such absolute demand upon men. We regret, we condemn, we may infinitely deplore sexual irregularity in son, or brother, or husband, or father, or friend, but we do not ostracize;—we may forgive, we may honour, we may even glorify the offender in spite of his offense. But for the female dissolute there is no forgiveness, however we may extra-socially pity or even admire. . . . For the offense of man is individual and limited, while that of the woman is general, and strikes mortally at the existence of the family itself.[29]

Smith acknowledges that white men's violation of the miscegenation taboo is regrettable, but white women's is unforgivable; this disparity demonstrates that the system of white supremacy depends on controlling the traffic in women and, consequently, paternity so as to allocate the power derived from paternal law and represented through the Name-of-the-Father. Nevertheless, as Faulkner's novel demonstrates, racial mixing—whether or not the children of such unions threatened legal lines of inheritance—ultimately smudged the color line. As Eric

Sundquist writes, "Sexuality is the principal site of racial contention in the South, presided over by the mulatto/a who, in his or her 'mongrel' flesh, announces the scandalous absence, contrary to the official story, of barriers."[30] Moreover, the privileged position within the southern chivalric code of white women's sexual purity *depends*, in part, on the institutionalized sexual availability of black women for white men.[31] Thus, the collapse of racial distinctions is built into the very structure and ideology of the slavery system; the tacitly accepted miscegenation between white men and black women, though excluded from the aegis of paternal Law, ultimately works to sabotage the dominant fiction of strict racial categories.

Although Sutpen commits his original act of miscegenation unknowingly, the site and circumstances explicitly signal how the structure of the slave system encourages miscegenation—despite any professed opposition—and thereby ensures the eventual collapse of its own ideological underpinnings. Haiti represented the threat to slavery not only of rebellion, but of sanctioned miscegenation—a more insidious, corrosive force. Caribbean colonies were especially notorious for according people of mixed blood a Europeanized sociolegal status discrete from and superior to that of "blacks."[32] Thus, Anglo-Americans—with their "one drop" definition of blackness—tended to "associate creoles . . . with the colonialist site of slavery, miscegenation, and political and cultural degeneration."[33] Sutpen is implicated in this colonial system, as his miscegenation with the Haitian heiress—however involuntary—attests. But it is Sutpen's adherence to America's ideology of racial purity, rather than his engagement in miscegenation itself, that ensures the downfall of his white empire.[34] Attempting to bleach the stain of black blood from the line of descendants he hopes to found, he declines to recognize his son. But, in bastardizing Bon, Sutpen makes his first son a subject of indeterminate paternity and racial identity, thus enabling Bon to later insinuate himself with Sutpen's "white" children and wield the threat of incest and miscegenation. As Snead observes, "[T]he main characters in the Sutpen story, by following logical steps forward from illogical premises, have created the sort of chaos they were hoping to dispel."[35] This is only one instance in which America's racial ideology, articulated through the family for purposes of maintaining control over the mode of production, sets the stage for its own defeat.

The text's indeterminate narrative structure mirrors the effects of an American racial ideology that represses bonds of kinship between blacks and whites. Referring to the multiple narrators who provide conflicting and fragmented aspects of the Sutpen history, Peter Brooks writes,

> [I]n this novel which preeminently concerns fathers, sons, generation, and lines of descent, there seems to be no clear authority . . . for the telling of the story. . . . [N]ot only does the identity of all the important characters seem to be in question, but the very discourse about identity seems to lack authority."[36]

Like Brooks, Snead argues that the narrative's purposefully elliptical structure embodies the fracturing of the patrilineal lines of descent it represents; it "reveals a social law through a narratological insight."[37] But, unlike Brooks, Snead reveals the textually submerged element of race to be that which interferes with masculine, as well as narrative, authority: "The absenting of society's repressed member [the African American] becomes the place of greatest structural weakness in the social narrative that Shreve and Quentin, in the later part of the novel, try to reconstruct, seam by seam."[38] In other words, the unknowable gaps in the Sutpen story that Shreve and Quentin must fill in to explain, for example, Sutpen's objections to Bon or what Sutpen must have said to Henry in his efforts to turn Henry against Bon, reflect the repression of blackness that brings down the Sutpen family line and that frustrates the passing down of its story:

> Whatever is of consequence in *Absalom, Absalom!* lies in seams—not in what speakers say, not in the stream itself, but in what remains unsaid, what must be left to speculation. An entire area of Faulkner scholarship has grown up around trying to determine who knew what, and when, and how. What Faulkner has done is to bury the intense racial theme (and, by implication, the Southern theme) deep within those seams. He has bypassed questions of fairness, justice, and equality in favor of the historical and traditional role race played in a region that fought and died to preserve a way of life that cannot be glamorized because it included slavery.[39]

The novel's narrative withholding revolves around the epistemological uncertainty of racial identity. In fact, the text's lacunae have spurred an endless critical debate about whether Bon is black, a debate analogous to the characters' obsessions with finding out black blood and symptomatic, as well, of the very difficulty of fixing racial identity—a difficulty the novel structurally replicates.

In writing that "the destiny of Sutpen's family . . . would be the land's catastrophe too," Faulkner suggests that Sutpen's obsession with establishing and maintaining a racially pure plantation dynasty is symbolic of the South's regional ideology and America's nationalist expansionism (89). First, the dominant fiction of masculinity and the family, which consolidates Southern identity, hinges primarily on race: "[R]ace enters Faulkner's texts as a practice whereby, through segregating a certain group of people from the category of 'whiteness,' Yoknapatawpha society finds the chief proof of its authority, integrity, and communal identity."[40] Second, by mythically representing the great man and the great war, the novel links the white supremacist story of the nation's birth to its constituent national ideal of the individualist, self-made man. Sundquist writes,

> If Faulkner never found a clear way to articulate the links between midcentury international politics and American race relations, . . . he nonetheless intuited the power of allegorical form to reveal the historical forces at play in a provincial moment or event."[41]

The coincidence between the self-destruction of Sutpen's family and the South's defeat in the Civil War signals the beginning of the collapse of the dominant fiction of racial binaries and gender roles that justified the southern socioeconomic structure. As in Silverman's framework, the larger social reality is condensed within and effected through the forms of the family.

The Primal Scene of Class Difference

If Sutpen's plan to establish himself as patriarch of a socially prominent, slaveholding family embodies the terms of the South's dominant fiction, then by what mechanism is Sutpen accommodated to this ideology as social reality? Although not revealed until more than halfway through the novel, the determining event of Sutpen's life occurs when, as a boy, he knocks on a plantation door—intent on delivering a message to its wealthy owner on behalf of his employee father—only to be rebuffed by a black slave who tells him to go around to the back door. Put in his place by the slave, who has evaluated his ragged appearance in order to monitor class divisions among whites, the young Sutpen discovers that not all white men are considered equal and, moreover, that distinctions are made according to accumulated wealth:

> He had learned the difference not only between white men and black ones, but he was learning that there was a difference between white men and white men not to be measured by lifting anvils or gouging eyes or how much whiskey you could drink then get up and walk out of the room. (282)

Manhood is conferred, in other words, neither by honor nor courage, nor simply by whiteness and maleness. The masculine privilege he had assumed was his birthright—had simply lived as his identity—is snatched away. Although he was able to accept the division of men according to racial distinctions, class distinctions are beyond his conceptual grasp:

> [H]e had never even heard of, never imagined, a place, a land divided neatly up and actually owned by men who did nothing but ride over it on fine horses or sit in fine clothes on the galleries of big houses while other people worked for them; he did not even imagine then that there was any such way to live or to want to live, or that there existed all the objects to be wanted which there were, or that the ones who owned the objects not only could look down on the ones that didn't, but could be supported in the down-looking not only by the others who owned objects too but by the very ones that were looked down on that didn't own objects and knew they never would. (276)

This passage catalogues the elements of a capitalist economy that have become properties of masculinity: individual property and land ownership, accumulated surplus wealth, and alienated labor. It is not that there are different sorts of men, some with money and others without, but rather that only those with money, slaves, and leisure are truly men. It dawns on Sutpen that, although "he had actually come on business, in the good faith of business which he had believed all men accepted," "the rich man (not the nigger) must have been seeing [his family] all the time—as cattle" (291, 293). From this point on, Sutpen determines to conduct his business in the common currency of masculinity.

Race plays an instrumental role in this critical scene, which constitutes Sutpen's class identity. In the moment when the slave tells Sutpen to go to the back door—treating him as he deems only blacks should be treated—Sutpen discovers his own lack in relation to the mode of production. Racial difference—represented by the plantation slave—

both introduces class difference to Sutpen's self-conception and comes to signify that difference. Sutpen associates his "lack" in terms of class (and masculinity) with contamination by blackness. His later marriage to the mixed-blood heiress ameliorates his actual class position but literalizes this racial contamination. Experiencing his class position as a threat not only to his racial identity, but to his patriarchal authority, Sutpen develops a "castration fear" signaled by a hysterical compulsion to cleanse his wife's black blood from his family line.

The exchange between slave and white boy, which triggers Sutpen's epiphany and the ensuing meditation on notions of masculinity, is often—if rather casually—termed a "primal scene." But in what particular ways does this drama of class identification follow Freud's model of the instantiation of gender difference? Like Freud's primal scene, which helps achieve the oedipal phase's task of inserting the child into the social order, Sutpen is thereby positioned within the divisions of the society he inhabits. This scene inserts him into the sociosymbolic order not in terms of sex and gender, however, but in terms of class position. This is not to say that sexual difference is insignificant in *Absalom,* but rather that gender identity is not at stake for Sutpen, who does not experience the blow to his masculine ego as a feminization; he is never in doubt, for example, that his sisters occupy a different and inferior position to his own. So although an early phase of gender differentiation seems to have already taken hold (and an earlier phase of racial differentiation, too, since he accepted the inferiority of blacks), prior to the scene the boy lives in a naive and earthy world of undifferentiated white male equality—a world steeped in mythic images of a rugged, individualist, frontier America. Sutpen's Adamic fall from "innocence" into the knowledge of class difference forever changes his social reality. (Faulkner employs the very term "fell" to describe Sutpen and his family's "descent" from the isolated hills of west Virginia into the cultured and cultivated Tidewater plains where the scene occurs.) It is as if by being barred from crossing the physical threshold of the plantation house, he is shunted across a symbolic one.

To compare this scene with the specular dramas of the Oedipus complex, I will briefly recap the two central acts of witnessing in Freud's descriptions of how children come to know and accede to the "realities" of sexual difference. First, the child catches sight of the opposite sex's genitals, a vision understood by Freud as obvious proof of women's castration. Girls, he claims, recognize the "fact" of sexual difference and their own inferiority instantly, while boys disavow the sight, accepting its "truth" only when later impressed with the threat of castration. (This story naturalizes and biologizes the different social positions accorded men and women.) If the boy achieves his disavowal of women's "castration" by substituting another object or trait for the "missing" penis, a sexual fetish originates. The second visual crisis that precipitates sexual differentiation is the primal scene, wherein the boy (Freud gives examples only of boys) watches his parents engage in coitus and, supposedly understanding his mother's castration in relation to the father's superior sexual position, renounces the possibilities of having her or taking her place so as to avoid castration at the father's hands. The boy instead identifies with the conventionally masculine role of his father. The primal scene, then, convinces the boy of the fact of sexual difference, which he had earlier disavowed.

We might discuss Faulkner's scene in relation to each of these acts of witnessing that effect gender differentiation. Sutpen's trajectory of identification blends the positions of girl and boy. Like Freud's girl-child, who realizes her castration instantly, Sutpen immediately apprehends his inferior position in relation to the planter. Sutpen's "lack" in terms of class, however, is at odds with the masculine sufficiency that had earlier characterized his gender identity. But, unlike the girl, who has no way of obviating her socially devalued gender, Sutpen

> rejects his father as a model and adopts the plantation owner as his surrogate father, as his model for what a man should be. And Sutpen feels the same ambivalence toward him that a son would feel for a father. At first, he considers killing him, but then he realizes that he doesn't want to do away with the plantation owner, he wants to become the plantation owner.[42]

Economic lack—unlike anatomical difference—is not (in this context) essentialized, and Sutpen can *choose* power; that is, he can manipulate his position within the dominant fiction. Moreover, Sutpen's choice to become, rather than to kill, the powerful patriarch reveals the oedipal struggle, mythologized as a fight to the death between father and son, to be a more mundane psychosocial system for perpetuating patriarchal power.

In a brilliant reprise of John Irwin's influential psychoanalytic reading of the novel, Carolyn Porter demonstrates how Sutpen's crisis brings into focus the mechanism that perpetuates patriarchal power. Porter argues that Sutpen's crisis is not only an instance of the Freudian oedipal struggle in which the son must take the father's place, but

> the very *model* of that dilemma itself. In other words, it is not only that Sutpen "incorporates into himself the patriarchal ideal . . . in much the same way" that the generalized Freudian "mechanism" demands of all sons who would be fathers, but that this mechanism is precisely what is set in relief as the operating rule of patriarchal authority when the boy Sutpen is portrayed as literally incorporating "the patriarchal ideal."

The representation of Sutpen's trauma constitutes an abstracted model because it "systematically foregrounds the very distinction between the 'personal father' and the 'mastery of fatherhood'" on which the mechanism depends.[43] The son's task is to "overcome the mastery of the personal father while maintaining the mastery of fatherhood" so that the goal of taking the father's place can remain valuable.[44] By "demanding that the son 'internalize' as his 'superego' an impersonal image, the patriarchal model thus ensures that the 'mastery of fatherhood' itself will remain secure." Moreover, the preservation of the impersonal indicates "not only the 'internalization' but the very emergence of the 'figure of mastery,' what Lacan designates as the 'Law' of the 'Father.'"[45] In other words, this scene shows how patriarchy is perpetuated through the unconscious processes of the Oedipus complex and how the subject is accommodated to the Name-of-the-Father.

Significantly, in Faulkner's account, oedipal processes do not involve a struggle over the mother; normative masculinity is signaled instead by the possession of slaves, land, and capital—by control of the mode of production. If masculine identity is defined through the economy, then economic standing is similarly defined according to the terms of idealized masculinity since Sutpen's obsession with establishing a line of descent indicates that wealth alone cannot confer social standing. The material aspects of class, in other words, are embedded within the symbolic system of paternal Law and effected by way of the dominant fiction of the family. The preservation of the abstract figure of mastery serves as the mechanism through which masculinity "denies" subjective lack.[46]

The planter's *patriarchal* power is explicitly defined in relation to the class-race structure of the antebellum South.[47] America's capitalist economy, embodied by the leisured planter who "spent most of the afternoon . . . in a barrel stave hammock between two trees, with his shoes off and a nigger who . . . did nothing else but fan him and bring him drinks" had been gradually impressing its terms upon Sutpen's "innocent" consciousness prior to his interview with the slave at the plantation door (282). This social structure does not penetrate Sutpen's consciousness, however, until he experiences discrimination personally:

> When he was a child he didn't listen to the vague and cloudy tales of Tidewater splendor that penetrated even his mountains . . . and when he became a boy he didn't listen to them because there was nothing in sight to compare and gauge the tales by . . . and when he got to be a youth and curiosity itself exhumed the tales which he did not know he had heard and speculated about them, he was interested . . . but without envy or regret, because . . . it had never once occurred to him that any man should take any such blind accident as [luck of rich birth] as authority or warrant to look down at others, any others. So he had hardly heard of such a world until he fell into it. (277–78)

In other words, what Sutpen discovers in a "flash" he had been discerning gradually, if unconsciously. Before the slave has even finished telling Sutpen to use the back door, the boy is revisiting and reevaluating his past in his mind's eye (286–87). The boy Sutpen's delayed understanding of his class inferiority, despite ample exposure to information, also follows the Freudian trajectory of a boy's acceptance of the "fact" of women's castration through witnessing the primal scene. Just as I argued in chapter 2 that Freud's primal scene represents and compresses the gradual process by which the boy internalizes ideologies of sexual difference, so here the plantation door scene dramatically represents how the white boy internalizes a subject position within the ideologies of class difference.[48] The individual mechanism of patriarchy that Porter delineates is nestled within a cultural context saturated with corresponding images of class, race, and masculinity.

In one striking aspect, Sutpen's formative drama does not seem to fit Freud's classic primal scene. The plantation manor "scene" does not appear to be a dramatic, visual crisis: Sutpen is a central participant in a two-person dynamic between himself and the slave, rather than a voyeuristic observer in a triangulated configuration. But it so happens that the scene is triangulated and specular in two different ways. First, the planter, who is not actually there, is all the more present for having the black slave stand in for him. Sutpen fantasizes that the planter is watching him; he imagines that

> the man who did not even have to wear the shoes he owned, whom the laughter which the balloon [his imaginative figure for the slave]

> held barricaded and protected from such as he, looked out from whatever invisible place he (the man) happened to be at the moment, at the boy outside the barred door in his patched garments and splayed bare feet. (293)

The planter's very absence signals his function as the symbolic father and Sutpen's fantasy that he is the surveillant subject who knows.[49] The black slave performs the symbolic labor of representing the gap between the planter and the boy.

The second triangle is constituted by a splitting within Sutpen himself that occurs at the moment of the trauma, so that there is the slave and the two Thomas Sutpens: "[B]efore the monkey nigger who came to the door had finished saying what he did, he [Sutpen] seemed to kind of dissolve and a part of him turn and rush back through the two years they had lived there" (286–87). Through a newly formed double consciousness, Sutpen sees himself as the black slave sees him and as the white man would see him. He actually imagines that he is looking out at himself from within the head of the slave:

> The nigger was just another balloon face slick and distended with that mellow loud and terrible laughing so that he did not dare to burst it, looking down at him from within the half closed door during that instant in which, before he knew it, something in him had escaped and—he unable to close the eyes of it—was looking out from within the balloon face. (292–93)

Seeing himself through the eyes of others who adjudge him with "amused contempt and pity," Sutpen experiences the Du Boisian double consciousness associated with African American subjectivity.

Displacing Class onto Blackness

If Sutpen's primal scene shows that he comes to identify with normative masculinity in order to compensate for his own class castration, it does not explicitly indicate that he displaces his lack onto the image of blackness. Faulkner repeatedly emphasizes that Sutpen's resentment is toward the wealthy ruling class and not toward the black slaves themselves, although the slaves are the visible representatives of the white planter power. Immediately following the slave's rebuff, Sutpen mentally reviews several occasions on which black slaves stood in for white owners. For example, he suddenly realizes that when a black coachman had practically run over his sister and he had thrown clods of dirt at the carriage "that it had not been the nigger coachman that he threw at at all" (288). This scenario blends into a memory of his father reporting that he and his cronies had "whupped one of Pettibone's niggers," and when the boy asked which one and what he had done to deserve it, the father could only repeat that the black man belonged to a white man: "Hell fire, that goddamn son of a bitch Pettibone's nigger" (289). In fact, the narrative repeatedly stresses that blacks are *not* of concern: "[Y]ou knew that you could hit them [the slaves]. . . . But you did not want to, because they (the niggers) were not it" (287). "*But I can shoot him.* (Not the monkey nigger. It was not the nigger anymore than it had been the nigger that his father had helped to whip that night" (292). "[T]he rich man (not the nigger) must have been seeing him all the time" (293). "*The nigger never give me a chance to tell him what it was and so he (not the nigger now either) won't know it*" (296). This parenthetical tic insisting that it is "not the nigger" suggests that blacks are always in the line of sight, but thought to matter not at all. Such constant awareness of something, the significance of which is repeatedly disavowed, discursively enacts the place of blackness in the South's racialized ideology.

As Snead notes, until Quentin and Shreve factor in the missing quantity of blackness, the story as it has been passed down makes no sense:

> The "shadows" and "ghosts" of Rosa's narrative are the blacks that narrative precision (actually "*im*precision") has rendered invisible, and whose invisibility finally thwarts all efforts to understand the "why" of Sutpen's life. . . . The repetition of blacks' absence makes the exactly transmitted narrative incredible until Quentin and Shreve, as a last resort, restore the black, whose import as repeated absence everyone had overlooked all along.[50]

Quentin's father says as much: "Yes, Judith, Bon, Henry, Sutpen: all of them. They are there, yet something is missing; . . . you bring them together in the proportions called for, but nothing happens" (124). The topic of race and, more specifically, miscegenation (in cases that threaten to "pollute" lines of inheritance) is unspeakable and incomprehensible in Sutpen's time; it requires the relatively historical perspective of Shreve and Quentin. Sutpen cannot reveal aloud the aspect of his first wife that "voided and frustrated the central motivation of his entire design," even when he seeks reassurance from General Compson about having put her aside (328). The whites' inability to see the relevance of blackness to the story is symptomatic of a collective belief that denies the relation between whites and blacks—a denial represented in the text by the "failure to recognize" the blood relation between Bon and the Sutpen.[51] In other words, the "narrational regimen," as Snead terms it, that repeatedly omits the crucial relations between blacks and whites, all the while seeming to "see" blacks, mimics the chimera of a racial epistemology that relies on vision to detect the illusory difference between "black blood" and "white blood."

The narrative's missing term of blackness, which signals both the categorical indeterminacy and cultural instability of race, is matched by the vagaries of Sutpen's "design." Sutpen's design is the condensate with which he emerges from the crucible of the primal plantation scene. The composition of Sutpen's design remains, however, beyond definite knowledge, and—like Henry's reason for killing Bon—subject to various, if overlapping, definitions. General Compson rambles that it is "Sutpen's fierce and overweening vanity or desire for magnificence or for vindication or whatever it was" (43–44). Sutpen's design has a "secret end" which no one knows (44). Rosa conjectures that "what [Sutpen] fled from must have been some opposite of respectability too dark to talk about" (16). But if, as General Compson learns, the design's intent is "the vindication of a past affront" (62), its content is most often said to include a wife. For example, Sutpen says that to accomplish his design he "should require money, a house, a plantation, slaves, a family—incidentally of course, a wife" (329). But though he proclaims the wife incidental, she is clearly instrumental since she alone (in the case of the first wife) makes an "ironic delusion" (328) of his aims despite the fact that he has acquired the other necessary items. Rosa also realizes that a wife provides Sutpen with something he needs more than upper-class trappings. She says it is not that Sutpen

> wanted to be [a gentleman], or even be taken for one. No. That was not necessary since all he would need would be Ellen's and our father's names on a wedding license (or any other patent of respectability) that people could look at and read just as he would have wanted our father's (or any other reputable man's) signature on a note of hand because our father knew who his father was in Tennessee and who his grandfather had been in Virginia and our neighbors and the people we lived among knew that we knew and we knew they knew we knew. (15)

And Mr. Compson backs up Rosa's claim that Sutpen needed the legitimacy conferred by marrying the daughter of a reputable man: "In fact, Miss Rosa was righter than she knew: he did want, not the anonymous wife and the anonymous children, but the two names, the stainless wife and the unimpeachable father-in-law, on the license, the patent" (59). Marriage is spoken of in the language of commerce, in terms of money and contracts, patents and licenses—a vocabulary that lays bare the skeleton of a kinship Law based on the exchange of women that underlies the fiction of romantic love and family. Through "the shield of a virtuous woman"—whom, it goes without saying, must be white—Sutpen will establish affiliations of kinship that enable him to compensate for his own obscure origins and accrue status for his name (13). As a player in the game of the Name-of-the-Father—that is, having conjoined the actual and symbolic fathers—Sutpen will be able to restore a sense of masculine sufficiency. Sutpen's design depends on, even if it does not end with, the right wife—to be obtained through contractual and economic exchange between men.[52]

Sutpen does not conform to the dominant fiction of the family so much through the psychic ties of oedipal affection as through a perversely literal desire to observe the Law of Kinship. He obeys the letter of paternal Law rather than its spirit, designing his family according to a prescribed formula of economic exchange that is not cloaked in the fantasy and fiction of romantic love. Devoid of compassion and affection, Sutpen conceives of his familial transactions "like the ingredients of pie and cake and once you had measured them and balanced them and mixed them and put them into the oven it was all finished and nothing but pie or cake could come out" (328). His dogmatic approach to building alliances of kinship according to the dictates of white paternal Law allows Sutpen to deny familial relations in abandoning his first wife and child. This literal adherence to the father's name, as it operated in the slaveholding South, dictated "the logical steps by which he had arrived at a result absolutely and forever incredible" (328–29).

Although Sutpen's design depends on establishing the social currency of his name through the operations of kinship Law, his design is not complete until he anchors a dynasty with that name. His own poor class standing is signaled by the absence of information surrounding his "obscure origin." Like many slaves, "he didn't know just where his father had come from" nor "within a year on either side just how old he was" (278, 283). So to compensate for his "dark" origins and rootless present, conditions all too characteristic of the natal alienation of slavery, he tries to establish himself as a genealogical point of origin, a primal father. But, as we have seen, Sutpen's desired object, a white heir, is beyond his grasp; the twisted racial logic of his will to paternal power renders his family "doomed" and "cursed" to destroy itself (17, 20). As Snead writes, "racial separation destroys rather than creates order."[53] So Sutpen's design, the product of his traumatic discovery of lack, remains not only unarticulated but unfulfilled. And as that object which the subject imagines to be fully satisfying, yet which is inevitably beyond satisfaction, Sutpen's design is Sutpen's desire.

The object of Sutpen's desire arises from the trauma of differentiation. The pivotal role of sexual differentiation in the discourses of psychoanalysis is, in *Absalom,* supplanted by a class differentiation experienced through the dominant fiction of gender. The class lack that interpellates Sutpen at the plantation manor door dissolves his prior masculine sufficiency. He discovers, in a sense, that his penis is not equal to the phallus. He disavows the knowledge of this "castration" by projecting it onto blacks, just as the male disavows subjective lack by projecting it onto feminine subjectivity. In Sutpen's psychic process of disavowal, race stands in for class, and Sutpen's desire for social status and masculine sufficiency manifests itself as an obsession with whiteness. The process whereby race is substituted for class bears relation to the mechanism of substitution that Freud says is integral to fetishism. Freud's fetishistic male is able simultaneously to maintain belief in women's castration and to repress such knowledge through a process of substitution:

> It is not true that, after the child has made his observation of the woman, he has preserved unaltered his belief that women have a phallus. He has retained that belief, but he has also given it up. . . . Yes, in his mind the woman *has* got a penis, in spite of everything; but this penis is no longer the same as it was before. Something else has taken its place, has been appointed its substitute, as it were, and now inherits the interest which was formerly directed to its predecessor.[54]

But since Sutpen is in the process of disavowing his own lack, not that of women or blacks, he makes a substitution for *his* missing part. To preserve belief in his own phallic sufficiency, Sutpen substitutes whiteness for his low socioeconomic status, obscure origins, and alienated labor. Whiteness becomes the fetish allowing him to preserve the image of masculine sufficiency "that the little boy once believed in and—for reasons familiar to us—does not want to give up."[55] The obsession with the racial purity of his family's line that characterizes Sutpen's design displays the "extraordinary increase" of interest typical of fetishes because "the horror of castration has set up a memorial to itself in creation of this substitute."[56] And, like the fetish that serves as "a token of triumph over the threat of castration and a protection against it," Sutpen's fetishized whiteness is meant to surmount and protect against his class lack.[57] Just as Silverman showed that "traditional masculinity emerges . . . as a fetish for covering over the castration upon which male subjectivity is grounded," Sutpen's specifically white masculinity emerges as a fetish that defends against the economic lack upon which his subjectivity is grounded.

If whiteness is a fetish that covers over the lack characteristic of subjectivity in general, then the actual condition of being is, within these terms, blackness. Such a common blackness is one way to understand Shreve's final, enigmatic, and confusingly retroactive vision of a future in which all inhabitants of the western hemisphere—whether black or white in appearance—will have derived from black blood:

> I think that in time the Jim Bonds are going to conquer the western hemisphere. Of course it wont quite be in our time and of course as they spread toward the poles they will bleach out again like the rabbits and the birds do, so they wont show up so sharp against the snow. But it will still be Jim Bond; and so in a few thousand years, I who regard you will also have sprung from the loins of African kings. (471)

This vision of a bleak future race simultaneously sprung from African kings and degenerate idiots suggests Faulkner's ambivalence toward the loss of the South's myth of white masculine sufficiency. *Absalom* sounds the modernist lament for the humanist subject even as it exposes the racist fictions on which it had rested. Unlike Mitchell's Scarlett who, despite her unreconstructed racism, refuses to mourn the past and looks toward an industrial New South, Faulkner's novel—to a vastly greater degree—confesses the wrongs of slavery but imagines no alternative.[58]

The next chapter considers another history of slavery told through the frame of family and kinship. Like *Absalom, Absalom!* Toni Morrison's *Beloved* retells the history of slavery through a collective narrative composed of individual memories. Morrison's novel, however, voices perspectives largely absent from Faulkner: the feminine, maternal, and African American.

CHAPTER 5

Rites and Responsibilities: Toni Morrison and Object Relations

In the relatively few years since its publication, Toni Morrison's *Beloved* has generated much critical comment. As Barbara Christian notes, "[T]he number of critical essays published on this novel rivals those written on only a few other contemporary African American novels."[1] Christian outlines several critical trends, including psychoanalytic readings of the mother/daughter relationship at the center of the novel and African Americanist studies of the novel's revision of the history of American slavery. Christian argues, however, that neither of these approaches explores how Morrison fashions a literary "fixing ceremony" from the traditional African belief in "ancestor worship" in order to heal the "psychic rupture" caused by the "holocaust" of the Middle Passage. The novel re-members those lost in the Middle Passage—in the double sense of recovering their memory and remembering their embodiedness—in accordance with the West African worldview that remembering and paying tribute to the dead is critical to a sense of "personal being and, beyond that, of the beingness of the group."[2] Although Christian aims to distinguish this Africanistic reading from the others, I want to consider the connections among these three ways of reading: a West African cosmological perspective, a psychoanalytic reading of the mother/daughter relationship, and an African Americanist study of the novel's historic revision of slavery.[3] It is, of course, the novel's genius that it tangles these themes so inextricably as to join continents, cosmologies, and eras. Christian's own terms of analysis dovetail with psychoanalytic and historical interpretations: she repeatedly characterizes the novel as an exploration of the "psychic ruptures," "psychic horror," and "psychic wounds" caused by the repressed American holocaust of slavery and the Middle Passage. Because Morrison thematizes the relationship between individual subjectivity (the psychic) and collective history (the holocaust of slavery), the novel addresses one of the structuring tensions between psychoanalytic and African Americanist discourses. In other words, Morrison explores the double consciousness inherent in the fraught relationships between memory and history, individual and collective, trauma and politics.[4]

I want to begin this discussion of how the novel represents the relationship between individual and collective identity and between the shared history, but individual experience, of American slavery by way of Morrison's comments about the political significance of *absence* to her literary project. Morrison suggests that it is precisely the pointed absence of African Americans from canonical nineteenth-century American literature that shapes the tradition's concern with race. She writes that

> invisible things are not necessarily "not there"; that a void may be empty, but it is not a vacuum. In addition certain absences are so stressed, so ornate, so planned, they call attention to themselves; arrest us with intentionality and purpose like neighborhoods that are defined by the populations held away from them.[5]

Analyzing the mechanisms of exclusion through which a normative whiteness is constructed will, she suggests, yield the traces of blackness, the "ghosts in the machine," that drive "the choices, the language, the structure—the meaning of so much American literature" (379). If the representational absence of African Americans effectively structures American literature, it is telling that Morrison describes her own writing as an attempt to depict invisibility, to describe absence, and to write the shape of silence. Rather than simply filling in the raced omissions of American literature, Morrison outlines the absences effected by America's ideology of whiteness. Through "the silent center" of Pecola's self in *The Bluest Eye*, the already long-gone neighborhood that begins *Sula,* or Hagar's uncanny missing navel in *Song of Solomon,* Morrison's narratives center on meaningful negative spaces, representational echoes that signify not only the past silences of literature, but the losses of African American experience and history.

Morrison's novel *Beloved* figures the multiple absences wrought by America's history of slavery in the liminal presence of a ghost. Although the ghost, Beloved, indicates the baby girl murdered by her escaped slave mother to prevent the girl's return to slavery, metaphorically she is also, as Marianne Hirsch notes, "memory itself, she is the story of slavery, the memory of slavery come back to haunt the community."[6] The ghost functions as a floating signifier of slavery's effects, representing Sethe's killed daughter, the psychic reality of Sethe's "unspeakable" memories of slavery, and slavery's legacy to the nation. Beloved's capacity to embody both a collective history of slavery and an individual child provides a mechanism for mapping out an African American community's individual relationships to a common past. Shape-shifting from specific person to cultural concept, Beloved makes the collective history of slavery intelligible on the level of subjective experience; her mutability binds the personal to the political, individual desire to the social symbolic, and memory to history. The ghost's symbolic resonance also allows Morrison an indirection useful for rendering representation's approximate relationship to the experience of slavery—that is, to question the possibility of direct historic knowledge within the novel's form. As Valerie Smith has noted, to write about slavery as the collective past of African Americans, to represent history and individual suffering in language is always to risk eliding the gap between the lived experience of individuals and representation.[7]

The tensions between individual and collective, history and memory, are played out in the shifting address of the word "beloved." In the dictionary, "beloved" is classified first as an adjective and only second as a noun. As the title of Morrison's novel, its sense as a modifier calls attention, before the first sentence, to an absence—the absence of the thing it modifies: who or what is beloved? The beloved one is, indeed, missing since the term refers to the daughter Sethe killed to keep her from a life of slavery. But as the name of the murdered girl's ghost, "Beloved" also designates the presence that concentrates the energy of her absence. Thus, the word describes the condition of the girl: she is beloved by her mother, and yet it is the girl's proper name (it is the only one she is called in the novel). Named for her significance to Sethe, the girl's being short-circuits back to her relation to her mother. Her status follows the mother's condition, so to speak, and she lacks a center or self in her own right.

The convergence in Beloved's name of her self and her meaning for her mother signals that although the ghost is Sethe's killed daughter with her own—albeit not fully developed—subjectivity, she is also a figure of the self-division Sethe experiences in relation to her unspeakable past. As Sethe endures a fragmentation of self, a radical lack of agency enforced by the system of slavery, she incorporates her daughter into her own identity. Sethe lays claim to her daughter as a function of her own desire, a claim staked most forcefully in the act of killing Beloved so that the slavers will not "dirty my best thing" (251). The difficulty of establishing boundaries of the self, signaled here by Sethe's struggle to balance autonomy with maternal responsibility, represents the problem posed to subjective integrity by slavery. In other words, enslavement problematizes the production of bodily and subjective coherence necessary to engender both individual desire and intimate relations with others. Sethe's paralyzing possession by traumatic memories, even after abolition, signals a continuing split within her self experienced as an invasion of something Other. This structure of traumatic memory as alienation from within is doubled by Beloved's haunting of Sethe. Once an infant whose survival depended on her mother, the ghostly Beloved is a separate being who nevertheless claims Sethe's existence as her own. Sethe's relation to her past, then, is figured as an inadequately individuated relationship between mother and daughter. And the struggle to establish subjective agency in the wake of slavery's historic trauma is akin to the process of individuation between mother and daughter.

Representing the historic trauma of slavery through the vicissitudes of a mother-daughter relationship, *Beloved* forges a link between the feminine and the collective identity. Even as the narrative bears down on questions of Sethe's subjectivity as an African American woman, mother, and former slave, the personal circles back to the communal. Another twist to the shifting address of the name "Beloved" delineates this movement from the individual to the social. Sethe takes the name Beloved from what she remembers of the traditional rite spoken at the girl's funeral:

> She had not thought to ask [the engraver] and it bothered her still—that for twenty minutes, a half hour say, she could have had the whole thing, every word she heard the preacher say at the funeral

> (and all there was to say surely) engraved on her baby's headstone: Dearly Beloved. But what she got, settled for, was the one word that mattered. (5)

This seems to imply that the words spoken over the grave, "Dearly Beloved," are addressed to the dead. In fact, the funeral rite (which is not actually reproduced in the novel) addresses not the dead, but the mourners of the dead: "Dearly Beloved, we are gathered here to mourn. . . ." So the address "Beloved" shifts syntactically away from the absent child who is a figure of the past to the community of former slaves who survive her. The girl and the community are linked by this shared address, which shuttles between specific horrors of slavery and their collective legacy.

The endless deferral of presence suggested by Beloved's name marks the multitude of losses wrought by America's history of slavery. As the shape of desire left in slavery's wake, this signifying absence propels the narrative—like the baby ghost shifts the furniture in 124 Bluestone Road, or the otherworldly girl drives Paul D from the upstairs bedroom, to the keeping room, to the outside shed, and finally away from the house altogether. The syntactic layers of the word "beloved" mark the uneven continuities between past and present, self and other, individual and collective.

Symbolizing both a particular person (Sethe's daughter) and a common body (the sixty million who died in the middle passage), Beloved embodies a tension between specificity and representativeness in writing on slavery that goes back to slave narratives. Slave narrators grappled with representing as *universal* the inhumanity of slavery and the humanity of blacks through *individual* accounts of their development of a recognizably American identity. Significantly, slavery violated constructs of gender and slave narratives strained to reconstruct normative gender identity. Paradigmatic male narrators such as Frederick Douglass represent the journey from slavery to freedom as running a parallel course to the attainment of an idealized masculinity. His escape is justified and enabled because he acquires literacy, economic self-sufficiency, and pugilistic prowess; his self-representation satisfies the foundational American ideal of individualism in the literary tradition of Emersonian self-reliance.

Following this literary and ideological model of self-reliance posed different problems for former slave women negotiating the gap between conditions of their lives and normative femininity. Slavery precluded black women from conforming to models of feminine sexuality and maternity—less acceptable literary topics than the loss of control of one's labor and intellectual growth. How, then, could women testify to slavery's violations and violence without implying their failure to satisfy the terms by which femininity and, therefore, their very humanity were determined? Moreover, women's more *relational* identity and material circumstance, stemming in part from conditions of childbearing and motherhood, means that the autobiographical project itself, as it has been defined in terms of individual self-creation, might be an inherently gendered form not suited to women's experience or modes of self-definition.

Slave women's lives were unrepresentable, not only because the forms of victimization they experienced composed an unspeakable topic, but because violations of normative femininity were sometimes the result of their own *choices*. In her slave narrative, Harriet Jacobs discusses her relationship with a white man who was not her master and to whom she was not married, as if desire played no part. She represents her decision to engage in this relationship as a means of escaping the sexual coercion of her master. She insists that her own escape from slavery, which forced her to leave her children for a number of years, was a form of maternal self-sacrifice intended to force the children's father to free them. Of course, Jacobs's choices were severely constrained by her slave status and her stated motivations were, undoubtedly, central. Nevertheless, she feels compelled to justify her limited autonomy only in terms of sexual purity and maternal duty. Thus, women slave narrators such as Jacobs developed narrative strategies of indirection, ellipsis, and allegory; the unspeakable desires of slave women compose another set of absences in the history of slavery.[8]

Like many women's slave narratives, *Beloved* contains a silent center of violated gender norms: a mother's murder of her own child. By contrast, however, the novel's narrative movement is precisely the work of reconstructing and articulating the effects of this silence.[9] Notwithstanding Douglass's equation of physical escape and the construction of a free identity, in *Beloved* slavery continues to inhibit agency even after escape and Emancipation. The former slaves inhabit freedom cautiously—as if they have it on temporary loan. Legal freedom does not guarantee self-possession since "[f]reeing yourself was one thing; claiming ownership of that freed self was another" (95). So the term "Reconstruction" signifies a process of psychic—as well as civic—recovery, of processing memory and history in order to build a habitable self and society.[10] Like Sethe, the members of the community must acknowledge their intimate relations to the violences of the past before they can build connections with each other. As Smith writes, "There is no journeying forward without a journey back"; remembering and telling the secret stories of past abuse is a "narrative process that leads to self-knowledge because it forces an acceptance of the past."[11] Because Beloved's death is the ever-present, but untold, story that spurs the former slaves to tell their own histories in slavery, Beloved figures as the portal between their slave past and their free—if scarred—present, between impotence and agency.[12]

The difficulty of this "journey back" is figured centrally by Sethe's relationship to Beloved, the daughter she killed and the figure of her past enslavement. At the outset of the novel, Sethe has not incorporated her past into the present; the past insinuates itself regardless: "She worked hard to remember as close to nothing as was safe. Unfortunately her brain was devious" (6). As long as Sethe is trying not to remember she is always and only remembering: "Her brain was not interested in the future. Loaded with the past and hungry for more, it left her no room to imagine, let alone plan for the next day" (70). The insistent irruption into consciousness of the details of slavery deadens Sethe to the present and frightens her from imagining a future. Not only is Sethe still psychically bound by slavery, she constantly re-experiences it physically. The *thought* of loving Beloved elicits the *sensation* of the cool tombstone Sethe laid against while trading sex to the engraver (4–5). Sensory perceptions that shut down at the time of Beloved's death (of color, of the preacher's words at the funeral, of the sequence of events surrounding Beloved's death) are pieced together only later. This piecemeal reconstruction of memories is paralleled by a piecing together of her body; Sethe needs to be bathed in parts to heal the wounds of her escape.[13] By fragmenting the coherence of both memory and body, slavery impedes self-knowledge. Sethe must integrate her memories of slavery and the murder before she can engage her own desire to plan a free future and form meaningful relationships with her surviving daughter, Denver, with Paul D, and with her community.[14]

Sethe's failure to incorporate the absences of the past into her present life is signaled not only by her dislocating memories and disintegrating body, but by her paralyzing silence on the "unspeakable" subject of Beloved's death. Although she does not speak of the past to others, she relives it daily in her head. When Sethe stops keeping strict silence, she can only explain herself ineffectually. She compulsively tries to justify her actions to an unforgiving Beloved, and "circles the subject" when she tells Paul D about Beloved's death. Sethe's inability to articulate a self in relation to her actions as a mother is, moreover, characterized through the merging of her identity with Beloved's. The dynamics of their relationship reflect an uncanny doubling and inadequately differentiated subjectivity. When Sethe thinks of why she killed Beloved rather than see her recaptured and raised in slavery she thinks, "The best thing she was, was her children. Whites might dirty *her* all right, but not her best thing—the part of her that was clean" (251). And Beloved says Sethe's face is hers: "I am not separate from her there is no place where I stop her face is my own and I want to be there in the place where her face is and to be looking at it too" (210). Pronouns as well as body parts are intermingled; the blurred boundaries of identity are inseparable from the lack of bodily boundaries. When Beloved's ghost materializes in the flesh, Sethe gives over herself so completely that her own flesh wastes away as Beloved fattens. Sethe withdraws further from an active life and the community: "Whatever is going on outside my door ain't for me. The world is in this room. This here's all there is and all there needs to be" (183).

Sethe's struggle between merging with and individuating from Beloved suggests the difficulty of articulating desire from the maternal position, a position immeasurably complicated by conditions of slavery. Defining herself solely as a maternal body, Sethe cannot find her own desire or the boundaries of her self.[15] In order to conceive of herself other than as a function of her children, Sethe must question "the hierarchy of motherhood over selfhood on which her life had rested."[16] The communal exorcism of Beloved at the narrative's conclusion suggests that Sethe will come to see herself as separate from her children as she finds a way to live with the losses of the past. The exorcism, which signals the community's tacit decision to withhold judgment about Sethe's actions as a mother, allows Sethe to (re)integrate her body, memory, and identity and allows the community to (re)unite around the effort to heal the historic trauma of slavery. Paul D assists at the birth of Sethe's selfhood, telling her, "You your best thing, Sethe." And Sethe is able to use this interpellation to name a self—specifically, to articulate a self in relation to an other through her interlocutory iteration, "Me?"

The Experience of Memory

Although it is commonly understood that *Beloved* is about the experience of American slavery, the novel is set during Reconstruction so that we "see" slavery only through the lens of characters' memories. By doubly filtering the representation of slavery, Morrison highlights the inherently mediated nature of historic knowledge—even as she emphasizes the crucial role such partial knowledge plays in charting a course for contemporary life. Just as the characters understand slavery through the medium of memory, we know it through the medium of history, the collective memory of culture. The narrative structurally enacts the slippery substance and flow of memory by destabilizing the spatial opposition between absence and presence, collapsing the temporal distinction between past and present, and erasing the subjective differentiation between self and other. Although memories are a form of mental representation of the past, in their vivid recurrence, they can seem like actual experience. Memories of slavery bleed into the present to influence the present lives of the former slaves—a process analogous to the way that the legacy of slavery shapes our contemporary culture.

Sethe's involuntary possession by "devious" memories that revisit her with the force of actual occurrence corresponds to the pathology of trauma "which consists . . . solely in the *structure of its experience* or reception: the event is not assimilated or experienced fully at the time, but only belatedly, in its repeated *possession* of the one who experiences it."[17] Because a traumatic event is first experienced only after an initial forgetting, traumatic remembering is, in a sense, a form of experience; it is "the literal return of the event against the will of the one it inhabits."[18] The experiential force and literalness of traumatic memory, of "rememory," is evidenced in Sethe's insistence that images of slavery persist as dangerously tangible entities:

> I was talking about time. It's so hard for me to believe in it. . . . I used to think it was my rememory. . . . But it's not. Places, places are still there. . . . What I remember is a picture floating around out there outside my head. I mean, even if I don't think it, even if I die, the picture of what I did, or knew, or saw is still out there. . . . Someday you'll be walking down the road and you hear something or see something going on. . . . And you think it's you thinking it up. . . . But no. It's when you bump into a rememory that belongs to

> somebody else. . . . The picture is still there and what's more, if you go there—you who never was there—if you go there and stand in the place where it was, it will happen again; it will be there for you, waiting for you. (35–36)

This booby trap of a memory actually alters dimensions of space and time; a reality inheres in the image that

> cannot be interpreted, simply, as a distortion of reality, nor as the lending of unconscious meaning to a reality it wishes to ignore, nor as the repression of what once was wished . . . [I]t is not a pathology, that is, of falsehood or displacement of meaning, but of history itself.[19]

In other words, Sethe's memories bear a materiality that cannot be relegated to a realm of *psychic* reality (of projection, desire, or fantasy) once-removed from *social* reality. And if you can be trapped by *other* people's memories, then even damage done to an individual subject carries a certain historic force. The physical presence of these memory-images is the cultural work slavery performs, even after abolition.

If the delay in knowledge of an event that characterizes the psychic structure of trauma is similar, as Cathy Caruth argues, to history's belated and mediated relation to the "truth" of experience, then *Beloved* explicitly links the pathology of individual trauma and the problem of inherently belated historic knowledge of slavery.[20] This linkage suggests not only that there is a structural similarity between individual trauma and history, but that the subjective perspective is crucial to understanding the history of slavery. Dori Laub and Shoshana Felman argue that the core experience marked by trauma's initial absence of knowledge can be approached only through personal testimony:

> The victim's narrative—the very process of bearing witness to massive trauma—does indeed begin with someone who testifies to an absence, to an event that has not yet come into existence, in spite of the overwhelming and compelling nature of the reality of its occurrence. While historic evidence to the event which constitutes the trauma may be abundant and documents in vast supply, the trauma . . . has not been truly witnessed yet. . . . The emergence of the narrative which is being listened to—and heard—is, therefore, the process and the place wherein the cognizance, the "knowing" of the event is given birth to. The listener, therefore, is a party to the creation of knowledge *de novo*.[21]

When the traumatic event is "not a story to pass on," the site of knowledge shifts to the *process* of narration, rather than to a body of evidence produced by the telling. This narrative process aligns the production of history with the formation of identity: "The narrator herself does not know any longer who she was, except *through her testimony.* . . . In itself, this knowledge *does not exist,* it can only *happen* through the testimony: it cannot be separated from it."[22] Psychoanalysis's claim that giving testimony is crucial to consolidating identity after trauma dovetails with the emphasis in African American literary theory on the role of storytelling in recovering a usable past for black identity and community.[23]

If giving testimony is the "journey back" that will consolidate Sethe's identity in the wake of slavery's trauma, the therapeutic process is frustrated by the doubleness of her maternal subjectivity. Her self is split by her child's claim to it. Social proscriptions of maternity frustrate her ability to assign meaning to her choices as a mother. Both inhibited and compelled by her own guilt and by the condemnation of others, Sethe refuses to speak of the past, yet cannot stop explaining her actions. In fact, she has erected a monument to her eternally interrupted explanation: the tombstone with the fragmented message telling her daughter she is beloved and naming her daughter Beloved ("For another ten minutes could she have gotten the whole thing?"). To Sethe the epitaph is apostrophic, a calling to and a naming of the child, the beginning of the explanation for why Sethe killed her.[24] But though she claims to want to soothe Beloved with explanations, Sethe continually stimulates her:

> [Denver] had begun to notice that even when Beloved was quiet, dreamy, minding her own business, Sethe got her going again. Whispering, muttering some justification, some bit of clarifying information to Beloved to explain what it had been like, and why, and how come. It was as though Sethe didn't really want forgiveness given; she wanted it refused. (252)

Locked in the circular logic of justifying an act that is loving and violent, violating and protective, Sethe welcomes the haunting to forestall the finality of Beloved's death. Sethe's perseverating explanation to Beloved traps her in the past and cuts her off from her network of relationships. She tolerates the haunting of the baby ghost in her house and when Beloved returns in the flesh, Sethe gives over her life to her daughter's "presence": "Beloved ate up her life, took it, swelled up with it, grew taller on it. And the older woman yielded it up without a murmur" (250). Each sets her account of violence, abuse, and abandonment against the other's.

In "Apostrophe, Animation, and Abortion," Barbara Johnson also argues that the particular relation between maternity and death invites the discursive mode of apostrophe. Analyzing several poems in which the lyric speaker addresses a child not born because the speaker had an abortion, Johnson asks,

> If apostrophe is said to involve language's capacity to give life and human form to something dead or inanimate, what happens when those questions are literalized? What happens when the lyric speaker assumes the responsibility for producing the death in the first place. . . ?[25]

The grammar of this apostrophe, she answers, collapses interpersonal boundaries so that the speaker is "eternally addressed and possessed by the lost, anthropomorphized other" (189). As in the standoff between Sethe and Beloved in 124 Bluestone Road, Johnson notes a suspension of resolution and a lack of individuation between mother and child expressed through metaphors of devouring:

> The speaker's attempt to absolve herself of guilt depends on never forgetting, never breaking the ventriloquism of an apostrophe through which she cannot define her identity otherwise than as the mother eaten alive by the children she never fed. . . . The children are a rhetorical extension of the mother, but she . . . has no existence apart from her relation to them. (192)

The poem's structure of address thus enacts the impossibility of distinguishing between the conflicting claims of mother and child—which is, argues Johnson, the point of undecidability in the conflict over abortion. This lack of clear distinction frustrates the maternal subject's narrative self-construction.

The effect of Sethe's overidentification with Beloved is double-edged: the sense of oneness that led Sethe to kill Beloved compels her, upon Beloved's ghostly return, to sacrifice herself to Beloved's demands. And Beloved, with her two-year-old's needy subjectivity, cannot tolerate her mother's separateness. First killed by Sethe's love, Beloved begins to kill Sethe out of her own infantile desire to possess her mother absolutely. Denver watches the convergence of their positions:

> Her eye was on her mother, for a signal that the thing that was in her was out, and she would kill again. But it was Beloved who made the demands. Anything she wanted she got, and when Sethe ran out of things to give her, Beloved invented desire. . . . The job she started out with, protecting Beloved from Sethe, changed to protecting her mother from Beloved. (240, 243)

Johnson also notes a transposition of mother/child roles in the apostrophes of her lyric speakers. The mother's call to the child echoes back to the mother such that the speaker is "simultaneously eclipsed, alienated, and confused with the addressee. It is already clear that something has happened to the possibility of establishing a clear-cut distinction . . . between subject and object, agent and victim" (189). In Sethe's protective murder of Beloved, the good mother converges with the monstrous—a convergence that is doubled in much recent feminist theory, which outlines something inherently monstrous in the mother-daughter relationship. Largely based on psychoanalytic object relations theory (for which Nancy Chodorow's *The Reproduction of Mothering* serves as the foundational text), feminist critics have "posited that the female self is less individuated then the male self since both are formed in relation to the mother, but the male self has the fact of sexual difference to institute and ensure differentiation."[26] The monstrousness of the mother-daughter relationship lies in the incompleteness of differentiation between the two individuals; mother and daughter are not the same, but neither are their identities wholly separate from each other. Describing this monster as a double-headed being "whose multiple parts are neither totally merged nor totally separate," Jane Gallop asks, "Who is the monster? The mother or the self? The inability to answer that urgent question is certainly tied to the difficulty in separating mother from self. As we have seen, the monster *is* the difficulty."[27] Indeed, who is the monster? The ghost, Beloved, or the murderous mother, Sethe?

Like the poets Johnson considers, Sethe's apostrophic testimony is mired in the intersubjective mother-child relationship that frustrates discrete self-construction. Her finally silent surrender ("without a murmur") cedes the apostrophic position to Beloved. The discursive mode of apostrophe is, Johnson suggests, the purview of the child since language acquisition and subjectivity originate with the demand to the mother following the loss of maternal plenitude. And if language originates in this infantile subject position, there is an inherent difficulty in "elaborating a discursive position other than that of child":

> If apostrophe is structured like demand, and if demand articulates the primal relation to the mother as a relation to the Other, then . . . the figure of apostrophe . . . comes to look like the fantastically intricate history of endless elaborations and displacements of the single cry, "Mama!" The questions these poems are asking, then, is what happens when the poet is speaking *as* a mother, a mother whose cry arises out of—and is addressed to—a dead child? (198–99)

For *Beloved,* the question is not only what happens when Sethe speaks as a mother to her dead child, but also how does her address to Beloved speak to the larger African American community and the sixty million and more dead? How does this mother's attempt to construct an autonomous identity while maintaining a caring relation to her daughter do justice to the broadest questions of African American identity and the shared history of slavery?

That Sethe's murder of Beloved poses a problem for delineating not only her own identity, but the community's ethical codes suggests that the self can come into being only within a social context. Paradoxically, Sethe's desperate attempt to fulfill the role of mother within the constraints of slavery actually violates codes of maternal behavior. Without the support of her community and family, Sethe is suspended in the gap between her failure at Motherhood and her actions as a mother, between societal expectations and the conditions of her particular life. The oxymoron of Sethe's "murderous love" deconstructs the binary of good mother/bad mother and poses the question of what it means to be a good mother in conditions such as slavery. Does the killing represent a supreme act of maternal responsibility or a perverse disregard for Beloved's autonomous existence? When does protection devolve into domination? In posing these questions, the novel places maternity within a specific racial, historical, and national context—thereby countering notions of a transcendent, universal motherhood. The condition of maternity, wherein the child is wholly dependent on the mother, radically problematizes "the relations between subjectivity, autonomy, interconnectedness, responsibility, and gender."[28] As a nexus for these relations, Sethe's story exposes the structures and assumptions of the community's moral system.

Object Relations and Race

A wealth of feminist theory, primarily growing out of the psychoanalytic discourse of object relations, examines how the social meaning and experience of maternity divides gender roles, shapes subjectivity, and constructs ethical codes. This theoretical framework maps out critical issues underlying Sethe's lack of autonomy from her children and the community's opprobrium of Sethe as a mother.

Object relations maintains that a child's subjectivity forms in relation to the primary caretaker, usually the mother, rather than in submission to paternal law. In focusing on the mother-child relationship, object relations departs from Freudian and Lacanian theories, which locate identity formation in the father's disruption of the bond between mother and child, which, ostensibly, sends the child on the way to independence and individuality. Locating identity construction within, rather than at the point of rupture of, the mother-child bond recalibrates theories of identity in several ways. First, object relations grounds "the production of gendered subjectivity in historically specific and socially variable caretaking arrangements," rather than in the transcultural symbolic of Lacan or the oedipal structure of Freud.[29] As a theoretical apparatus sensitive to cultural context, object relations can respond to differences of race, class, and culture—as well as gender—in describing the constitution of subjectivity. Second, in recognizing the significance of the preoedipal phase—that is the relation with the mother—as crucial to individual development, object relations refigures the structure of subjectivity. While Freudian/Lacanian psychoanalyses, as well as dominant modernist and postmodernist discourses, have redrawn humanism's unified subject as split, fragmented, alienated, or constituted through lack, object relations imagines identity as negotiated, multiple, or intersubjective.[30] The individual subject is constituted through and within relationships to others. By reformulating the self as relational rather than autonomous, object relations challenges the Western cultural priority accorded individuality over collectivity and counters the notion that immediate personal connections must be transcended in order to engage in sociopolitical work.[31] Third, by displacing paternal law from its determinate role in subject formation, object relations dethrones the phallus from its sovereign position in symbolic representation. This displacement clears space in the social symbolic for nonphallic representations of desire.

If identity develops out of relation to, rather than splitting by, then we might imagine the subject—in spatial terms—as linked to a web or network of others, rather than as split within itself. This relational, negotiated self, although "historically produced through 'discursive' and ideological formations, nevertheless has a material existence and history in actual human relationships, beginning crucially with those between infant and caretakers at the start of life."[32] The identities of both boys and girls form in proximity to the mother (as primary caretaker), but gender norms differentiate the process. In *The Reproduction of Mothering,* Chodorow argues that boys must learn masculinity by differentiating from the mother as the primary object, while girls learn femininity by identifying with the mother. Because girls become subjects by identifying with rather than against the primary object, the female self is less individuated or separate from others—especially the mother—than the male self.[33] And boys' "repudiation of the primary identification with and dependency on the mother . . . leads to an individuality that stresses . . . difference as denial of commonality, separation as denial of connection."[34] Thus, women experience subjectivity as constituted in relation to others more directly than do men. Object relations' model of a self-in-relation finds a parallel in the "relational, dispersed, collective concept of identity which emerges" in the writings of many contemporary women.[35] Feminist object relations theory, then, has challenged the equation of full subjectivity with autonomy, a definition that grew out of models of masculine development.[36]

In terms of theme and structure, *Beloved* indicates the vicissitudes of developing in relation to the mother. Sethe and Beloved's consuming need for each other displays the "permeable ego boundaries"[37] that can result from gender identification between mother and daughter. The narrative's nonsyntactic passages—reminiscent of Kristeva's presymbolic maternal chora—intertwine the subjectivities of Sethe, Beloved, and Denver. And Sethe's intergenerational relations to other women, such as Baby Suggs, Denver, and even Mrs. Garner, figure centrally—as does the absence Sethe feels for having been deprived of a relationship with her own mother. Anchoring this relational model of identity in specific historical, social, and racial coordinates, *Beloved* works as a specimen text for theorizing the relevance of object relations theory to racial politics. Moreover, as a maternal discourse concerned primarily with Sethe's experience, the text provides a dimension missing in the greater part of psychoanalytic feminism that "can add the female child to the male, allowing women to speak as daughters, [but] has difficulty accounting for the experience and the voice of the adult woman who is a mother."[38] Because the narrative traces the process through which Sethe carves out a space for her own desire apart from her role as a mother, feminist psychoanalytic critics have declared *Beloved* a breakthrough narrative of maternal subjectivity.[39] This maternal voice, moreover, politicizes issues of desire and subjectivity by situating maternity within the historical context of American slavery and Reconstruction. In other words, psychoanalytic critics have suggested that *Beloved* provides the opportunity to ground discourses of feminine and maternal subjectivity in a specific cultural context that takes into account components of identity other than gender alone.[40] Although object relations helps explain the problems of maternal subjectivity presented by the text, *Beloved*'s linking of intersubjective identity to communal identity—within a racially specific historical context—could help extend the parameters of relational subjectivity beyond the individual and the feminine.

In suggesting a relationship between aspects of racial identity and object relations theory, I face not only skepticism about the usefulness and appropriateness of any psychoanalytic discourse to the politics of race, but also charges from psychoanalytic feminists themselves that object relations embraces essentialist, normative conceptions of gender, sexuality, family structure, and parenting roles. Acknowledging such criticism, Elizabeth Abel writes that object relations, "while avoiding the homogeneity of the Lacanian symbolic . . . has tended to homogenize gender by implying that children learn within the family a single uniform masculinity or femininity." She distinguishes, however, between the value of object relations as a theoretical framework and the limited application to which it has been put. Although object relations has, in practice, "confined itself to the Western middle-class nuclear family and has bracketed all variables other than gender," its grounding in the social endows the theoretical apparatus with the capacity to address a range of social and gender relations. The unimaginative positing of two fixed, heterosexual genders arose from the theory's implementation, rather than its intrinsic limitations: "To foreground . . . diverse social arrangements would entail not a revision of this theory but, rather, a fulfillment of its claims to explain" how the construction of a self-in-relation varies with culture, race, class, and historic moment.[41] Similarly, Denise Segura and Jennifer Pierce, authors of "Chicana/o Family Structure and Gender Personality: Chodorow, Familism, and Psychoanalytic Sociology Revisited," argue that object relations has construed the social in the particular terms of an Anglo, middle-class, nuclear family:

> Many Chicana/o scholars have characterized the existence of multiple mothering figures as a distinctive feature of life in Chicana/o families. Yet this feature goes unnoticed in white feminist accounts of "mother-centric" families, most notably in Nancy Chodorow's classic *The Reproduction of Mothering.* Chodorow argues that the development and reproduction of gender identity—that is, of "masculine" and "feminine" personality—arise from a "universal" nuclear family structure in which one heterosexual female parent is primarily responsible for the exclusive mothering of children.[42]

However, these authors also defend the usefulness of object relations as a theoretical framework for analyzing family structure and gender roles in varying cultural and racial contexts:

> [W]e take issue with the complete dismissal of Chodorow's theory that often accompanies such critiques. . . . The usefulness of Chodorow's theoretical framework . . . should not be obscured by the limitations of her empirical account. . . . Chodorow's theory actually provides a useful framework for studying racial and ethnic differences in the acquisition of gender identity because it emphasizes the socially specific context in which mothering takes place.[43]

I am interested not only in how racial and ethnic differences affect the acquisition of gender identity, but in how such differences affect our notions of identity-in-relation. Specifically, I want to think about the links between an individual's relational identity and group identity. Although object relations' model of development has been devised, primarily, in tracking the development of girls and the subjective experience of mothers, both of which were relatively neglected by Freud, we might ask, what are the implications of a relational identity beyond the family? In extrapolating from the interpersonal to the collective, I want to ask if the concept of relational identity is useful for describing the political cohesion of a larger group.

Freud's and Lacan's models of autonomous identity reflect a Western "ideology of individualism" that permeates social structures within and beyond the family. Whereas Johnson's analysis of apostrophic poems explores the unresolvable difficulty of distinguishing absolutely between the competing claims of mother and child, Jessica Benjamin argues that Western society has met this difficulty by negating the claims of the mother while exaggerating, for the child, the value of individuality, independence, and separation. From infancy, an "ideology of individualism" institutes a drive toward separation and autonomy as the task of development. To combat the fear of dependency and in order to appear self-sufficient, the child denies his/her dependency on the primary caretaker, traditionally the mother or another woman:

> The intention is not to do without her [the mother] but to make sure that her alien otherness is either assimilated or controlled, that her own subjectivity nowhere asserts itself in a way that could make his dependency upon her a conscious insult to his sense of freedom.[44]

This denial of dependency requires that the mother have no desire of her own, that she appear selfless, so that the child will not be faced with an unmet need that would ripple the illusion of self-sufficiency. Independence is won at the expense of the mother's recognition as a subject:

> The repression of the initial fusion with the mother is the condition of the construction of the subject. . . . Although she produces and upholds the subject, she herself remains the matrix, the other, the origin. And the child's own narrative—the narrative of our culture—rests on that "othering."[45]

Children learn to see the mother as an object or extension of themselves, rather than as a full subject.

Because the ideology of individualism requires suppression of the mother's subjectivity so as not to disturb the child's sense of autonomy, it has contributed both to relations of domination and to the cultural inability to represent and articulate women's desire. Women's independent desire, potentially threatening to the child, becomes antithetical to conceptions of femininity and maternity. Mothers are subjected to a code of self-sacrificing behavior, the normative weight of which is rendered invisible because social conceptions of maternity are naturalized. Synthesizing a long tradition of feminist theory that has tried to show that the personal is, indeed, political, Benjamin argues that a Western ideology of individualism locates social struggle outside the realm of personal relationships and recognizes the contributions only of those who transcend the pull of personal relationships to act autonomously. This definition of political agency as inimical to personal ties has worked to exclude women, who have been less able or less likely to act apart from their personal and familial obligations.

Object relations' hypothesis that, where women are the primary caretakers of children, relation is emphasized in feminine development and autonomy is stressed in masculine development has thus prompted revisions of the standard psychoanalytic tenet that autonomy is the single goal of development. In contrast to an ideal of individualism, feminist psychoanalytic theory has suggested that "individuality is properly, ideally, a balance of separation and connectedness, of the capacities for agency and relatedness."[46] Adding this model of female development to the male has also spurred challenges to the conventions of moral theory, which has ranked regard for individual rights over concern for responsibility to others. Feminist psychoanalytic theory, then, has challenged the equation of full subjectivity and complete moral development with autonomy.

Maternity and Morality

The conjunction of maternity with issues of morality, racial character, public opinion, and social norms—although not racially specific—bears specific precedent and ideological weight in the history of racial formation in the United States. As Hortense Spillers writes, slavery made the black female

> the principal point of passage between the human and the non-human world. Her issue became the focus of a cunning difference—visually, psychologically, ontologically—as the route by which the dominant male decided the distinction between humanity and "other." At this level of radical discontinuity in the "great chain of being," black is vestibular to culture.[47]

The line of inheritance drawn by slavery—that children of slave women follow the condition of the mother—excludes the black father and excuses the white. This "problem" of black family structure enables the othering of African Americans through articulations of gender and family. Spillers points out that the "absence" of the black father, though accomplished by "violent historical intervention that, for all intents and purposes has *banished* the father, if not in fact *murdered* him," occasions guilt in African Americans, who feel "called upon to 'explain,' make excuses for his 'absence.'"[48] Moreover, the phenomenon of absent fathers is distorted and exaggerated in the service of pathologizing the black family and demonizing black mothers. The resulting images of the emasculating black matriarch (of the Moynihan

Report, for example) and the wanton "welfare queen" (of the Reagan 1980s and Gingrich 1990s) accrue the blame for the unequal socio-economic conditions of African Americans:

> According to Daniel Patrick Moynihan's celebrated "Report" of the late sixties, the "Negro Family" has no father *to speak of*—his Name, his Law, his Symbolic function mark the impressive missing agencies in the essential life of the black community, and it is, surprisingly, the fault of the Daughter, of the female line. This stunning reversal of the castration thematic, displacing the Name and the Law of the Father to the territory of the Mother and Daughter, becomes an aspect of the African-American female's misnaming.[49]

Attacks on the African American community for what is perceived as an atypical and immoral constitution of the family reveal the insecurity of the keepers of paternal law. The exclusion of African Americans from patrilineage may have *enabled* slavery, but it also exposed the cultural underpinnings of seemingly natural structures of family, paternity, and patriarchy. In Spillers's words, "This articulated problematic [of black family structure] comes nearer the 'truth' because it plants ambiguity at the heart of an interpretation of the father's law."[50] The historical exclusion of black men from the legal family structure thus presents an opportunity to challenge the uniformity of paternal law. However, it also deals a blow to African American men, who do not enjoy the same male privilege as white men. Because the persistent inequities between black and white Americans are so often blamed on the African American family structure, it has been frequently suggested that the social ills of African Americans would be cured if only black men were ensconced in the same patriarchal privilege enjoyed by white men.[51] Corollary to such anxiety about the father's absence and/or impotence is horror of the mother's power.[52] This horror underlies the community's ostracism of Sethe because they believe that in killing her own child, in violating "maternal instinct," Sethe has made herself, and therefore all blacks, susceptible to the challenge from whites that blacks are not human. When Paul D learns that Sethe killed her own child, he criticizes her simply by saying, "'You got two feet, Sethe, not four'" (165); she is satisfying Schoolteacher's expectation that blacks manifest animal characteristics.[53] In judging Sethe, the community adopts the normative definition of maternal behavior—despite the fact that conditions of slavery inherently denied the possibility of "normal" choices and behavior. Sethe's inability to imagine a self separate from her child is exacerbated by society's and her community's expectations of maternal behavior. Maternal self-sacrifice dictates that Sethe do nothing to harm Beloved, yet Sethe's choices, when the slavers come to recapture her, do not include any that save Beloved from harm. At the moment of crisis, Sethe chooses between the two possible evils; afterward, she cannot reconcile her choice to kill Beloved with her conception of maternal care. Caught between the passivity of allowing harm to come to Beloved or the activity of harming Beloved to prevent others from harming her, she is paralyzed in both thought and action.[54]

Sethe's seemingly impossible "choice" between two courses of events, each of which will result in harm, is similar, in some sense, to the dilemma women face in deciding whether to have an abortion. Carol Gilligan's influential study of gender differences in conceptions of morality, *In a Different Voice,* focuses on women's decisions about whether to have an abortion as a test case that sharply illustrates "the conflict between self and other [that] constitutes the central moral problem for women."[55] Gilligan found that women tend to make moral decisions according to an "ethic of care" that puts a premium on resolving conflict so that no one will be hurt (65). Because a woman's decision to continue or abort a pregnancy "affects both herself and others and engages directly the critical moral issue of hurting," it "catches up issues that are critical to psychological development. These issues pertain to the worth of the self in relation to others, the claiming of the power to choose, and the acceptance of responsibility for choice" (71, 94). Women's concern with responsibility for others stems from both women's experience of relationships as sustaining rather than threatening, and from cultural expectations that women be self-sacrificing. In its most positive form, this "ethic of care" fosters empathy, social connection, and nonviolence, but in combination with normatively feminine characteristics of self-sacrifice and passivity, it can inhibit women from acting independently and making responsible choices. If women do not extend the obligation of care to include the self as well as others, then any self-interest seems selfish and at odds with responsibility toward others.

"It is precisely this dilemma—the conflict between compassion and autonomy, between virtue and power—which the feminine voice struggles to resolve in its effort to reclaim the self and to solve the moral problem in such a way that no one is hurt" (71).

Many of the women Gilligan interviewed initially construed the abortion decision as a choice between selfishness (to abort) and responsibility (to continue the pregnancy). These women came to realize, however, that continuing the pregnancy might harm both others to whom they felt responsible and their own interests. In the process of resolving this problem, wherein "responsibilities conflict and decision entails the sacrifice of somebody's needs," the women Gilligan interviewed underwent a sequence of development that refined their ethic of care (74). They distanced themselves from social norms of feminine self-sacrifice, extended the ethic of care to include themselves, and so dissolved the disparity between selfishness and responsibility. In the case of pregnancy, "the conflict between self and other remains, [but] the moral problem is reconstructed in light of the realization that the occurrence of the dilemma itself preludes nonviolent resolution" (94).

Recasting the dilemma from a choice between right and wrong to a choice between evils allows women to consider the social injustice that a particular problem may reflect, that is, to identify "the violence inherent in the dilemma itself, which is seen to compromise the justice of any of its possible resolutions" (101). This contextual, rather than abstract and systematic, approach to moral judgments excludes women from the standard descriptions of moral development, which rank a concern for rights (which Gilligan associates with a masculine conception of morality) over an ethic of responsibility. To provide a balance between autonomy and care, Gilligan advocates an integration of rights and responsibilities.

Although not about abortion, *Beloved* also traffics in the murky moral realm where a woman's choice is a matter of life and death for her child and where even the most considered maternal decision cannot defend against guilt. Sethe faces an inherently violent dilemma, generated by the injustice of slavery, between killing her child to keep her from slavery or letting her live the life of a slave. Although the dilemma, in this instance, is not between the mother's interests and those of the child but rather between outcomes for the child, Sethe's overidentification with Beloved endows her act of murder with a kind of self-interest that is cast as selfishness by those who judge her. Paul D censors Sethe for self-indulgence when he says that her "love is too thick" (164). Sethe does not abrogate maternal responsibility at the crucial moment—though the killing is represented more as a reflex than a considered choice. But later, if Sethe does not exactly doubt the justice of her action, at least she cannot face its effect.[56] Like the women in Gilligan's study who have not learned to temper ideals of self-sacrifice with self-protection, Sethe renounces agency and autonomy in the face of Beloved's needy recriminations.[57] To transcend this self-negating stance, Sethe must allow that the circumstances of slavery precluded nonviolent resolution, that her own interests are as legitimate as Beloved's, and that—since she cannot undo the harm done to Beloved—she cannot expect Beloved's understanding.

Whereas Gilligan implies that women learn to weigh their own interests alongside their responsibilities to others through an increased "understanding of the psychological logic of relationships," in *Beloved* the interpersonal and psychological are always embedded within the communal. Sethe does not make the transition to a fully individuated identity alone. Rather, Sethe's surviving daughter, Denver, ventures into the community to bring help. Until her desperate forays for help beyond the yard of 124 Bluestone Road, Denver had withdrawn into a private world so as not to face her family's history or the community's scorn. Because she did not try to understand the circumstances of Sethe's "crime" and her father's disappearance, she remained unaware of the history of slavery and resentful toward her mother for the family's isolation and deprivation. But despite her fear and resentment of Sethe, her mother remains the moving force of Denver's small universe; like Beloved, Denver lacks appropriate autonomy and individuation. She begins to differentiate herself from her mother through learning her mother's story of the experience of slavery, which she has, until now, disliked hearing.[58] Although Denver does not have memories of slavery, she must learn to negotiate her way through the memories of her mother and her community to arrive at a point of understanding and autonomy, a point the infantile ghost can never reach.

Denver's quest for help, which leads her to the women of her community, "inaugurated her life in the world as a woman" (248). She brings help in the body of women who come to exorcize the ghost from Sethe's home. In effect, they serve as midwife, come to deliver Sethe of Beloved in a rebirth that will allow Sethe an adequately individuated identity. In the decision to help Sethe, the community members, as well as Denver and Paul D, recognize the limits to passing moral judgments on others. Ella, considering the fact that she let a baby die who was the issue of repeated rape by her slave master and his son, suspends judgment of Sethe because she would not want her own choices to be judged. Sethe's crisis of decision and memory comes to be framed by the unspeakable stories of the other former slaves, such as Stamp Paid and Ella. If "[n]ot a house in the country ain't packed to the rafters with some dead Negro's grief," if each former slave has an unspeakable story, then the slave system's radically personal violations preclude systematic moral judgment of those affected (5). The novel, in fact, suggests the significance of what Gilligan calls "the contextual particularity" of a moral problem, which "allows the understanding of cause and consequence which engages the compassion and tolerance repeatedly noted to distinguish the moral judgments of women" (100). The community takes responsibility for care of one of their number and so acknowledges that judgment should not be passed without consideration of circumstance. The women's own, Paul D's, and Denver's belated acceptance of Sethe—without explanation of her unspeakable story—allows Sethe, finally, to let the past flow into her consciousness, albeit painfully, like blood flowing back to a numbed limb. With sensation returned, she can begin to imagine a future, to make use of her acquired agency. Sethe's newly born self, though more clearly differentiated, is still situated interdependently within relationships to Denver, Paul D, and her community.

Insisting on individuality and context, the text demonstrates that only a fully elaborated history of the experience of slavery—fleshed out like the ghost returned as a girl—can inform judgments of racial issues and individual actors. At the same time, however, the narrative's unfilled gaps (What, finally, happened to Halle?), its suspended resolutions (Should Sethe have killed Beloved?) insist on the limits of knowledge. *Beloved*'s paradox of telling an "unspeakable" story asks the reader to recognize our inherently mediated relationship to history, to memory, and to the stories of others. Because interpretation and moral choice are, in the end and within reason, individual acts, Sethe's story can be told but not explained. When Sethe does speak to Paul D about the day Beloved died, "the circle she was making around the room, the subject, would remain one. That she could never close in, pin it down for anybody who had to ask, if they didn't get it right off—she could never explain" (163). The case of maternity, in particular, forces a confrontation with the radical individuality of moral choice; as an example of ineluctable gender difference, biological maternity highlights the fact that individuals necessarily occupy different positions in relation to ethical decisions.[59] Referring to Gilligan's study of abortion decisions, Johnson meditates on the incommensurability of gendered positions in relation to motherhood:

> Why, I wondered, would an investigation of gender *differences* focus on one of the questions [whether to have an abortion] about which an even-handed comparison of the male and the female points of view is impossible? Yet this, clearly, turns out to be the point: there is difference *because* it is not always possible to make symmetrical oppositions. As long as there is symmetry one is not dealing with difference but rather with versions of the same. Gilligan's difference arises out of the impossibility of maintaining a rigorously logical binary model for ethical choices. Female logic, as she defines it, is a way of rethinking the logic of choice in a situation in which none of the choices are good. (190–92)

Johnson wonders, then, how a moral *system* can account for such individual *differences* of position and context.[60] In putting forth a contextual and personal morality that neither condemns nor sanctions Sethe's killing, the novel allows for differences of gender and race, experience and history. In addition to emphasizing the individual, the novel stresses the interdependence of individuals and communities: Amy Denver's help is crucial to Sethe, Stamp Paid's self-image depends on assisting escaping slaves, and Paul D decides to risk emotional vulnerability to make a life with Sethe. Significantly, ideals of care and relation complement rather than preclude respect for autonomy and individuality.

The interdependence of identity between Sethe and the community that judges her actions as a reflection on itself resembles the mother-daughter identification of Sethe and Beloved. In other words, the conflict between group and individual over membership and independence can be seen as a relational identity parallel to the mother-daughter intersubjectivity described by object relations. I would argue, then, that the terms of monstrous doubling that feminists have used to describe the mother-daughter relationship also describe the tensions that individual African Americans experience in their relationship to the larger—if diversely constituted—African American community. Gallop likens the relational identity of daughter and mother to the relation between an individual feminist critic and the larger community of feminist critics. Each feminist critic, she argues, negotiates her degree of autonomy and identity within feminism, just as daughters negotiate in relation to mothers.[61] Similarly, in yet another form of double consciousness, an African American writer would negotiate the relation of his/her work to the collective body of African American culture and society. This is not to say that all African American writers identify themselves or should be identified primarily in terms of race. But if the dominant culture identifies individual blacks with a collective body of African Americans, then racial attitudes help create issues of individuation between a group and its members.

Commenting on contemporary race relations in an interview with the *New York Times,* historian John Hope Franklin implies just such a continuing tension between the individual and the collective:

> We're always talking about blacks as a group and whites as individuals. Susan Smith is talked about as an individual, a crazy woman in South Carolina. This little boy who was killed in Chicago, 11 years old killed by another one who was 9 or something, that's regarded as the encapsulation of a trend, a reflection of the kind of things that whites have tried to do for blacks, and this is what happens. What would people say about black people if Susan Smith were black? They would be poised to write a whole book, "The Bell Curve" or something, as a result of it.[62]

If, as Franklin says, we are always talking about blacks as a group, then the actions of any one individual stand in for the collective body. There is, in other words, a metonymic relationship between the individual and the group, the part standing in for the whole. The knowledge that the actions of one are, in effect, the actions of all contributes to double consciousness, that "sense of always looking at one's self through the eyes of others" that Du Bois explained in 1903. Franklin's comment suggests that—despite changes in race relations since the early part of the twentieth century—if you are black, you must worry that your actions reflect directly on your fellow African Americans and that you will be judged not by your own actions or character, but by the actions and character of some other individual who is considered representative of the group. You are, then, refused the individuality that serves as a hallmark of the American conception of democracy. This is not to say that all African Americans experience the legacy of slavery or the construction of racial or gender identity similarly, but that individuals continually face the imposition of similitude.

What is striking about Franklin's observation, in addition to the split he notes between the inherent individuality of whiteness and the typology of blackness, is the example he uses to demonstrate this difference of perception: a case of maternal infanticide. Susan Smith, a southern white woman who claimed that a black man had kidnapped her two young sons, was found to have killed them herself. While I agree with Franklin that the dominant culture extrapolates from the particular to the general in reference to African Americans (when the particular is negative), the example of Susan Smith does not, in itself, demonstrate the different interpretations accorded the actions of whites and blacks since the Smith case has no celebrated black counterpart in the contemporary moment. What interests me, in particular, about Franklin's example is that a mother's murder of her child should, here also, raise the specter of moral condemnation of African Americans as a race.

An/Other Signifier of Desire

Through the test case of maternity—a position particularly destabilized by the confluences of body and subjectivity, self and other, symbolic and social, individual and collective—*Beloved* suggests the ways that slavery systematically and institutionally destroyed bodily coherence and subjective agency. However, the mutability of the figure of the ghost connects the singular and paradigmatic infanticide to the range of violations experienced by the other slaves. Born out of his or her deepest deprivation, Beloved takes the shape of each character's particular struggle with identity and relation. To Denver, she is the sister who, in the father's absence, acts as a third term that loosens the strictures of the mother/daughter dyad, who provides a buffer between Denver and the terrifying power of her mother. Beloved's siren call to Paul D to "touch me. On my inside part. And you have to call me my name," echoes his own need for recognition of and by an other in order to animate his dormant capacity for intimacy, to open his heart, which is rusted shut like a tobacco tin (117). Embodying each character's demon of desire, Beloved is both vanquished at the moment of personal fulfillment and ever-present—like "weather"—as that part of need that remains beyond satisfaction.[63] The figure of Beloved, in her various guises, links the effects of slavery to the force of desire.

If Beloved signifies the lack resulting from the subject's insertion into a symbolic system articulated not only through the grammar of speech, but through the grammar of slavery, then the novel redraws the relation between the unconscious and the social, between language and the body, gender and race, the phallus and desire. I would suggest that, as a signifier of desire, Beloved poses an alternative to the phallus while yet signaling individual lack in relation to a symbolic system.

As such, the figure forges a link between the claims and demands of both Lacanian and object relations psychoanalytic feminism, specifically in relation to the problem of phallocentrism. *Beloved* fulfills the promise of object relations to demonstrate a nonphallic order of symbolization that accommodates women as full, desiring subjects. To the extent that it represents subjectivity as formed out of lack or absence and the resulting desire as that which exceeds demand, *Beloved*'s vision is Lacanian. The subjective lack in *Beloved,* however, comes not from an ahistorical, universal oedipal tableau, but from the laws of kinship that uphold slavery and construct both racial and sexual difference. As Abel suggests, perhaps an infusion of the social and, in particular, a consideration of the exigencies of race in the American context can effect a rapprochement between these discourses of psychoanalytic feminism, "so sharply and hierarchically split over the last decade" and guilty, in either case, "of privileging a decontextualized gender as the constitutive factor of subjectivity" (186). Toward this end, Abel reads Spillers's essay "Mama's Baby, Papa's Maybe" as politicizing Lacan "by highlighting the fissures between the social and symbolic realms within the culture of slavery, in which the Name of the Father establishes not gender but property [so that] slave children . . . have a distinctive relation to the patriarchal symbolic register" (188). This deployment of a socially grounded Lacanian vision retains the significance of the patriarchal symbolic register while tacitly affirming object relations' relocation of "the origin of the social subject in the maternal rather than the paternal function" (189). *Beloved* similarly underscores the role of the symbolic order even as it suggests flexibility in the distribution of the father's Name. The novel, furthermore, highlights the importance of the maternal function and relational identity, representing them as compatible with paternal law.[64]

The split between object relations and Lacan centers on the role of the phallus as signifier of desire and of castration or paternal law as the instrument of gender differentiation.[65] Although both Lacanians and object relationists connect phallocentrism (that is, the structuring of representation, desire, and symbolic meaning in reference to an attribute associated with masculinity) to the problem of women's social subordination,[66] each proposes a different solution: "Feminists [object relationists fall in here] think we must alter the phallocentrism of discourse in order to alter women's lot in society. Lacanians would simply separate the symbolic phallus from the penis."[67] Despite the reductionism of assigning particular feminists to either side of such a sweeping duality—or, for that matter, of opposing feminists to Lacanians—I would like to consider, albeit briefly, a representative of each position. The former intervention—that is, altering the phallocentrism of discourse—requires establishing a nonphallic signifier of desire in order to articulate a femininity defined as the subject rather than the object of desire; this approach implies that changes toward gender equality effected in culture and ideology will be mirrored in the symbolic system. Representative of this position, Benjamin contends:

> So far, women do not have an equivalent [to the phallus] image of desire; the existing equation of masculinity with desire, and femininity with object-of-desire, reflects a condition that does exist. . . . It is a real appearance . . . but only apparently essential, rather a manifestation of deeper causes. This condition, then, is not inevitable but has come into being through forces we intend to understand and counteract. . . . [W]e only have to argue that how biological givens are psychically organized is partly the work of culture, of social arrangements, which we can change or redirect.[68]

In the second case, that class of theorists who would separate the penis from the phallus maintains that the subject can come into being only through submission to a fixed paternal law and a universal symbolic system; however, this realm of signification might be separated from the actual relations of power between men and women:

> For if patriarchal culture is that within which the self originally constitutes itself, it is always already there in each subject as subject. Thus how can it be overthrown if it has been necessarily internalized in everybody who could possibly act to overthrow it? . . . It is not patriarchal culture, but the biologistic reduction of the Law of the Dead Father to the rule of the actual, living male that must be struggled against.[69]

This tack presumes a separation between linguistic/symbolic systems and social structures.

Neither object relations nor Lacanian feminism has, of yet, yielded a workable solution to the dominance of the phallus in conceptions of signification and the resulting problem of feminine desire. Gallop objects to the feminist call for a nonphallic mode of representation on the grounds that it entails occupying a stance outside the symbolic system and denies rather than confronts the phallocentrism of our culture: "Such positioning ignores the subject's need to place himself within the signifying chain in order to be anyplace at all."[70] Benjamin, in fact, does seem to deny the necessity of signification in her attempt to crack the seemingly closed system of phallocentric representation. She dismisses altogether "the representational level, which has been organized and dominated by the phallus" and exhorts feminists to find instead "an alternative mode of structuring the psyche, not just a symbol to replace the phallus."[71] Responding to her own challenge, she posits "the intersubjective mode of desire [which] has its counterpart in spatial rather than symbolic structures."[72] Benjamin not only evades the current power structure of our symbolic system, but circumvents the psychic dimension of representation altogether.

The attempt to separate the phallus from the penis also falls short since, as its own proponents concede, such separation is impossible. Gallop notes,

> [W]henever any Lacanian set out to clear up the confusion between phallus and penis, she or he inevitably fell into the same sort of confusion the effort was meant to remedy. . . . I believe it to be a symptom of the impossibility, at this moment in our history, to think a masculine that is not phallic.[73]

This even as she considers "that very impossibility to be nonetheless an urgent necessity."[74] Gallop seems to contradict herself. On the one hand, she exposes the mechanism through which the phallus is idealized in Lacanian psychoanalysis:

> Now, certainly, when Lacan talks about the "castration" entailed by the subject's being in language, in the symbolic order, a good way to understand that castration is that one is always deprived of signifying the referent. . . . But to say that *phallus,* a signifier forming part of our language, is the name of that unreachable, unspeakable referent constitutes phallus as some fundamental, transcendental truth.[75]

But, on the other, she demands that "phallus" continue to designate that "unspeakable referent," thereby begging the question, why and where from paternal law? How, then, given Gallop's own critique of the phallus's transcendent truth status in Lacanian psychoanalysis, can the phallus be retained as signifier of the "unreachable, unspeakable referent" of language without preserving its always already primacy, without short-circuiting its referentiality back to the penis?

I am not interested in merging Lacan and object relations purely for the sake of creating a unified feminist family. Rather I want to retain certain insights of each discourse while untying the theoretical knots between them in order to create a more flexible and responsive analytic framework. If the phallus is entrenched as signifier of desire because of Lacan's insistence on the transcendence of paternal law, then we can destabilize its universality by showing that the subject's development in relation to the Name-of-the-Father varies according to the specificity of material culture. But, unless we can formulate a relation between the social and the symbolic system, there is no room for individual agency or cultural difference in relation to processes of subject formation.[76] One way to contextualize the process of the individual's insertion into the symbolic order is to identify a mechanism other than paternal Law (or a variation of paternal law) that ensures differentiation between mother and child. But if the father and the phallus do not interrupt the mother-child dyad as the agent of desire, who or what does? And if paternal law does not obtain universally, how, then, does cultural context impinge on sexual difference? In *Beloved,* slavery's violation of kinship networks and the perversion of patrilineage shift the rule of symbolic order under which the enslaved are socially positioned. The father's physical and symbolic exile under slavery exaggerates identification between mother and child, producing a dangerous loss of boundaries between Sethe and Beloved's selves. Without the protection of the Name-of-the-Father within a symbolic order dominated by paternal law, Sethe's nameless child is marked "slave." In her reading of Spillers, Abel writes that in the slave economy, where "kinship, gender, and the body are deconstructed" and where the slave mother is denied claim to her children,

> seizing the power to name . . . is both an imperative of survival and the condition of possibility for a new social subject undetermined by either the dichotomy phallus/castration that has vexed the efforts of Lacan's feminist heirs to theorize the place of "the feminine" in "language" or by the conventions of domesticity that have produced the Anglo-American "gendered female."[77]

In *Beloved,* Sethe claims the right to name her child, but can wield this power only at the cost of Beloved's life. Maternal power is not ensured by the absence of paternal sanction, and slavery, in effect, separates the *mother* as well as the father from the child—with the result that Beloved's development is arrested at a presubjective stage in which she still looks to her mother for the mirroring necessary to constitute the infant's sense of self. Beloved's infantile demand constitutes Sethe as the Other of desire, as "already possessing the 'privilege' of satisfying needs, that is to say, the power of depriving them of that alone by which they are satisfied."[78] Although Sethe is—in Lacan's terms—the phallic mother, Beloved is not yet subject to paternal law, so that symbolizing her desire in terms of the phallus seems arbitrary rather than descriptive. For Sethe, Beloved symbolizes a fragmenting of self, not in relation to a transcendent Symbolic imposed through language and defined in terms of sexual difference, but rather as articulated through the body and language and defined by the historic contingencies of both race and gender. The separation between mother and child repeats Sethe's loss in infancy of her own mother (who was kept working in the fields while Sethe's care was delegated to another slave), a loss that seems to contribute to her extreme, compensatory sense of maternal duty.

Thus the household of women at 124 Bluestone Road is not the safe space of intersubjective recognition that allows articulation of feminine desire imagined by Benjamin, but rather a yawning gap of raw desire unsanctioned by language and the social order, and without the luxury of mutual recognition of selfhood. Who or what, if not the father or paternal law, will rupture this overidentification of mother and daughters, bringing them back into the realm of the social? When the community of women insist on Beloved's necessary absence and Sethe's return to community life, they demand the regulation of desire that, for Lacan, is the work of the symbolic Father, the phallus. Sethe's awakening of self—literally in Paul D's arms and figuratively in the cradle of the community—recalls Benjamin's intersubjective space, that is a space created between self and "a holding other whose presence does not violate one's space but permits the experience of one's own desire, who recognizes it when it emerges of itself."[79] But despite the exorcism and Sethe's rebirth, Beloved remains:

> Everybody knew what she was called, but nobody anywhere knew her name. Disremembered and unaccounted for, she cannot be lost because no one is looking for her, and even if they were, how can they call her if they don't know her name? Although she has claim, she is not claimed. (274)

Her intangible presence signals that even Sethe's and the community's laying to rest of the violent past cannot seal over the absences of history, losses that remain beyond stories as desire remains beyond demand. Sethe's nascent experience of self suggests, then, a subjectivity of workable agency and coherence, but not without the crevices of the unconscious.[80]

The resolution of the conflict between Sethe's individual choices and the community's moral code depends on understanding the relation between social structure and identity. Unless we understand history's impact on the unconscious, the violences of the past will continue to structure the selves of subsequent generations just as Denver grows out of the shape of her mother's experiences. And our responses to others will be determined by our own guilt and self-doubt in the same way that Paul D challenges Sethe's humanity because he fears his own behavior ("the calves of his youth") has consigned him to the animal realm (165). Thus, the narrative explores the importance of its own telling by demonstrating the necessity of passing down the memories and experiences of slavery. The poverty of understanding, the willful political amnesia, that our contemporary culture brings to the continuing impact made by our long history of slavery and racism makes itself apparent in the intolerance, condemnation, and denial of responsibility that so many Americans bring to problems associated with some—especially poor—African American communities. Although rhetoric about the laziness of "welfare mothers" and the burdens of self-doubt that affirmative action ostensibly imposes on minorities seems to acknowledge the role psychology plays in sociopolitical issues, it is only by ignoring the larger social context of race that pundits and politicians can blame social problems on the *individual* failure of will they suggest is endemic to a race. In no way does a call to both blacks and whites for understanding and care, a call I hear in Beloved's name, obviate the need for personal responsibility. *Beloved* is no "victim discourse"; it explores the possibilities for individual agency from within a set of social and ideological conditions. Nonetheless, historical events leave psychological imprints and these, in turn, bear material weight.

Perhaps the novel's insistence on the suspension of judgment necessitated by our inherently mediated knowledge of history and its effects is most evident in the novel's address to the reader. In using a figure as unbelievable, as unspeakable as a ghost, Morrison overtly challenges the impulse to judge Sethe's story. Because Beloved is unambiguously and unabashedly a "real" ghost, she cannot be dismissed as simply local color or folk tradition; she "is no projection of a neurotic observer, no superstitious mass delusion."[81] The reader is compelled to come to terms with a finally incomprehensible story, just as individual characters must come to terms with their histories of slavery. "One of its purposes," Morrison has written about the supernatural element of *Beloved*, "is to keep the reader preoccupied with the nature of the incredible spirit world while being supplied a controlled diet of the incredible political world."[82] It is a strategy to give the reader no time to disbelieve.

AFTERWORD

Biracial/Multiracial—New Subject?

As the prohibitive force of the miscegenation taboo wanes in American law and culture, we might expect the binary opposition between white and black to collapse. Although racial constructions are remarkably intransigent, the recent emergence of "biracial" and "multiracial" categories might herald a significant shift. The term "biracial" primarily describes individuals with parents who each identify as a different race (as those races have been traditionally defined). For example, in her groundbreaking collection of interviews, *Black, White, Other: Biracial Americans Talk about Race and Identity,* Lise Funderburg defines as biracial those individuals who "have one biological parent who identified as black and one who identified as white" (15). The term is not limited to those who have a black and a white parent, but recognizes individuals whose parents are of any two different races. Recent memoirs, oral histories, and autobiographical fictions about biracial identity include, in addition to Funderburg's book, Rebecca Walker's memoir, *Black, White, and Jewish: Autobiography of a Shifting Self,* and Danzy Senna's novel *Caucasia.*[1]

Not just literary phenomena, biracialism and multiracialism have permeated the culture—from the disciplines and discourses of psychology to popular culture to the media. Internet discussion and support groups abound. For example, "My Shoes," a chat group hosted by a licensed psychologist, supports "multiracial children, adolescents, and adults who have a white appearance."[2] In 1998, a PBS *Frontline* documentary focused on biracial identity; in 2000, *Newsweek* devoted a cover story to "Redefining Race in America," with a section on multiracialism titled "The New Face of Race."[3] Tiger Woods famously coined the term "Cablinasian" to characterize his own mixed heritage from his black father and Thai mother, refusing the conventional racial designations the press has tried to assign him. Advocacy groups such as Project Race lobby for "a multiracial classification on all school, employment, state, federal, local, census and medical forms requiring racial data."[4] The relatively broad application of the terms "biracial" and "multiracial" helps break down rigid racial categories, as it also helps form a larger constituency of multiethnic Americans.

The post–civil rights movement terms "biracial" and "multiracial" seem to have arisen as forms of self-definition meant to resist the state's imposition of unitary racial categories.[5] Perhaps the greatest indicator of their effect is that in 2000, for the first time, the U.S. census allowed respondents to check off more than one box to identify their race.[6] Writing for the *New York Times,* Steven A. Holmes quipped, "The four words on the census form, 'check all that apply,' sound more bureaucratic than revolutionary. Yet when used in a question asking people to describe their race, those words represent the latest shake-up in the way the country views itself racially."[7] This change in how the federal government classifies citizens by race came largely in response to lobbying by groups such as Project Race.[8] The 2000 census included six single races, any combination of which the respondent could check. These choices provided for fifteen combinations of two, twenty combinations of three, fifteen blends of four, six groupings of five, and one combination of all six—sixty-three possible combinations in all.[9] About seven million people chose the new option of picking more than one racial category to identify themselves.[10] Even as the Census Bureau counted race, it acknowledged that racial categories are nonfactual: the census telephone help line included a menu option for people with "questions about the meaning of race." It featured a recorded voice saying,

> The concept of race reflects self-identification. It does not indicate any clear-cut scientific definition which is biological or genetic in

> reference. The data for race represents self-classification by people according to the race or races with which they most closely identify.[11]

Of course, choosing more than one race for self-identification doesn't solve the problem of categorization. No set of races can account for the historical, geographic, and cultural factors that shape identity, and the groupings still reflect our ideological and political conceptions of race. Consequently, numerous commentators criticized the new census policy for offering inadequate choices. In a *Washington Post* column, Courtland Milloy archly described his confusion in filling out the census in order to highlight its categorical contortions:

> The race category on the census that really caught my eye was the one that supposedly applied to me. It came with three names attached: "Black, African Am./Negro." I thought all of those were separate categories, with African Am. being some kind of airline. African American, on the other hand, is the name most "people of color" prefer, according to recent opinion polls; black is no longer the in word. And speaking of the n-word, what about all of the black rappers who go by that? I can already smell an undercount. As for "Negro," I hadn't seen one of them since 1968.

An op-ed column in the *Boston Globe* also pointed out the limits of the census form's racial smorgasbord, noting that it broke down formerly homogenizing categories such as Asian into a number of subcategories, but left other sweeping categories intact—specifically those for whites and blacks.[12]

Controversy over the census and its implicit politics of racial affiliation generally played out between civil rights groups (concerned with maximizing minority political power and economic resources) who opposed the census change and advocacy groups (focused on individual choice) who supported it. Some civil rights groups interpreted biracial self-identification as a disavowal of minority racial identity. Many also expressed concern that biracial and multiracial self-identification on the census would result in lowered tallies for particular racial groups and, consequently, reduced voting power and allocations of federal aid.[13] As an article from the *Boston Globe* reported,

> To many mainline civil rights groups, the new census is part of a multiracial nightmare. After decades of framing racial issues in stark black and white terms, they fear that the multiracial movement will

> break down longstanding alliances, weakening people of color by splintering them into new subgroups.[14]

Civil rights groups that opposed or registered concern over the change included the NAACP, the Congressional Black Caucus, the Urban League, the National Council of La Raza, and the National Asian Pacific American Legal Consortium.[15] To address the potential political consequences of lower minority counts, the Clinton administration, which oversaw the 2000 census, determined that any people identifying themselves as both white and members of a racial minority would be counted as members of the minority. But critics on the right characterized this policy as a resurrection of the "one-drop" rule, arguing that "politicians and race hustlers" could use it to inflate minority counts for the purposes of manipulating voting districts and affirmative action.[16]

While numerous civil rights groups opposed the census change, many advocacy groups championed it as a victory for individual choice. Biracial individuals and parents of biracial children celebrated the opportunity to identify themselves and their children in ways that accounted for their family makeup. One woman, the daughter of a white, Jewish mother and a Chinese father, explained, "As a child I was very confused. I had to pick either 'Chinese,' 'White,' or 'Other.' It never seemed to work out."[17] Project Race's Web site echoes this frustration with unitary race categories: "Being forced to choose only one race forces us to deny one of our parents," it states. In another biracial manifesto, Maria P. P. Root, Ph.D., author of several books on biracial identity and a clinical psychologist, penned a "Bill of Rights" for biracial individuals. I quote it in its entirety:

> I have the right:
> Not to justify my existence in this world
> Not to keep the races separate within me
> Not to be responsible for people's discomfort with my physical ambiguity
> Not to justify my ethnic legitimacy.
>
> I have the right:
> To identify myself differently than strangers expect me to identify
> To identify myself differently than how my parents identify me
> To identify myself differently than my brothers and sisters
> To identify myself different in different situations.

> I have the right:
> To create a vocabulary to communicate about being multiracial
> To change my identity over my lifetime—and more than once
> To have loyalties and identify with more than one group of people
> To freely choose whom I befriend and love.[18]

Root lays claim to the power of self-definition to break free of conventional racial categories implicitly based on "one-drop" ideologies and binary conceptions of race. But if Root conceives of race as contingent rather than essential, this is not the case for all proponents of biracialism and multiracialism. Project Race, for example, asserts that adding biracial and multiracial categories to all official forms requiring racial designation (school, government, medical, employment) will produce a more accurate accounting of a person's race. The group's statement of purpose claims that forms requiring individuals to choose only one race for identification require us

> to do something illegal, since we are defining ourselves as something we are not.
>
> Multiracial people should have the option of recognizing *all* of their heritage. "Multiracial" is important so that children have an identity, a correct terminology for who they are. "Other" means different, a label that no person should bear. Also, without proper racial and ethnic classifications, multiracial people are "invisible" in the health care system.[19]

Project Race's appeal to discourses of law, medicine, and "terminology" implicitly argues that multiracial classifications are objectively accurate rather than more culturally attuned. This rhetoric does little to recognize the inherently social and contingent nature of all racial categories. Thus, the move toward bi- and multiracialism does not necessarily herald the dissolution of "race."[20] It does, perhaps, signal a change in the politics of racial affiliation.

Though the federal government's recognition that racial identities are neither unitary nor mutually exclusive is, in some ways, a positive development, we might also read the shift as part of a trend toward the "privatization of U.S. citizenship [which] help[s] devalue political identification itself for U.S. citizens."[21] Describing this trend, Lauren Berlant writes that "since '68, the sphere of discipline and definition for proper citizenship in the United States has become progressively more private, more sexual and familial, and more concerned with personal morality"

(177). Berlant sees this privatization of citizenship operating in cultural fantasies that represent the typical American citizen of the future as a multiracial woman. We have all seen this computer-generated, phantasmatic model American; her face is a morphed amalgamation of races and she inhabits those magazine articles that foretell the day when whites will be a minority. Exemplifying America's future, her cyborg-beautiful face has graced the covers of *Time, Mirabella,* and the *National Review.* These mainstream media magazines respond to anxieties over America's multiethnic citizenry with the fantasy of a multiracial, but nonracially specific, national subject. As Berlant writes, she "has been cast as an imaginary solution to the problems of immigration, multiculturalism, sexuality, gender, and (trans)national identity that haunt the U.S. present tense" (176). In part because this imagined multiracial citizen of the future is not obviously of any one or even any identifiable combination of races, she is wholly assimilable to a Euro-dominant and consumerist American culture. She threatens neither racial difference nor racial specificity. How, then, could she be organized according to racial identity politics? In effect, this future-perfect American, this multiracial Galatea, embodies the fantasy that racial difference could be eliminated through miscegenation. She mediates between the "seemingly private world of personal affect, intimacy, and reproduction and the public realm of social exchange."[22]

Will biracial and multiracial designations similarly contribute to a depoliticizing privatization of citizenship? Or will they offer new possibilities for agency and self-determination? The answer is probably both.

Notes

Introduction

1. W. E. B. Du Bois, *The Souls of Black Folk* (New York: Penguin, 1989), 5, hereafter cited in the text as *Souls*. Du Bois first published the chapter containing the passage on double consciousness as an essay titled "Strivings of the Negro People" in the August 1897 issue of the *Atlantic Monthly* (Lewis, *W. E. B. Du Bois: Biography of a Race*, 279).

2. Although contemporary critical discourse often quotes Du Bois's statement that "the problem of the Twentieth Century is the problem of the color-line" (1), Arnold Rampersad writes that "the central metaphor both of black existence and of the book [is] 'the Veil'" (*The Art and Imagination of W. E. B. Du Bois*, 70).

3. In accordance with the conventions of his time, Du Bois refers to African American identity in the universal male singular "the Negro." In my own attempts to analyze racialization, I do not mean to suggest there is any unitary racial or gender subjectivity. For more on the "need to complicate unitary subjectivities," see Davies, *Black Women, Writing and Identity: Migrations of the Subject*, 41. See also Loomba, *Colonialism/Postcolonialism*, 166.

4. Diana Fuss credits Gates with having "done the most to open the floodgates for poststructuralist Afro-American literary theory, primarily through his editorship of . . . *Black Literature and Literary Theory* and *'Race,' Writing,*

and Difference" (*Essentially Speaking*, 81). For foundational work in American studies that analyzes the racialization of American national identity, see Kaplan and Pease, *Cultures of United States Imperialism,* and Moon and Davidson, *Subjects and Citizens: Nation, Race, and Gender from Oroonoko to Anita Hill.*

5. Abel, Christian, and Moglen, introduction to *Female Subjects in Black and White: Race, Psychoanalysis, and Feminism,* 5.

6. Despite psychoanalysis's long neglect of race, recent work begins to correct that blind spot. See Abel, "Race, Class, and Psychoanalysis? Opening Questions"; Abel, Christian, and Moglen, *Female Subjects in Black and White*; Eng, *Racial Castration: Managing Masculinity in Asian America;* Fuss, "Interior Colonies: Frantz Fanon and the Politics of Identification"; B. Johnson, *The Feminist Difference: Literature, Psychoanalysis, Race, and Gender*; Lane, *The Psychoanalysis of Race;* Pellegrini, *Performance Anxieties: Staging Psychoanalysis, Staging Race;* Seshadri-Crooks, *Desiring Whiteness;* Spillers, "Mama's Baby, Papa's Maybe: An American Grammar Book," "'The Tragic Mulatta': Neither/Nor—Toward an Alternative Model," "'The Permanent Obliquity of an In[pha]llibly Straight': In the Time of the Daughters and the Fathers," and "'All the Things You Could Be by Now, If Sigmund Freud's Wife Was Your Mother': Psychoanalysis and Race"; Tate, *Psychoanalysis and Black Novels: Desire and the Protocols of Race;* and Walton, *Fair Sex, Savage Dreams: Race, Psychoanalysis and Sexual Difference.* In the area of film studies, see Doane, "Dark Continents: Epistemologies of Racial and Sexual Difference in Psychoanalysis and the Cinema"; J. Gaines, "White Privilege and Looking Relations: Race and Gender in Feminist Film Theory"; Kaplan, *Looking for the Other: Feminism, Film, and the Imperial Gaze;* and Rony, *The Third Eye: Race, Cinema, and Ethnographic Spectacle.*

7. Cooke, *Afro-American Literature in the Twentieth Century,* 72. Other notable works containing stock scenes of racial discovery include Zora Neale Hurston's *Their Eyes Were Watching God* (1937), Lillian Smith's *Strange Fruit* (1944), and Walter White's *A Man Called White* (1948).

8. Wald, "Becoming 'Colored': The Self-Authorized Language of Difference in Zora Neale Hurston."

9. Bruce, "W. E. B. Du Bois and the Idea of Double Consciousness," hereafter cited in the text. For a brief discussion of medical sources for Du Bois's concept of double consciousness, see also Rampersad, *The Art and Imagination of W. E. B. Du Bois,* 74. For a discussion of the Germanic influences of Goethe and dialectical philosophy possibly absorbed during Du Bois's two years of study in Germany, see Lewis, *W. E. B. Du Bois: Biography of a Race,* 281–82. For a discussion of the influence of Hegel's *Phenomenology of Spirit,* see Zamir, *Dark Voices: W. E. B. Du Bois and American Thought, 1888–1903,* and Siemerling, "W. E. B. Du Bois, Hegel, and the Staging of Alterity." For a discussion of double consciousness as derived from the tradition of American pragmatism, see West, *The American Evasion of Philosophy.*

10. For a discussion of historical links between, and theoretical implications of, Du Bois's concept of double consciousness and the origins of psychoanalysis, especially Freud's notion of trauma, see Zwarg, "Du Bois on Trauma: Psychoanalysis and the Would-Be Black Savant."

11. For a cogent discussion of whether Du Bois conceived of race as biological or cultural, see Appiah, "The Uncompleted Argument: Du Bois and the Illusion of Race."

12. J. Johnson, *The Autobiography of an Ex-Colored Man,* hereafter cited in the text. For a discussion of Du Bois's influence on Johnson and another discussion of double consciousness in this novel, see Gilroy, *The Black Atlantic,* 130–33.

13. The publisher's preface to the anonymous 1912 edition promises that "in these pages it is as though a veil had been drawn aside: the reader is given a view of the inner life of the Negro in America, is initiated into the 'freemasonry,' as it were, of the race" (vii). In thus promising to draw aside the "veil" and initiate whites into the "freemasonry" of African American life through a true story of passing, only to deliver a fiction that underscores the cruelty and irrationality of segregation, Johnson manages another sly reversal of the racial hierarchy. Playing on white desire for the repudiated Other, he implies that it is whites, not blacks, whose vision is occluded by the veil of segregation. This vision problem, which we might consider a form of white double consciousness, recurs in the prologue to Ralph Ellison's *Invisible Man,* wherein whites are so blinded by fantasies of racial prejudice that they cannot see actual African Americans before their eyes (3–5).

14. Douglass, *Narrative of the Life of Frederick Douglass, An American Slave,* 107.

15. See Freud, "The Dissolution of the Oedipus Complex," "Fetishism," "From the History of an Infantile Neurosis," and "Some Psychical Consequences of the Anatomical Distinction between the Sexes."

16. Lacan, *Écrits,* 1–7.

17. Freud, "Totem and Taboo." For critiques of Freud's concept of "the primitive," see Doane, "Dark Continents: Epistemologies of Racial and Sexual Difference in Psychoanalysis and the Cinema," 209–12; Seshadri-Crooks, "The Primitive as Analyst: Postcolonial Feminism's Access to Psychoanalysis," 194; and Fuss, *Identification Papers,* 35–36.

18. Doane, "Dark Continents," 210.

19. Walton, *Fair Sex, Savage Dreams,* 12.

20. "Race" also haunts early psychoanalysis in Freud's ambivalent relationship to racial constructions of Jewishness. See Boyarin, "What Does a Jew Want?; or, The Political Meaning of the Phallus," 211–40; Gilman, *Freud, Race, and Gender;* and Santner, *My Own Private Germany: Daniel Paul Schreber's Secret History of Modernity.* Another line of inquiry into race and early psychoanalysis would be to analyze racialized constructions of class in

bourgeois European society. Both of these areas are beyond the scope of this study.

21. Walton, *Fair Sex, Savage Dreams,* 5. For criticisms of feminist theory's omission of race in revising psychoanalytic discourses of subject formation, see also hooks, *Black Looks: Race and Representation,* 206–13; J. Gaines, "White Privilege and Looking Relations: Race and Gender in Feminist Film Theory," 61; Seshadri-Crooks, "The Primitive as Analyst," 187–92; Kaplan, *Looking for the Other,* 99–130; and Bergner, "Politics and Pathologies: On the Subject of Race in Psychoanalysis," 222.

22. For example, Kaja Silverman writes, "The unconscious articulation of racial and class difference is facilitated, however, by the articulation of an even more inaugural difference, which we also need to conceptualize ideologically—sexual difference" (*Male Subjectivity at the Margins,* 23). For a discussion of the same privileging of sexual over racial difference in the work of Joan Copjec, see Walton, *Fair Sex, Savage Dreams,* 6–7.

23. Resistance to psychoanalysis might also stem from the fact that psychiatry and psychoanalysis often pathologized black identity. I have discussed the tensions between psychoanalysis and African American literary and cultural theory previously in "Politics and Pathologies," 219–25. See also Walton, *Fair Sex, Savage Dreams,* 1–2. For a lengthy study, see Mama, *Beyond the Masks: Race, Gender, and Subjectivity.*

24. Christian, "The Race for Theory," 37.

25. Abel, Christian, and Moglen, introduction to *Female Subjects in Black and White,* 1.

26. Ibid., 2.

27. Morrison, "Unspeakable Things Unspoken: The Afro-American Presence in American Literature," 370.

28. Morrison, preface to *Playing in the Dark,* v; "Unspeakable Things Unspoken," 370.

29. Davies, *Black Women, Writing and Identity,* 41. See also West, "Black Culture and Postmodernism," 91.

30. Gates, "Criticism in the Jungle," 4–5.

31. Davies, *Black Women, Writing and Identity,* 42.

32. Radhakrishnan, "Ethnic Identity and Post-Structuralist Difference," 50.

33. Bergner, "Politics and Pathologies," 222.

34. Fanon, *Black Skin, White Masks,* 10–11.

35. Vergès, "Chains of Madness, Chains of Colonialism: Fanon and Freedom," 49.

36. Hall, "The After-life of Frantz Fanon: Why Fanon? Why Now? Why *Black Skin, White Masks*?" 17.

37. Judith Butler, *Bodies That Matter,* 94. See also Silverman, *Male Subjectivity at the Margins,* 6.

38. Silverman, *Male Subjectivity at the Margins*, 23. See also Walton, *Fair Sex, Savage Dreams*, 7, and Loomba, *Colonialism/Postcolonialism*, 148.

39. Silverman, *Male Subjectivity at the Margins*, 35, hereafter cited in the text.

40. Lévi-Strauss asserts that the incest prohibition marks the "threshold of culture" itself; it "provides the means of binding men together" by "ensuring the total and continuous circulation of the group's most important assets, its wives and its daughters" (*The Elementary Structures of Kinship*, 12, 480, 479).

41. See Rubin, "The Traffic in Women," 157–210.

42. As Judith Butler warns, "one might rearrange kinship relations outside of the family scene, but still discover one's sexuality to be constructed through more deep-seated constraining and constitutive symbolic demands. What are these demands? Are they prior to the social, to kinship, to politics? If they do operate as constraints, are they for that reason fixed?" (*Bodies That Matter*, 96).

43. Lévi-Strauss does remark in passing that "incest proper, and its metaphorical form as the violation of a minor (by someone 'old enough to be her father,' as the expression goes), even combines in some countries with its direct opposite, inter-racial sexual relations, an extreme form of exogamy, as the two most powerful inducements to horror and collective vengeance" (*Elementary Structures*, 10).

44. This is not to say that the incest and miscegenation taboos are completely analogous. For a pertinent and provocative discussion of how racial and sexual difference are not analogous, see Sedinger, "Nation and Identification: Psychoanalysis, Race, and Sexual Difference," 52–61.

45. Seshadri-Crooks, *Desiring Whiteness*, 3–4.

46. Seshadri-Crooks also asserts that "[w]hiteness represents complete mastery, self-sufficiency, and the *jouissance* of Oneness" (7). However, her formulation of how racial and sexual difference intersect differs somewhat from mine. For a critique of the claim that race, like gender, is organized in relation to the phallus as signifier, see Sedinger, "Nation and Identification," 42–45.

47. Although the "one-drop rule" did not become the uniform law of the land until the early twentieth century, racial classification laws designating white and nonwhite groups have been in operation since colonial times. Moreover, as Naomi Pabst acknowledges in her investigation of black/white mixed identity, historic classifications assumed "the basic 'nonwhiteness' of black/white interracial subjects" ("Blackness/Mixedness: Contestations over Crossing Signs"). For a sociological history of racial classification in the United States, with comparison to other countries' systems of racial classification, see Davis, *Who Is Black?*

48. Before abolition, not every colony, state, or region adopted the one-drop rule that defined anyone with any amount of known African heritage as

black. Some regions, such as Charleston, South Carolina, and New Orleans, Louisiana, had a three-tiered system of whites, mulattos, and blacks (Davis, *Who Is Black?* 36). Other areas followed a de facto, if not de jure, one-drop rule. Still others maintained a binary race system but used different criteria for distinguishing between white and black, such as declaring individuals to be black if they had one black grandparent or great grandparent or great great grandparent. However, from the 1850s on there was a general trend toward adoption of the one-drop rule in order to shore up slavery in the face of increased pressure from abolitionists and fear of insurrection (49). Not until the end of the era in which segregation was institutionalized—about 1915—was the one-drop rule followed throughout the nation (77).

49. Davis traces antimiscegenation laws back to colonial times, noting that the colony of Virginia passed its first such law in 1662 (*Who Is Black?* 33).

50. Although I want to extend psychoanalysis's focus beyond the family and the Oedipus complex, the family matrix remains an important site of racialization. It would be important to consider, for example, the influence of African American caregivers ("mammies" and maids) on the racialization of white children. For a brief discussion of the psychic significance of this dynamic, see Blassingame, *The Slave Community: Plantation Life in the Antebellum South,* 266–68.

51. Mannoni, *Prospero and Caliban: The Psychology of Colonization.*

52. Following Fanon's model, postcolonial critics such as Homi Bhabha, Gayatri Spivak, and Stuart Hall have made use of psychoanalytic theory to analyze the psychic dimensions of colonial power and representational discourses. For an overview of issues related to postcolonialism and psychoanalysis, see Loomba, *Colonialism/Postcolonialism,* 133–51.

53. Somerville, *Queering the Color Line,* 13.

54. Others have begun to use psychoanalytic theory to examine the racialization of white subjects. See, for example, Walton, *Fair Sex, Savage Dreams,* and Seshadri-Crooks, *Desiring Whiteness.*

1. Who Is That Masked Woman?

1. All Fanon quotations are from *Black Skin, White Masks.*

2. Henry Louis Gates Jr., "Critical Fanonism," 458, hereafter cited in the text. Previous to this resurgence, discourses of African and Caribbean liberation, Marxism, and American black nationalism had consistently taken up the philosophies of class struggle and anticolonial revolution advanced in Fanon's later works but had—for the most part—passed over *Black Skin, White Masks*'s psychoanalytic paradigm of the colonial relation. In later works such as *The Wretched of the Earth,* Fanon aligns himself with the Algerian anticolonial revolution. Serving as a sort of Gramscian organic intellectual, he posits a cohesive revolutionary identity for Algeria's and other colonized

regions' disparate cultural and ethnic groups. His strategic nationalism is especially compelling because it eschews simple essentialism. *Black Skin, White Masks,* though influential, was not seen as central to this "discourse of liberation," and the work was often cited as a source of autobiographical information on Fanon rather than as an autobiographically informed theory of the psychology of colonial relations.

3. See Homi K. Bhabha, "The Other Question: Difference, Discrimination and the Discourse of Colonialism"; "Remembering Fanon: Self, Psyche, and the Colonial Condition"; and "Interrogating Identity: The Postcolonial Prerogative."

4. Although psychoanalytic theory does not inherently preclude a radically constructionist perspective, Freud often assumes individual development is a response to psychobiological reality, rather than to sociopolitical conditions. Though he recognizes culture's repressive effect on individuals, he presumes that social arrangements and their psychic effects are essentially similar across cultures and thus, oxymoronically perhaps, *natural* to *culture.* He writes, for example, that "[a]lthough the majority of human beings go through the Oedipus complex as an individual experience, it is nevertheless a phenomenon which is determined and laid down by heredity and which is bound to pass away according to programme when the next pre-ordained phase of development sets in. This being so, it is of no great importance what the occasions are which allow this to happen" ("The Dissolution of the Oedipus Complex," 174). Without a more explicit critique of the cultural matrix, patterns of individual development appear inevitable.

5. More recently, feminist revisions of psychoanalysis (dating from Juliet Mitchell's pivotal 1975 work, *Psychoanalysis and Feminism*) have also politicized psychoanalysis by linking the development of "normal" femininity to the demands of patriarchy. For excellent arguments on the political relevance of psychoanalysis for feminism, see Rose, *Sexuality in the Field of Vision,* and Elliot, *From Mastery to Analysis.*

6. Fanon uses the masculine pronoun generically, but his descriptions are, for the most part, specific to men, as I show below. The impossibility of generalizing from this masculine universal to the feminine is, to a large extent, the subject of this chapter. For the moment I am caught within Fanon's terms, as is anyone who uses *Black Skin, White Masks,* without considering his elision of the feminine.

7. Parry, "Problems in Current Theories of Colonial Discourse," 29.

8. Sander Gilman has also addressed the intersections of race and psychoanalysis in documenting the construction of Jews as a racial other in nineteenth- and early twentieth-century Germany—the milieu that spawned Freud's psychoanalysis. Presenting a wealth of historical images and texts, Gilman shows that anti-Semitism, like other racisms, locates racial difference in sexuality, in the body, and in language. Gilman is less interested than I am, however,

in tracing the intersections of gender and race. He groups constructions of race, gender, and sexual orientation under a "general code of otherness" that allows him to focus exclusively on the case of race (*Jewish Self-Hatred,* 11). In his book *Freud, Race, and Gender,* Gilman actually replaces gender with race in psychoanalytic discourse by claiming that Freud's theories of femininity are constructed as a defense against anti-Semitism, that Freud appropriates "a specific image of the feminine onto which the qualities of the male Jew were projected" (37). This assertion seems to invalidate the psychoanalytic model of gendered subject formation and to preclude the possibility of using that model to describe non-Jewish racial identity. See also Eilberg-Schwartz, "Freud as a Jew," and Gilman, *The Case of Sigmund Freud.*

9. Mary Ann Doane suggests that blackness and femininity share a space in the Western symbolic system and the Western psychoanalytic text: "The force of the category of race in the constitution of Otherness within psychoanalysis should not be underestimated. When Freud needs a trope for the unknowability of female sexuality, the dark continent is close at hand" ("Dark Continents," 211). Doane also discusses gender in *Black Skin, White Masks,* focusing on Fanon's representation of white women, whereas I examine his account of black women.

10. Bhabha, "Remembering Fanon: Self, Psyche, and the Colonial Condition," 134.

11. For analyses of how Freud asks this question not of women, but of his male colleagues, silencing women on and as the subject, see de Lauretis, *Alice Doesn't: Feminism, Semiotics, Cinema,* 111; Felman, "Rereading Femininity," 19; and Doane, "Film and the Masquerade," 227–28.

12. Bhabha, "Remembering Fanon," 135.

13. Although I refer to the first-person narrator as "Fanon," I do not attribute autobiographical referentiality to this voice.

14. Bhabha, "Remembering Fanon," 135.

15. I am not suggesting that an essential self is violated when the subject encounters racial categories or that a nonracial self instantaneously "falls" into race. It is significant, however, that racial subject formation is represented as coming into being in a dramatic instance.

16. Doane stresses that this crisis of racial subject-formation bears a "perverse" similarity to "the Althusserian process of interpellation or hailing" ("Dark Continents," 224). I will return to this similarity in chapter 3.

17. Freud explains most fully how "primal scenes" introduce notions of sexual difference in "From the History of an Infantile Neurosis." For Freud's argument that the boy does not initially "believe in the threat [of castration] or obey it in the least" and comes to belief only through a visual crisis—"the sight of the female genitals"—see "The Dissolution of the Oedipus Complex."

18. Freud, "From the History of an Infantile Neurosis," 25.

19. Ibid., 38n6.

20. Freud, "Some Psychical Consequences of the Anatomical Distinction between the Sexes," 253.

21. Bhabha, "Remembering Fanon," 135, my emphasis.

22. Rose, *Sexuality in the Field of Vision,* 226, my emphasis.

23. Ibid., 227.

24. Even if the girl-child's instant recognition or the boy-child's disavowal and subsequent acknowledgment of women's castration is a rendering of culturally acquired notions of symbolic power relations, patriarchy's scopic regime nevertheless sets women up as the visual repositories of lack.

25. In discussing this scene, Bhabha makes a telling slip. He writes that "a white *girl* fixes Fanon in a look and word as she turns to *identify with her mother*" ("The Other Question," 321, my emphasis). But nowhere does Fanon say that the child is a girl. Moreover, he seems to refer to the child's gender on the next page: "[T]he handsome little *boy* is trembling because he thinks that the nigger is quivering with rage" (114, my emphasis). And the mother, at least in this instance, apologizes for her son's outburst. Bhabha's slip suggests that preconceptions of how race, gender, and sexuality intersect run deep.

26. The importance of visibility to determinations of race has not been described only in psychoanalytic terms. Cornel West, for one, traces the origin of Western racism to early European phenomenology, which privileged observation and held to a "normative gaze" based on classical aesthetics and promoted through the science of natural history (*Prophesy Deliverance,* 53–55).

27. According to Jane Gallop, the phallus always connotes the penis, despite claims by Lacan and his explicators that the phallus is detached from both the penis and the masculine since it belongs to the order of language and since all subjects are alienated in language. Gallop notes that "this confusion will support a structure in which it seems reasonable that men have power and women do not" (*Thinking through the Body,* 127).

28. Furthermore, black men are castrated in terms of social power, but are imagined as overendowed in terms of sexual anatomy. White women and black men disturb the white male imago on the level of sexual anatomy, but not in the same way.

29. Doane, "Film and the Masquerade," 231.

30. Ibid., 231.

31. Since the publication of "Film and the Masquerade," Doane and other feminist film theorists have begun to take on questions of racial difference. See n. 4 of the Introduction.

32. Rubin, "The Traffic in Women."

33. Irigaray, *This Sex Which Is Not One,* 170, hereafter cited in the text.

34. Fanon's argument about the psychosexual dynamics of race does not mention the long-standing abuse of black women by white men. Doane discusses this omission in "Dark Continents."

35. Although it has often been argued that restoring black men as "heads of household" would redress the effects of racism and slavery, this position merely substitutes a domestic domain of patriarchal privilege for racial equality and neglects altogether black women's claims to racial and gender equality. For a critique of this masculinist position, see Spillers, "Mama's Baby, Papa's Maybe."

36. Doane, "Dark Continents," 219.

37. *Je suis Martiniquaise* is the autobiography of Mayotte Capécia, a Martinican who is the chapter's representative black woman and who was, for a time, the mistress of a white French naval officer. "Nini" is a fictional text by Abdoulaye Sadji, published in the African periodical *Présence africaine;* the title character, a mulatta, takes offense at the attentions of a black suitor, whom she considers her inferior. The main character of René Maran's novel *Un homme pareil aux autres* is a black man educated in France who wants to marry a white woman but who worries that his race makes him an unacceptable suitor.

38. Doane, "Dark Continents," 219.

39. T. Denean Sharpley-Whiting takes issue with my analysis of Fanon's treatment of Capécia in "Fanon and Capécia." She argues, with some justice, that Capécia is not compelled by dire economic straits to take up with a white man and also that Capécia seems to have internalized colonial attitudes regarding the superiority of whiteness. For these reasons, we cannot celebrate Capécia as a champion of black women's self-determination. I would maintain, however, that even as Capécia valorizes whiteness, she is at the same time critical of the colonial project and its racism. Thus, despite its inconsistencies and Capécia's problematic racial politics, *Je suis Martiniquaise* remains an instructive account of a black woman's effort to carve economic and sexual autonomy out of a society that narrowly circumscribes women's self-determination. My point is not so much that Capécia represents an ideal as that Fanon is markedly less tolerant of her desire for whiteness than he is of Maran's male protagonist's.

40. According to Fanon, the black family is free of neuroses unless contaminated by white, Western culture (151–52, 143–44).

41. Doane, "Dark Continents," 220.

42. Although I repeat Fanon's singular terms "the woman of color" and "the black woman," I do not accept the idea of uniformity within—or a fixed definition of—the category.

43. Bhabha, "Remembering Fanon," 147–48.

44. Relegating gender to a subsidiary position within a "broader" class of oppression has a long history. For example, traditional Marxist theory long argued that economic class is the overarching determinant of social status and therefore advocated that an analysis of patriarchy be subordinated to a critique of capitalism. As a result, traditional Marxism never adequately addressed women's oppression.

45. Toni Morrison uses the phrase to name the "[a]ctive but unsummoned presences" of blackness in canonical American literature that "can distort the workings of the machine and can also *make* it work" ("Unspeakable Things Unspoken," 13).

2. Myths of Masculinity

1. Grosz, *Jacques Lacan: A Feminist Introduction,* 38.

2. I use the masculine pronoun in this paragraph to mimic this assumption that the male is the universal subject.

3. Douglass, *Narrative of the Life of Frederick Douglass, an American Slave, Written by Himself,* hereafter cited in the text.

4. William Andrews writes, "Douglass's account of his rise from slavery to freedom fulfills certain features of the jeremiad's cultural myth of America. . . . [T]he rebellion of a fractious individual against instituted authority is translated into a heroic act of self-reliance, a reenactment of the national myth of regeneration and progress through revolution" ("The Performance of the *Narrative,*" 166).

5. Cunningham, "'Called Into Existence': Desire, Gender, and Voice in Frederick Douglass's *Narrative* of 1845," 109.

6. McDowell, "In the First Place: Making Frederick Douglass and the Afro-American Narrative Tradition," 192.

7. Critical praise for Douglass's 1845 autobiography from both contemporary reviewers and more recent scholars of African American literature reveals something of a paradox: Douglass's text is perceived as the *truest* testimony to African American identity under slavery because it is the most *literary* of the slave narratives. Valerie Smith articulates this formulation as "the paradox that by fictionalizing one's life, one bestows a quality of authenticity on it" (*Self-Discovery and Authority in Afro-American Narrative,* 2).

8. McDowell, "In the First Place," 194.

9. Smith, *Self-Discovery and Authority,* 21.

10. McDowell, "In the First Place," 192–97.

11. Cunningham, "'Called into Existence,'" 111.

12. McDowell writes, "In choosing autobiography as a form, Douglass committed himself to what many feminists consider an androcentric genre" ("In the First Place," 198). Furthermore, women's slave narratives modeled on "feminine" literary forms have been ignored or disparaged as less accurate, convincing, and well-written. Harriet Jacobs's narrative, *Incidents in the Life of a Slave Girl,* has been criticized for its lapses into the language and tropes of women's sentimental writing. See, for example, Stone, "Identity and Art in Frederick Douglass's *Narrative,*" 64; and Franchot, "The Punishment of Esther: Frederick Douglass and the Construction of the Feminine," 148.

13. Silverman, *Male Subjectivity at the Margins,* 17.

14. McDowell, "In the First Place," 194–95.

15. Douglass represents the processes of acquiring literacy and freedom, which culminate in the writing of the *Narrative*, as essential to identity itself. Critics also emphasize that Douglass weaves together freedom, literacy, identity, and authorship; James Olney represents a succinct example: "The social theme, the reality of slavery and the necessity of abolishing it, trifurcates on the personal level to become subthemes of literacy, identity, and freedom which, though not obviously and at first sight closely related matters, nevertheless lead into one another in such a way that they end up being altogether interdependent and virtually indistinguishable as thematic strands" ("'I Was Born': Slave Narratives, Their Status as Autobiography and as Literature," 156).

16. Silverman, *Male Subjectivity*, 15–16.

17. Lubiano, foreword to *(Dis)Forming the American Canon*, xxi.

18. Frederick Douglass, *My Bondage and My Freedom* and *The Life and Times of Frederick Douglass*.

19. For a concise and cogent explanation of why it makes sense to use psychoanalytic theory to analyze texts that predate the rise of psychoanalytic discourse and a defense against charges of psychoanalysis's antihistoricism, see Marshall, "Psychoanalyzing the Prepsychoanalytic Subject," 1207–16.

20. Obeyesekere, *The Work of Culture, Symbolic Transformation in Psychoanalysis and Anthropology*, 71.

21. Ibid., 24, 73.

22. See Parsons, "Is the Oedipus Complex Universal?" 278.

23. Obeyesekere, *The Work of Culture*, 71.

24. Ibid., 71. Freud subsumes issues of power within a theory articulated primarily in terms of sexuality because he lacks a critique of patriarchy as the locus of familial authority. In the cultural context of the European nuclear family, the father—as representative of social authority—has both power over the boy and exclusive sexual access to the boy's erotic object, his mother. Without a critique of the patriarchal power structure, the father's authority is so naturalized as to escape notice. It is not so much that Freud does not recognize the dimension of power in oedipal struggles, but that this dimension is always described through sexuality: the metaphor of castration.

25. Parsons, "Is the Oedipus Complex Universal?" 281.

26. Because Freud lacked a working theory of symbolic or ideologic transmission of cultural attitudes, he hypothesizes the occurrence of "primal scenes" as actual experiences that precipitate the subject's assumption of oedipal attitudes. I would argue that in staging the primal scene, Freud makes visible and concrete the intangible processes that construct desire.

27. Felman, *Jacques Lacan and the Adventure of Insight*, 103.

28. Lacan, *Écrits*, 67.

29. Butler, *Gender Trouble*, 76.

30. Noting the importance of the father's name to the genre of autobiography, Annette Niemtzow writes, "He struggles to define himself by the very terms established not only by white culture, but by autobiography itself. . . . An autobiographer, even a slave autobiographer or even a fictive autobiographer, must pay attention to the ideal of father, if the reader is to believe in the existence of that self" ("The Problematic of Self in Autobiography: The Example of the Slave Narrative," 117, 118). See also McDowell, "In the First Place," 198.

31. Cunningham, "'Called into Existence,'" 112.

32. In one of many observations that Douglass begins with the uncertainty of his own beginning, Henry Louis Gates Jr. writes, "[F]or Douglass, the bonds of blood and kinship are the primary metaphors of human culture." Family ties are more than a metaphor for this text, however; "laws" of kinship structure human society on symbolic and sociolegal levels, both of which have material effects on individuals. Gates himself notes, in the case of slavery, that "patrilinear succession of the planter has been forcibly replaced by a matrilinear succession for the slave" ("Binary Oppositions in Chapter One of the *Narrative*," 70).

33. Spillers, "Mama's Baby, Papa's Maybe," 455.

34. Douglass's lament that the breakdown of the system of paternity effected by irresponsible *white* fathers exposes the illogic of contemporary arguments that blame current racial inequality on irresponsible (absent) *black* fathers.

35. Cunningham, "'Called into Existence,'" 114.

36. Grosz, *Jacques Lacan*, 148.

37. During the Oedipus complex, the paternal metaphor (through the figure of the father) as a symbol of social authority is substituted for the child's love of the mother, which must be repressed according to the incest prohibition. Through this substitution (signified by the father's name and the phallus) the child obtains a place in the social order beyond the family (Grosz, *Jacques Lacan*, 104). This substitution of the father also constitutes the unconscious by interrupting the narcissistic mirroring dyad between mother and child. The introduction of a dominant third term outside the child's self (the father) comes to represent the Other. The father, as representative of the Symbolic, takes on a metaphorical function of authority signified by the phallus (Felman, *Jacques Lacan and the Adventure of Insight*, 105). The subject takes up his/her relation to the paternal metaphor, the signifier phallus, through a process of gender identification. And it is through this accession to the Symbolic, through the paternal metaphor, that the subject enters the system of language, which is determined by the Symbolic.

38. Franchot, "The Punishment of Esther," 141, 148, 144.

39. Douglass, *My Bondage*, 37.

40. Ibid. In his 1845 autobiography, Douglass acknowledges no close

contact with family members and thereby suggests that he is a self-made man; by contrast, the 1855 autobiography draws on conventions of sentimental fiction.

41. "The profound ambiguity of this relationship between father and son and master and slaver persists, if only because the two terms 'father' and 'master' are here embodied in one, with no mediation between them" (Gates, "Binary Oppositions," 70).

42. The rhetorical display of the abused slave woman, a convention of abolitionist literature, suggests that her body is invested with the truth about slavery. Using the image of the unveiled female form to signal the revelation of knowledge was common to nineteenth-century discourses of science and epistemology (see Jordanova, *Sexual Visions*). Sight became a privileged source of knowledge in the nineteenth century, in part because of scientific discoveries about the eye's physiology and the invention of visible technologies such as photographs, daguerreotypes, and stereoscopic cards, which were available to the middle class (see Burbick, *Healing the Republic)*.

43. Freud, "The Dissolution of the Oedipus Complex," 175, 176.

44. Freud, "Some Psychical Consequences of the Anatomical Distinction between the Sexes," 256.

45. Ibid., 252.

46. Ibid.

47. Interestingly, neither Douglass nor those who charge him with reconstituting feminine victimization through his very narration of the whipping scene note that the whipping is, in a sense, occasioned by an act of resistance on Hester's part: she had asserted sexual autonomy by meeting her lover despite the master's prohibition.

48. Franchot, "The Punishment of Esther," 142.

49. Freud, "From the History of an Infantile Neurosis," 210.

50. Ibid., 221.

51. Ibid., 231.

52. Cunningham, "'Called into Existence,'" 123.

53. Leverenz, *Manhood and the American Renaissance,* 109.

54. Franchot, "The Punishment of Esther," 153.

55. McDowell, "In the First Place," 203; ibid., 154.

56. Freud, "A Child Is Being Beaten," 179–204, hereafter cited in the text.

57. Silverman explains that the dominant ideology covers over subjective lack in the male: "[W]hen the Name-of-the-Father organizes the rules determining marriage, reproduction, lineality, abode, and inheritance, The Law of Kinship Structure exists in a contradictory relationship to the Law of Language. The Law of Language dictates universal castration, whereas our Law of Kinship Structure equates the father with the Law, and hence exempts him from it. . . . Our dominant fiction calls upon the male subject to see himself, and the female subject to recognize and desire him, only through the

mediation of images of an unimpaired masculinity. It urges both the male and the female subject, that is, to deny all knowledge of male castration by believing in the commensurability of penis and phallus, actual and symbolic father" (*Male Subjectivity at the Margins*, 42).

58. Franchot, "The Punishment of Esther," 154–55.

3. The Mulatto and the Miscegenation Taboo

1. I use the term "folk" in keeping with Hazel Carby's assessment that literature by urban African Americans in the 1920s represented "the masses of rural black Southern workers . . . as a metaphorical 'folk'" (*Reconstructing Womanhood*, 164).

2. Deborah McDowell writes that Helga is the "classic 'tragic mulatto'": "alienated from both races, she is defeated by her struggle to reconcile the psychic confusion that this mixed heritage creates" (introduction to *Quicksand and Passing*, xvii).

3. Hughes, "Cross," epigraph to *Quicksand and Passing*.

4. Bone, *The Negro Novel in America*, 102.

5. The stereotypic logic of "race" denies the very possibility of African American individuality. Consequently, every African American and every African American author is expected to represent the whole group while, paradoxically, dissolving stereotypes. As we saw with Frederick Douglass, slave narrators were bound to make their individual experiences represent the experiences of slaves in general. Douglass had to prove the humanity of blacks as a whole while also demonstrating his own exceptionalism. As a standard trope of African American literature, the tragic mulatto also bears this burden of representativeness.

6. Wall, *Women of the Harlem Renaissance*, 97.

7. Carby, *Reconstructing Womanhood*, 168.

8. McDowell, introduction to *Quicksand and Passing*, xviii. McDowell explains that, as a writer, Larsen faced the same dilemma in representing black women's sexuality: she had to figure out "[h]ow to write about black female sexuality in a literary era that often sensationalized it and pandered to the stereotype of the primitive exotic" while at the same time "giv[ing] a black female character the right to a healthy sexual expression and pleasure without offending the proprieties established by the spokespersons of the black middle class" (xvi).

9. duCille, *The Coupling Convention: Sex, Text, and Tradition in Black Women's Fiction*, 87. Like McDowell, duCille attests to the groundbreaking importance of desire, sexuality, and subjectivity in *Passing* given the political constraints on representations of black women's sexuality in the 1920s.

10. Washington, *Invented Lives: Narratives of Black Women 1860–1960*, 160.

11. Johnson, *The Feminist Difference: Literature, Psychoanalysis, Race, and Gender,* 42.

12. Tate, *Psychoanalysis and Black Novels: Desire and the Protocols of Race,* 124. Not surprisingly, the tension between these two strains of interpretation, the sociological and psychological, has structured the novel's reception since its publication. Tate summarizes this reception history well (126–29). It would be reductive, however, to label nonpsychoanalytic readings simply "sociological" or even "sociopolitical" when many do discuss the novel's representation of desire and subjectivity.

13. Ibid., 141.

14. Johnson, *The Feminist Difference,* 47, original italics.

15. Grosz, *Jacques Lacan: A Feminist Introduction,* 51.

16. Silverman, *Male Subjectivity at the Margins,* 32, hereafter cited in the text.

17. Lacan, "The Mirror Stage as Formative of the Function of the I," 2.

18. The resemblance between Althusser's concept of interpellation and Lacan's theory of symbolic accommodation should not be surprising given that Althusser draws directly from Freud and Lacan. He cites Freud in "Ideology and Ideological State Apparatuses" and takes terms such as *méconnaissance* from Lacan's essay on the mirror stage, which was published in France in 1966 ("Ideology and Ideological State Apparatuses," 164, 165), hereafter cited in the text.

19. Žižek, *The Sublime Object of Ideology,* 2–3, hereafter cited in the text.

20. Gallop, *Reading Lacan,* 86.

21. Ibid., 84.

22. Ibid., 89.

23. Fuss, *Identification Papers,* 2.

24. Althusser, "*Lenin and Philosophy" and Other Essays,* 163.

25. See Žižek, *The Sublime Object of Ideology,* 43; Silverman, *Male Subjectivity at the Margins,* 22.

26. The individual experiences lack or symbolic castration as s/he accedes to language and the symbolic order. The individual compensates for the lack instituted through language by desiring (the *objet a*), thus becoming a desiring subject. The desire for the *objet a* constitutes a fantasy/or misrecognition in that the subject "believes" the object can heal or fill the lack of being created by accession to the symbolic order.

27. To avoid perpetuating the error of Marxism's economic determinism (the principle that capitalism is the preeminent ideology that masks class conflict; eradicating capitalist ideology will solve all social inequalities) or substituting an alternative determinism, Žižek argues that ideological systems are historically and politically contingent and that they coexist (4). In this post-Marxist view, advanced by Ernesto Laclau and Chantal Mouffe in *Hegemony and Socialist Strategy: Towards a Radical Democratic Politics,* ideology is not

determined solely or even primarily by the mode of production. Although Žižek argues that there is, then, a plurality of social antagonisms (not just class), and any of them "can take over this essential role of mediator for all the others" (4), Silverman argues that the regime of sexual difference is the primary mediator of social antagonisms in Western ideology.

28. Elise Lemire argues that miscegenation functioned as *the* pivotal issue for those opposing black political rights between 1776 and 1865. In her analysis of political tracts, cartoons, and speeches from this time period, Lemire documents the ways in which abolition and black citizenship rights were synonymous with miscegenation in antiabolitionist political rhetoric and in the popular imagination, which held amalgamation, as race mixing was known until 1863, to be an unnatural crossing of species. See Lemire's *"Miscegenation": Making Race in America.*

29. Even in cases where white men wanted to marry black women with whom they had children or recognize their children with black women, laws against interracial marriage and manumission often made this difficult. Racial classification laws ensured that even mixed-race children recognized by white fathers would remain on the disenfranchised side of the color line. Such laws varied over time and by state.

30. Spillers, "'The Tragic Mulatta': Neither/Nor—Toward an Alternative Model," 147.

31. B. Johnson, *The Feminist Difference,* 38.

32. Bentley, "White Slaves: The Mulatto Hero in Antebellum Fiction," 198.

33. Ibid., 196, 197.

34. Somerville, *Queering the Color Line,* 77.

35. Somerville provides a fascinating analysis of the ways in which Hopkins's *Contending Forces* presents feminine sexual desire, specifically lesbian desire, even if it must ultimately be repressed for narrative resolution through the marriage plot (*Queering the Color Line*).

36. These nineteenth-century women writers also participated in "progressive" discourses of the period (as did Du Bois) that African and African American culture should advance through assimilation to white culture. See Somerville, *Queering the Color Line,* 79, and K. Gaines, "Black Americans' Racial Uplift Ideology as 'Civilizing Mission,'" 434.

37. Fuss, *Identification Papers,* 34.

38. Until the 1850s, some mulatto families and communities in certain areas had enjoyed privileges and status withheld from "blacks." But whites had increasingly withdrawn favor in the face of challenges to slavery and, after the Civil War, to white supremacy. At the same time, blacks became increasingly critical of mulattos who supported slavery and the white power structure. In the wake of segregation laws, the mulatto elites allied themselves with other blacks and helped lead the struggle for civil rights (Davis, *Who Is Black?*

77–78). At the same time, mulattos were a special target of white supremacist fears; witness their representation in D.W. Griffith's iconic film *The Birth of a Nation.*

39. Helga's *failure* to identify according to racial norms exposes the *usual* processes through which individuals accede to the requirements of the racial symbolic. Freud indicates that it is often those who deviate from the norm that make visible normativizing forces. Referring to his researches into normal narcissism in the process of ego formation, Freud writes, "Once more, in order to arrive at an understanding of what seems so simple in normal phenomena, we shall have to turn to the field of pathology with its distortions and exaggerations" ("On Narcissism," 82).

40. Lacan, *The Ethics of Psychoanalysis 1959-1960: The Seminar of Jacques Lacan, Book 7*, 319.

41. Butler, *Bodies That Matter,* 94–95, hereafter cited in the text.

42. Ibid, 99. See also Fuss, *Identification Papers,* 6–14, and Silverman, *Male Subjectivity at the Margins,* 6.

43. Freud, "Group Psychology and the Analysis of the Ego," 105, hereafter cited in the text.

44. Fuss, *Identification Papers,* 11.

45. Ibid., 12.

46. Butler, *Gender Trouble,* 63.

47. Fuss, *Identification Papers,* 12.

48. Freud, "The Uncanny," 220.

49. Todd, "The Veiled Woman in Freud's 'Das Unheimliche,'" 524.

50. Bergner and Plett, "Uncanny Women and Anxious Masters: Reading *Coppélia* against Freud," 166.

51. Hoffman, "The Sandman," 110, 114.

52. Bergner and Plett, "Uncanny Women," 166.

53. Du Bois, *The Souls of Black Folk,* 5.

4. Blackness and Class Difference in William Faulkner

1. Hailed as the Great American Novel, *Gone with the Wind* sold a million copies its first year in print and Margaret Mitchell won the Pulitzer prize. For an account of Mitchell's exclusion from and Faulkner's induction into the Southern Renaissance, see Pyron, "*Gone with the Wind* and the Southern Cultural Awakening." For a history and comparison of the novels' contemporary receptions, see Matthews, "The Civil War of 1936: *Gone with the Wind* and *Absalom, Absalom!*" For reevaluations of Mitchell's break with the tenets of traditional Southern ideology, see King, "The 'Simple Story's' Ideology: *Gone with the Wind* and the New South Creed," and O'Brien, "Race, Romance, and the Southern Literary Tradition."

2. Retamar, *Caliban and Other Essays,* 6.

3. Spillers, "Introduction: Who Cuts the Border? Some Readings on 'America,'" 3, 4.

4. Retamar, *Caliban and Other Essays,* 7.

5. Spillers, "Introduction: Who Cuts the Border?" 6.

6. Ibid., 9.

7. Godden, "*Absalom, Absalom!* Haiti and Labor History: Reading Unreadable Revolutions," 698.

8. Howe, "Letters on the Proposed Annexation of Santo Domingo," 369.

9. Barringer, "The American Negro: His Past and Future," 449.

10. Ibid., 449–50.

11. Godden's is an excellent analysis of Haiti's role in *Absalom* and, specifically, of Faulkner's anachronistic representation of Haitian plantation slavery in the 1820s, when it had become an independent nation by 1804.

12. Faulkner, *Absalom, Absalom!* 312, hereafter cited in the text.

13. Retamar, *Caliban and Other Essays,* 5–6, 14.

14. Genovese, *The Political Economy of Slavery,* xvi, 3, 28.

15. Silverman, *Male Subjectivity at the Margins*, 15, hereafter cited in the text.

16. Freud, "Fetishism" (1927), 152–53.

17. Silverman notes that "Freud himself broadens the concept of disavowal to include as one of its meanings the repudiation of something specific to the subject's own self in 'Some Psychical Consequences,' although he relies upon a female rather than a male example in doing so. It is, moreover, precisely upon castration that this disavowal is shown to turn" (46). I would suggest that he uses a female example because he imagines only women experience a sense of castration.

18. Freud, "Fetishism," 157.

19. Ibid., 154.

20. Carolyn Porter places Faulkner's concern with paternity in *Absalom* within the broader context of his interest in the family's relation to society as expressed in his complete works. She argues that Faulkner undertakes "a complex treatment of motherhood . . . in *The Sound and the Fury* and *As I Lay Dying*, where by any accounting the mother—whether dead or alive, woefully absent or dolefully present—figures centrally in the family economy of loss and desire. But as Faulkner's social canvas broadens with *Light in August* and his historical focus deepens with *Absalom, Absalom!* the critical pressure of his attention to the family gradually, and then decisively, shifts to the father." "[T]he question of the status and function of fatherhood that *The Sound and the Fury* poses and that *Light in August* begins to address more fully," continues Porter, "leads finally in *Absalom* to a concerned interrogation of fatherhood as the enigmatic source and vehicle of social identity and political sovereignty" ("*Absalom, Absalom!*: (Un)Making the Father," 169–70).

21. For a discussion of Sutpen as "deviant" seeker of the American dream, see ibid., 172–73.

22. The link between the incest taboo and miscegenation is expressed by an 1854 *Treatise on Sociology*, written by Mississippian Henry Hughes and quoted by Eric Sundquist: "'The same law which forbids consanguineous amalgamation forbids ethnical amalgamation. Both are incestuous. Amalgamation is incest'" ("*Absalom, Absalom!* and the House Divided," 97). Here, the incest taboo is invoked in order to stigmatize miscegenation ("ethnical amalgamation") and to naturalize the taboo against it.

23. Snead, "The 'Joint' of Racism: Withholding the Black in *Absalom, Absalom!*" 132. Sutpen's abandonment of his birth family and subsequent social ascent render him, according to Craig Werner, very like the protagonists of post–Civil War passing narratives ("Minstrel Nightmares: Black Dreams of Faulkner's Dreams of Blacks," 46). I would add that the potential for inadvertent incest between Bon and Judith that results from slavery's violation of conventional family structures and lines of descent also links *Absalom* to the passing novels that appeared after the Civil War.

24. In going to Haiti, "Sutpen thus joins the ranks of literary and historical figures for whom the colonial enterprise became the instrumental task in obtaining the object of their desires and establishing themselves as agents of destiny and subjects of history" (Saldivar, "Looking for a Master Plan: Faulkner, Parades, and the Colonial and Postcolonial Subject," 102–3).

25. That Sutpen's whiteness, established by gaining dominion over blacks, is inevitably compromised by the interracial intimacy required by the master/slave relation prompts Richard Godden to undertake a convincing Hegelian reading of the novel ("*Absalom, Absalom!* Haiti and Labor History: Reading Unreadable Revolutions," especially 690–95). For a similar but brief discussion of the master/slave relation, see also Genovese, *The Political Economy of Slavery,* 32–33.

26. Sutpen's daughter, Judith, is thus constructed "as the body on which the ideology of the South rests" (Roberts, *Faulkner and Southern Womanhood,* 37).

27. Sundquist, "*Absalom, Absalom!* and the House Divided," 100.

28. Smith, *The Color Line: A Brief in Behalf of the Unborn,* 62–63.

29. Ibid., 63–64.

30. Sundquist, "*Absalom, Absalom!* and the House Divided," 92.

31. Snead, "The 'Joint' of Racism: Withholding the Black in *Absalom, Absalom!*" 131.

32. Saldivar, "Looking for a Master Plan: Faulkner, Parades, and the Colonial and Postcolonial Subject," 104–5. For a thorough and historically detailed discussion of the significance of mixed-blood Creole culture in the Caribbean and Louisiana territory to burgeoning ideologies of American nationalism, see Ladd, "'The Direction of the Howling': Nationalism and the Color Line in *Absalom, Absalom!*"

33. Ladd, "'The Direction of the Howling,'" 529–30.

34. Porter also notes that "a strict obedience to the Law of the Father repeatedly undermines Sutpen's dynastic design" ("*Absalom, Absalom!*: (Un)Making the Father," 192). Werner notes that "Sutpen's attempts to manipulate the codes [of racial and gender classifications], which leads to his destruction by the poor white class he should have understood most clearly, reveals not so much his personal corruption as the absurdity of the codes" ("Minstrel Nightmares: Black Dreams of Faulkner's Dreams of Blacks," 47).

35. Snead, "The 'Joint' of Racism: Withholding the Black in *Absalom, Absalom!*" 134.

36. Brooks, "Incredulous Narration: *Absalom, Absalom!*" 110.

37. Snead, "The 'Joint' of Racism: Withholding the Black in *Absalom, Absalom!*" 136.

38. Ibid., 134. Despite his brilliant reading of the relation between the text's theme of an unstable paternal authority and its structure of unstable narrative authority, Brooks elides the issue of race. For discussions of the relation between the instability of racial categories and the elliptical structure of Faulkner's narratives, see Snead, "*Light in August* and the Rhetorics of Racial Division," and Sundquist, "Faulkner, Race, and the Forms of American Fiction."

39. Karl, "Race, History, and Technique in *Absalom, Absalom!*" 217–18.

40. Snead, "*Light in August* and the Rhetorics of Racial Division," 152.

41. Sundquist, "Faulkner, Race, and the Forms of American Fiction," 25. Many other, especially earlier, essays on the novel indicate the relation between the story of the Sutpens and the myths and history of the South as a whole. See, for example, Bjork, "Ancient Myths and the Moral Framework of *Absalom, Absalom!*"; Kartiganer, "The Role of Myth in *Absalom, Absalom!*"; Markowitz, "William Faulkner's 'Tragic Legend': Southern History and *Absalom, Absalom!*"; Sabiston, "Women, Blacks, and Thomas Sutpen's Mythopoeic Drive in *Absalom, Absalom!*"

42. Irwin, *Doubling and Incest/Repetition and Revenge*, 98.

43. Porter, "*Absalom, Absalom!*: (Un)Making the Father," 180, 181.

44. Irwin, quoted in ibid., 181.

45. Ibid., 181, 182.

46. Sutpen's transition from feelings of impotence to sense of purpose is marked by "an explosion—a bright glare that vanished and left nothing, no ashes or refuse: just a limitless flat plain with the severe shape of his intact innocence rising from it like a monument" (Faulkner, 297). Porter writes that in this movement from insulted boy to man with a plan, "Sutpen violently repudiates . . . his own impotence, an impotence whose discovery immediately produces the phallic monument in which it is at once enshrined and disavowed" ("*Absalom, Absalom!*: (Un)Making the Father," 190). In noting that Sutpen disavows castration, Porter links her description of the mechanism

that perpetuates patriarchy to Silverman's description of the process through which masculinity depends on disavowing subjective lack.

47. In her excellent analysis of class in *Absalom,* Myra Jehlen writes that "it is really the agrarian class conflict which initiates, motivates, and concludes Sutpen's career, with problems of race set, as it were, parenthetically within its broader context" (*Class and Character in Faulkner's South,* 67). I would modify this claim only to suggest that race is fully implicated in the class antagonisms. As Snead writes, "Faulkner's text illustrates that American caste and economic relations revolve around the black, the source of the paradoxes in Sutpen's story and American society's most volatile subject" ("The 'Joint' of Racism: Withholding the Black in *Absalom, Absalom!*" 134).

48. "Sutpen takes the incident at the front door of the plantation house in retrospect as the ***unique*** moment of subject formation, when in fact it is not unique but represents instead one in a *series* of social moments that together have shaped his life" (Saldivar, "Looking for a Master Plan," 99).

49. Porter writes of the planter's absent presence: "By detaching 'the paternal function' from its mere operation in the domain of images, what Lacan calls the 'imaginary,' and according it a transcendentalized status in the symbolic domain, the 'locus' of what he calls the 'Other,' Lacan enables us to see how the mechanism of patriarchy operates in order to perpetuate itself" ("*Absalom, Absalom!*: (Un)Making the Father," 182).

50. Snead, "The 'Joint' of Racism," 137.

51. Snead writes that the "errors of omission" reflect the "hoped for social order" ("The 'Joint' of Racism," 138). And Werner terms this denial of relation "the difficulty of acknowledging likeness," and cites as an example Rosa's hostility toward Clytie ("Minstrel Nightmares," 45).

52. The contractual, economic, and homosocial nature of marriage could not be made more obvious: it is five years before Sutpen "had speaking acquaintance with any white woman in the county, just as he had not furniture in his house and for the same reason: he had nothing to exchange for it them or her" (73). Rosa says that "since papa had given him respectability through a wife there was nothing else he could want from papa" (29).

53. Snead, "The 'Joint' of Racism," 138.

54. Freud, "Fetishism," 154.

55. Ibid., 153.

56. Ibid., 154.

57. Ibid., 154.

58. Richard King writes, "Nor did *Gone with the Wind* express the tragic ambivalence found in . . . Faulkner. Rather, it exemplifies the historical consciousness underlying the 'New South creed.' Though bearing its own share of nostalgia, the obscure object of the novel's desire is as much New South promise as it is Old South tradition. As Paul Gaston has noted, the New South advocates celebrated the antebellum South but also sanctioned industrial

development under the dispensation of laissez-faire capitalism. They shed no tears for the demise of the peculiar institution of slavery yet projected a South of white supremacy and black subordination, a sort of middle-class paternalism" ("The 'Simple Story's' Ideology," 170).

5. Rites and Responsibilities

1. Christian, "Fixing Methodologies: *Beloved,*" 363.

2. Ibid., 368.

3. Though I understand Christian's concern that "Western" readings of the novel have outstripped Africanist interpretations, I acknowledge that my own reading does little to correct this imbalance. My reading focuses on how the novel bridges discourses of history and subjectivity, the collective and the individual, even as I recognize that the novel also bridges Western and African worldviews.

4. Christina Zwarg fruitfully discusses the historic and theoretical relationships between Du Bois's notion of double consciousness—as a framework for conceptualizing the psychic effects of the trauma of slavery and segregation—and psychoanalysis's notion of trauma, especially its double structure of time, translation, and interlocution ("Du Bois on Trauma: Psychoanalysis and the Would-Be Black Savant," 1–39).

5. Morrison, "Unspeakable Things Unspoken: The Afro-American Presence in American Literature," 378. For more on Morrison's project of analyzing the "Africanistic presence" in American literature, see her book of critical essays, *Playing in the Dark.*

6. Hirsch, *The Mother/Daughter Plot,* 22.

7. V. Smith, "'Circling the Subject': History and Narrative in *Beloved,*" 343.

8. For more on Jacobs's strategies of narration, see Smith, "'Loopholes of Retreat:' Architecture and Ideology in Harriet Jacobs's *Incidents in the Life of a Slave Girl,*" and Yellin, introduction to *Incidents in the Life of a Slave Girl,* by Harriet Jacobs.

9. For a discussion of *Beloved* as a response to the omissions of slave narratives, see Holloway, "*Beloved:* A Spiritual"; Mobley, "A Different Remembering: Memory, History and Meaning in Toni Morrison's *Beloved*"; and Travis, "Speaking from the Silence of the Slave Narrative: *Beloved* and African-American Women's History."

10. Smith writes that Morrison's "characters understand who they are and what their lives mean when they can tell stories about how they came to be" (122).

11. V. Smith, *Self-Discovery and Authority in Afro-American Narrative,* 126, 122.

12. Enslaved individuals did not, of course, lack all agency (and free individuals are not without subjective constraint). Many of the novel's former

slaves acted to free themselves and to assist others in escaping slavery, for example. Nonetheless, the novel meditates on how slavery compromised psychic agency. Mr. Garner's supposedly kinder and gentler slavery is instructive on this count. Although he granted his male slaves more autonomy than most masters—calling them men, not boys, and allowing them to make some farming decisions, the novel demonstrates, especially through Paul D's story, how the institution still circumscribed their self-possession and their claims to normative masculinity.

13. The link between slavery's fragmentation of bodily autonomy and subjective incoherence is figured in Beloved's fear of bodily dissolution; her lost teeth announce disintegration rather than a baby's healthy growth (135). Baby Suggs tries to heal such fragmentation through preaching a catalogue that names the body's parts. She instructs her followers to love their bodies because "[y]onder they do not love your flesh. They despise it. They don't love your eyes; they'd just as soon pick em out. No more do they love the skin on your back. Yonder they flay it. And O my people they do not love your hands. . . . *You* got to love it, *you*!" (88). The conjunction of identity and the body, while not limited to the context of slavery, resonates with the ways blacks were equated with their bodies while stripped of control over them. The coupling of subjectivity and the body is replayed in Beloved's duality as ghost and flesh, girl and memory. Beloved's siren call to Paul D to "touch me. On my inside part. And you have to call me my name" reveals sexual, physical touch as a kind of naming or interpellation by an other in response to which subjectivity forms.

14. *Beloved* shares with Morrison's preceding works a focus on the individual's relation to the community. Writing before the publication of *Beloved*, Valerie Smith argues that Morrison's novels explore a communal sense of identity. In relation to *Song of Solomon* she writes, "The communal sense of identity that informs the earlier novels obtains here as well. Milkman's search for self-fulfillment is complete only when he recognizes that identity is a collective rather than an individual construct, and so defines himself in relation to a broad sense of history and community" (*Self-Discovery and Authority in Afro-American Narrative*, 136).

15. Wyatt, "Giving Body to the Word: The Maternal Symbolic in Toni Morrison's *Beloved*," 475.

16. Hirsch, *The Mother/Daughter Plot*, 7.

17. Caruth, introduction to the special issue "Psychoanalysis, Culture, and Trauma," 3.

18. Ibid.

19. Ibid., 3–4.

20. Caruth writes, "It is this inherent latency of the event that paradoxically explains the peculiar, temporal structure, the belatedness, of historical experience: since the traumatic event is not experienced as it occurs, it is fully evident only in connection with another place, and in another time" (ibid., 7).

21. Felman and Laub, *Testimony,* 57. Without comparing or equating the horrors of the Holocaust and slavery, I think it is safe to note that each was a socially and legally sanctioned system that denied the very humanity of a group of people in order to justify unimaginable brutality against them. Slavery, like the Holocaust, "created a world in which one could not bear witness to oneself . . . [and] when one's history is abolished, one's identity ceases to exist as well" (82).

22. Ibid., 51.

23. For a discussion of the importance of storytelling, personal narrative, and history to identity in Morrison's texts, see also Rushdy, "Daughters Signifyin(g) History: The Example of Toni Morrison's *Beloved.*" For a discussion of these themes in African American women's writing in general, see Henderson, "Speaking in Tongues: Dialogics, Dialectics, and the Black Woman Writer's Literary Tradition."

24. The psychic toll required by Sethe's attempts to explain and atone is matched by the physical sacrifice of her body ("open as any grave") to the engraver in return for the written message, "Beloved." The inscription and the self-sacrifice that paid for it serve as an explanation to the community as well as to Beloved: "She thought it would be enough, rutting among the headstones with the engraver, his young son looking on, the anger in his face so old; the appetite in it quite new. That should certainly be enough. Enough to answer one more preacher, one more abolitionist and a town full of disgust" (5).

25. Johnson, "Apostrophe, Animation and Abortion," 189, hereafter cited in the text.

26. Gallop, "The Monster in the Mirror: The Feminist Critic's Psychoanalysis," 15.

27. Ibid., 15, 16.

28. Ibid., 190.

29. Abel, "Race, Class, and Psychoanalysis? Opening Questions," 185.

30. The grounding of object relations in cultural arrangements not only bridges the gap between psychoanalysis and other theories of social change, but also reveals the similarities among psychoanalytic schools: "When difference is interpreted through a social as well as a linguistic framework the heterogeneity of the Lacanian subject seems insufficiently textured and less radically different from the intersubjectively constituted self of object relations" (ibid., 186). Arguing that both Lacanian and object relations discourses can be socially contextualized, Abel nonetheless claims that Lacanian psychoanalysis is structurally resistant to accounting for cultural variability "since this discourse collapses the social into a symbolic register that is always everywhere the same. While de-essentializing gender by relocating it in a cultural arena that is severed from biology, orthodox Lacanians essentialize a dehistoricized paternal law" (185). Notwithstanding Lacan's own rejection of

the sociological in psychoanalysis, I am not altogether willing to concede that Lacanian psychoanalysis structurally excludes social context.

31. Benjamin, "A Desire of One's Own: Psychoanalytic Feminism and Intersubjective Space," 78–80.

32. Waugh, *Feminine Fictions,* 14.

33. Chodorow, *The Reproduction of Mothering,* 93.

34. Benjamin, "A Desire of One's Own," 80.

35. Waugh, *Feminine Fictions,* 34–35. Teresa de Lauretis also distinguishes between poststructuralism's fragmented, split, and linguistically constructed subject and the more fluid, shifting, and multiple subject of much feminist theory. The political advantages of this feminist model of negotiated identity, argues de Lauretis, is that it can account for the differences of gender, race, and class through attention to "the personal, the subjective, the quotidian, as the very site of material inscription of the ideological" ("Feminist Studies/Critical Studies: Issues, Terms, and Contexts," 11).

36. "In psychoanalysis, it becomes more apparent that the celebration of individuality is a gender-related project. Indeed, the feminist critique of individualism has taken psychoanalysis itself to task both for its tendency to make independence and separateness the goal of development (as in the view that the ego develops from oneness to separateness) and for the idea that femininity is defined by the lack of the penis" (Benjamin, "A Desire of One's Own," 81).

37. Chodorow, *The Reproduction of Mothering,* 93.

38. Hirsch, *The Mother/Daughter Plot,* 12.

39. The following essays discuss *Beloved* as a narrative of maternal subjectivity: Hirsch, "Maternal Narratives: 'Cruel Enough to Stop the Blood'"; Mathieson, "Memory and Mother Love in Morrison's *Beloved*"; Moglen, "Redeeming History: Toni Morrison's *Beloved*"; and Wyatt, "Giving Body to the Word."

40. Morrison's novel has been helpful for adding theories of the body to psychoanalysis's language-based theories of subjectivity. Certainly, mothers' and blacks' social experience of the body share similarities. Historically, women have been identified with the bodily and biological, with discrimination proceeding from this perception and maternity representing the epitome of its practice: "Nothing entangles women more firmly in their bodies than pregnancy, birth, lactation, miscarriage, or the inability to conceive pregnancy" (Hirsch, *The Mother/Daughter Plot,* 166). And African Americans, both in constructions of blackness and in slavery, have been reduced to the bodily, defined and exchanged as bodies, and denigrated in terms of the construction of those bodies. Not only is experience of the maternal or black body mediated by socially constrained representations, but that experience of the body is that it is not your own. See also Henderson, "Toni Morrison's *Beloved*: Re-Membering the Body as Historical Text"; and Goldman, "'I

Made the Ink': (Literary) Production and Reproduction in *Dessa Rose* and *Beloved*."

41. Abel, "Race, Class, and Psychoanalysis?" 185–86, 185, 186.

42. Segura and Pierce, "Chicana/o Family Structure and Gender Personality: Chodorow, Familism, and Psychoanalytic Sociology Revisited," 62–63.

43. Ibid., 64.

44. Benjamin, "A Desire of One's Own," 80.

45. Hirsch, *Mother/Daughter Plot,* 167–68.

46. Benjamin, "A Desire of One's Own," 82.

47. Spillers, "Interstices: A Small Drama of Words," 76. Beloved's ghostly state also symbolizes her exclusion from the cultural and symbolic laws of patrilineage, which determine membership in social categories of the "human." The enslaved child who is excluded from the system "does become, under the press of a patronymic, patrifocal, patrilineal, and patriarchal order, the man/woman on the boundary, whose human status, by the very nature of the case, had yet to be defined" (Spillers, "Mama's Baby, Papa's Maybe," 469).

48. Spillers, "'The Permanent Obliquity of an In[pha]llibly Straight': In the Time of the Daughters and the Fathers," 157.

49. Spillers, "Mama's Baby, Papa's Maybe," 455.

50. Spillers, "'The Permanent Obliquity of an In[pha]llibly Straight,'" 157.

51. Morrison succeeds in representing the damaging effects of black men's historic exclusion from the sociolegal domestic economy of the dominant class without suggesting that instating black patriarchy will end the political and economic disenfranchisement of African Americans. Slavery's preclusion of black men from normative male gender identity is represented by Halle's crisis of witnessing—which precipitates his psychological breakdown—wherein he helplessly watches Sethe's abuse at the hands of Schoolmaster's nephews. Paul D meditates on the fragility of his sense of manhood under slavery since it was conferred only by the grace of his master, Garner, who eccentrically deigned to call his male slaves men rather than boys. Paul D's socially dislocated wandering across the American landscape before he reaches Sethe also ensues, in part, from slavery's exclusion of black men from familial systems. He is reincorporated into the family through his relationship with Sethe—a relationship that imagines a paternal and conjugal role for men based on mutuality rather than dominance.

52. The welfare reforms proposed and enacted since the term of the Republican-led 105th U.S. Congress, which created "marriage incentives," presume that poverty stems from breaking the norms of the patriarchal nuclear family structure.

53. In her discussion of poems about abortion, Johnson notes the political stakes of not reproducing children in the African American community: "The consequences of the death of a child ramify beyond the mother-child dyad to encompass the fate of an entire community. The world that has created

conditions under which the loss of a baby becomes desirable must be resisted, not joined. For a black woman, the loss of a baby can always be perceived as a complicity with genocide" ("Apostrophe, Animation, and Abortion," 195).

54. Reclaiming maternal discourse is important for rethinking issues of power; Hirsch writes that "the mother, in fact, is in the position of carrying all human fears and fantasies about power and authority. . . . A reconceptualization of power, authority and anger can emerge only if feminism can both practice and theorize a maternal discourse, based in maternal experience and capable of combining power and powerlessness, authority and invisibility, strength and vulnerability, anger and love" (*The Mother/Daughter Plot,* 166–67).

55. Gilligan, *In a Different Voice,* 70, hereafter cited in the text.

56. Sethe's guilt and sorrow over Beloved's death do not necessarily indicate that she regrets her choice of death over slavery for her daughter. Johnson explains the paradox of a woman's grief over an abortion that she nonetheless does not regret: "Readers of Brooks' poem ["The Mother"] have often read it as an argument against abortion. And it is certainly clear that the poem is not saying that abortion is a good thing. But to see it as making a simple case for the embryo's right to life is to assume that a woman who has chosen abortion does not have the right to mourn. It is to assume that no case for abortion can take the woman's feelings of guilt and loss into consideration, that to take those feelings into account is to deny the right to choose the act that produced them. Yet the poem makes no such claim: it attempts the impossible task of humanizing both the mother and the aborted children while presenting the inadequacy of language to resolve the dilemma without violence" ("Apostrophe, Animation, and Abortion," 191).

57. Gilligan observes that women who subscribe to rigid codes of feminine self-sacrifice often cannot face making any decision if all options entail hurting someone. In such cases, women construe themselves as passive, without agency: "The essence of moral decision is the exercise of choice and the willingness to accept responsibility for that choice. To the extent that women perceive themselves as having no choice, they correspondingly excuse themselves from the responsibility that decision entails" (*In a Different Voice*, 67).

58. That Denver learns to see her mother as a subject in her own right, rather than as a projection of her fears and fantasies, through listening to the story of her mother's experience, coincides with Hirsch's admonition that "[u]nless feminism can begin to demystify and politicize motherhood, and by extension female power more generally, fears and projections will continue. Feminism might begin by listening to the stories that mothers have to tell, and by creating the space in which mothers might articulate those stories" (*The Mother/Daughter Plot,* 167). Denver's success at resolving her own issues of individuation in order to develop empathy also illustrates Benjamin's claim that the capacity for recognition of others as subjects is what is at stake in

the mother-child relation as the matrix in which identity forms: "[T]he vital issue is whether the mother herself is able to recognize the child's subjectivity, and later whether the child can recognize the mother" ("A Desire of One's Own," 82).

59. Hirsch notes that feminist discourse, in its efforts to de-essentialize femininity, has been reluctant to discuss the physical and bodily experience of maternity and has, instead, privileged the cultural construction of mothering: "It is easy to grant that neither sex nor gender can be invoked as fixed or unproblematic categories. It is more difficult to assert that reproduction provides a radical arena of difference—and more than merely biological difference—and that it thereby challenges a positional, destabilized view of sex and gender more than perhaps anything else. The perspective of the maternal makes it difficult simply to reject the notion of biology and forces us to engage both the meaning of the body and the risks of what has been characterized as essentialist" (*The Mother/Daughter Plot,* 12). On the other hand, recent developments in the science and culture of reproduction (such as surrogacy) have further complicated any simple definition of biological maternity.

60. It may be necessary to stress that recognition of context and variability in relation to ethical choices does not render the concept of morality obsolete; neither does it render morality so flexible as to be meaningless. Gilligan's study shows a difference between moral frameworks, not the absence of moral standards. In other words, contextual rather than systematic morality uses different criteria for judgment; it does not lack criteria.

61. Gallop, "The Monster in the Mirror," 20–21.

62. Applebome, "John Hope Franklin, the Last Integrationist," 34–35.

63. Jacques Lacan, *Écrits,* 286.

64. In *Beloved,* subject formation is the exclusive product neither of the mother-child relation, nor the oedipal triad.

65. Both object relationists and Lacanians seem always to return to the phallus as the sticking point of psychoanalytic feminism. Benjamin writes that "the idealization of separation and the idealization of the phallus go together. We see that in Juliet Mitchell's argument that the phallus is the representative of the principle of individuation. That father and his phallus intervene to spring the child from the dyadic trap, the oneness with mother, forcing the child to individuate. This theme has been reiterated in myriad forms; indeed, the relationship to the father's phallus may be the indissoluble lump in the batter for a feminist version of psychoanalysis" ("A Desire of One's Own," 81). Gallop writes, "The debate over Lacan's, and beyond that, psychoanalysis' value for feminism itself centers on the phallus" (*Thinking through the Body,* 125).

66. Explaining how the phallic system of symbolization precludes articulation of feminine desire, Waugh writes, "In Lacan's system one cannot become a speaking subject at all, however, without entering the symbolic order and

accepting the phallus as the representation of the Law of the Father, repressing the desire for 'lost' wholeness which creates the unconscious. As desire moves in the unconscious ceaselessly from one signifier to another, seeking the impossible original lost object, the only hope of change offered to women by Lacan is through the impermanence of linguistic signifiers" (*Feminine Fictions,* 60). Hirsch similarly writes, "Both Freud and Lacan attribute to the mother a sole object of desire—the phallus. And since the phallus (as lack) is the tool of representation, and since the mother does not have it (in Lacan's terms, women lack lack), any other articulation of her own becomes an impossibility" (*The Mother/Daughter Plot,* 168).

67. Gallop, *Thinking through the Body,* 126.

68. Benjamin, "A Desire of One's Own," 84.

69. Gallop, *The Daughter's Seduction,* 14.

70. Ibid., 12.

71. Benjamin, "A Desire of One's Own," 92. When Benjamin suggests "finding an alternative to the phallic structures," it is not clear whether by "finding" she means identifying or inventing. Does her model of intersubjectivity describe women's actual social existence and psychic structures or a prescriptive version of them? Prescribing an alternative to the symbolic order as presently signified would be a significantly more ambitious task than displacing the phallus's singularity through identifying competing signifiers. I would suggest that much psychoanalytic feminism is not clear on this point.

72. Ibid., 94–95.

73. Gallop, *Thinking through the Body,* 128. For a discussion of the inevitable conflation of penis and phallus despite Lacanian assertions that men have the phallus no more than do women, see 125–31.

74. Ibid., 127.

75. Ibid., 128.

76. Lacan says the unconscious and its origin in humans' relation to language is unrelated to culture and ideology and operates according to some discrete and transcendent law: "It is not a question of the relation between man and language as a social phenomenon, there being no question even of something resembling the ideological psychogenesis with which we are familiar. . . . It is a question of rediscovering in the laws that govern that other scene (*ein andere Schauplatz*), which Freud, on the subject of dreams, designates as being that of the unconscious" (*Écrits,* 285).

77. Abel, "Race, Class, and Psychoanalysis?" 188.

78. Ibid., 286.

79. Benjamin, "A Desire of One's Own," 96.

80. The feminist model of a relational or negotiated identity neither suggests total self-knowledge, nor precludes the unconscious: "Much contemporary feminist fictional writing . . . has accommodated humanist beliefs in individual agency and the necessity and possibility of self-reflection and historical

continuity as the basis of personal identity. It has modified the traditional forms of such beliefs, however, in order to emphasize the provisionality and positionality of identity, the historical and social construction of gender, and the discursive production of knowledge and power. What many of these texts suggest is that it is possible to experience oneself as a strong and coherent agent in the world, *at the same time* as understanding the extent to which identity and gender are socially constructed and represented" (Waugh, *Feminine Fictions*, 13).

81. Edwards, "Ghost Story," 18.

82. Morrison, "Unspeakable Things Unspoken," 32.

Afterword

1. Walker, *Black, White, and Jewish: Autobiography of a Shifting Self*; Danzy Senna, *Caucasia*. Two other recent popular memoirs about biracial families, though the authors do not explicitly identify as biracial, are James McBride's *The Color of Water: A Black Man's Tribute to His White Mother*, and Gregory Howard Williams's *Life on the Color Line: The True Story of a White Boy Who Discovered He Was Black*.

2. "My Shoes." http://myshoes.com/MSMembership.html. April 30, 2003.

3. Meacham, "The New Face of Race," 38–41.

4. Project Race, www.projectrace.com/aboutprojectrace/. April 14, 2003.

5. The biracial and multiracial movement is, of course, only a recent permutation of a longstanding discourse on racial mixedness or hybridity. As Naomi Pabst warns, "[T]he tendency to overstate the historical ineluctability of the one-drop rule elides the a priori crisis of classification mulattoes have long presented within American discursive and cultural imaginaries." Discourses of mixed-race identity have long been used to undermine "rigid racist infrastructures," even though current expressions of multiracialism often imply their own originality ("Blackness/Mixedness: Contestations over Crossing Signs," 179, 181).

6. Racial categories have changed often over the course of census history and, at previous times, the census did include the category "mulatto." However, not until 1960 were individuals allowed to choose the racial category to which they belonged: "From 1930–1960, racial categories were still defined by the government, and undertrained, underpaid census-takers looked at people in order to determine their race. In 1960, self-identification became the rule" ("Race and the Census," 10). For an overview and analysis of the history of race categories used by the U.S. Census, see Goldberg, "Taking Stock: Counting by Race."

7. Holmes, "The Politics of Race and the Census," 3.

8. See Holmes, "The Confusion over Who We Are," 1, 5.

9. Murdock, "Separation of Race," 3.

10. Swift, "A Fresh Face on Race," 1; Trent, "'Multiracial' Category Is a Mixed Blessing," 39.

11. Milloy, "U.S. Census Cultivates Fiction of Race," 1.

12. Jacoby, "The Absurdity of Question 6," 3.

13. Holmes writes, "In contemporary America, the apportionment of political power on the basis of population, the use of race in the drawing of legislative districts, and racial bloc voting have prompted people to inflate their numbers. Or at least fear their dilution. That was why several civil rights groups and the Congressional Black Caucus opposed allowing people to choose more than one race on the 2000 census" ("The Politics of Race and the Census").

14. Rodriguez, "Civil Rights Groups Wary of Census Data on Race," 1.

15. Ibid.

16. Murdock, "Separation of Race." See also Lind, quoted in Holmes, "The Politics of Race in the Census."

17. Jen Chau, quoted in Graham, "Mixed Reaction to Census," 22.

18. Root, "Bill of Rights for Racially Mixed People," *Interracial Voice*, www.webcom.com/~intvoice/rights.html. May 26, 2003.

19. Project Race, www.projectrace.com/aboutprojectrace/. April 14, 2003.

20. Pabst comments on the potential problems of essentialism embedded within seemingly radical notions of racial hybridity: "A contention with this 'third space' to borrow Homi Bhabha's term, tactically disrupts binaries and places in relief borderlands, interstitial spaces, and contact zones that are too often disavowed. But it also risks reinscribing the very modes of classification it seeks to critique by establishing an additional category of belonging with its own dominant narratives, its own questions of belonging, its own issues of authenticity and essentialism, and its own policings and regulations" ("Blackness/Mixedness," 202–3).

21. Berlant, *The Queen of America Goes to Washington City: Essays on Sex and Citizenship*, 177, hereafter cited in the text.

22. Wiegman, "Intimate Publics: Race, Property, and Personhood," 860.

Works Cited

Abel, Elizabeth. "Race, Class, and Psychoanalysis? Opening Questions." In *Conflicts in Feminism*, edited by Marianne Hirsch and Evelyn Fox Keller. New York: Routledge, 1990.

Abel, Elizabeth, Barbara Christian, and Helene Moglen, eds. *Female Subjects in Black and White: Race, Psychoanalysis, and Feminism.* Berkeley and Los Angeles: University of California Press, 1997.

Althusser, Louis. *"Lenin and Philosophy" and Other Essays.* Translated by Ben Brewster. London: NLB, 1971.

Andrews, William L. "The Performance of the *Narrative.*" In *Frederick Douglass's Narrative of the Life of Frederick Douglass,* edited by Harold Bloom. New York: Chelsea House, 1988.

Appiah, Anthony. "The Uncompleted Argument: Du Bois and the Illusion of Race." In *"Race," Writing and Difference,* edited by Henry Louis Gates Jr. Chicago: University of Chicago Press, 1986.

Applebome, Peter. "John Hope Franklin, the Last Integrationist." *New York Times Magazine*, April 23, 1995, 34–37.

Barringer, P. "The American Negro: His Past and Future." In *Racial Determinism and the Fear of Miscegenation Pre-1900,* edited by John David Smith. New York: Garland, 1993.

Benjamin, Jessica. "A Desire of One's Own: Psychoanalytic Feminism and

Intersubjective Space." In *Feminist Studies/Critical Studies,* edited by Teresa de Lauretis. Bloomington: Indiana University Press, 1986.

Bentley, Nancy. "White Slaves: The Mulatto Hero in Antebellum Fiction." In *Subjects and Citizens: Nation, Race, and Gender from Oroonoko to Anita Hill,* edited by Michael Moon and Cathy N. Davidson. Durham: Duke University Press, 1995.

Bergner, Gwen. "Politics and Pathologies: On the Subject of Race in Psychoanalysis." In *Frantz Fanon: Critical Perspectives,* edited by Anthony C. Alessandrini. New York: Routledge, 1999.

Bergner, Gwen, and Nicole Plett. "Uncanny Women and Anxious Masters: Reading *Coppélia* against Freud." In *Moving Words: Re-writing Dance,* edited by Gay Morris. New York: Routledge, 1996.

Berlant, Lauren. *The Queen of America Goes to Washington City: Essays on Sex and Citizenship*. Durham: Duke University Press, 1987.

Bhabha, Homi. "Interrogating Identity: The Postcolonial Prerogative." In *The Anatomy of Racism,* edited by David Theo Goldberg. Minneapolis: University of Minnesota Press, 1990.

——. "The Other Question: Difference, Discrimination, and the Discourse of Colonialism." In *Literature, Politics, and Theory: Papers from the Essex Conference 1976–1984,* edited by Francis Barker, Peter Hulme, Margaret Iversen, and Diana Loxley. Colchester: Colchester University Press, 1983.

——. "The Other Question: The Stereotype and Colonial Discourse." In *The Sexual Subject: A Screen Reader in Sexuality.* New York: Routledge, 1992.

——. "Remembering Fanon: Self, Psyche, and the Colonial Condition." In *Remaking History,* edited by Barbara Kruger and Phil Mariani. Seattle: Bay Press, 1989.

Bjork, Lennart. "Ancient Myths and the Moral Framework of *Absalom, Absalom!*" In *American Literature* 35, no. 2 (1963): 196–204.

Blassingame, John W. *The Slave Community: Plantation Life in the Antebellum South*. Rev. ed. New York: Oxford University Press, 1972.

Bone, Robert. *The Negro Novel in America.* New Haven: Yale University Press, 1958.

Boyarin, Daniel. "What Does a Jew Want?; or, The Political Meaning of the Phallus." In *The Psychoanalysis of Race,* edited by Christopher Lane. New York: Columbia University Press, 1998.

Brooks, Peter. "Incredulous Narration: *Absalom, Absalom!*" In *William Faulkner's Absalom, Absalom!* edited by Harold Bloom. Chelsea: New York, 1987.

Bruce Jr., Dickson D. "W. E. B. Du Bois and the Idea of Double Consciousness." *American Literature* 64, no. 2 (1992): 299–309.

Burbick, Joan. *Healing the Republic.* Cambridge, England: Cambridge University Press, 1994.

Butler, Judith. *Bodies That Matter.* New York: Routledge, 1993.

——. *Gender Trouble.* New York: Routledge, 1990.

Capécia, Mayotte. *Je suis Martiniquaise.* Paris: Corrêa, 1948.

Carby, Hazel V., *Reconstructing Womanhood.* New York: Oxford University Press, 1987.

Caruth, Cathy. Introduction to the special issue, "Psychoanalysis, Culture, and Trauma." *American Imago* 48, no. 1 (1991): 1–12.

Chodorow, Nancy. *The Reproduction of Mothering.* Berkeley and Los Angeles: University of California Press, 1978.

Christian, Barbara. *Black Feminist Criticism: Perspectives on Black Women Writers.* Berkeley: Pergamon, 1983.

——. "Fixing Methodologies: *Beloved.*" In *Female Subjects in Black and White: Race, Psychoanalysis, and Feminism,* edited by Elizabeth Abel, Barbara Christian, and Helene Moglen. Berkeley and Los Angeles: University of California Press, 1997.

——. "The Race for Theory." In *The Nature and Context of Minority Discourse,* edited by Abdul R. JanMohamed and David Lloyd. New York: Oxford University Press, 1990.

Cooke, Michael G. *Afro-American Literature in the Twentieth Century.* New Haven: Yale University Press, 1984.

Cunningham, George P. "'Called into Existence': Desire, Gender, and Voice in Frederick Douglass's *Narrative* of 1845." *Differences* 1, no. 3 (1989): 108–36.

Davies, Carol Boyce. *Black Women, Writing, and Identity: Migrations of the Subject.* New York: Routledge, 1994.

Davis, F. James. *Who Is Black?* University Park: Pennsylvania State University Press, 1991.

Doane, Mary Ann. "Dark Continents: Epistemologies of Racial and Sexual Difference in Psychoanalysis and the Cinema." In *Femmes Fatales: Feminism, Film Theory, Psychoanalysis.* New York: Routledge, 1991.

——. "Film and the Masquerade." *The Sexual Subject: A Screen Reader in Sexuality.* New York: Routledge, 1992.

Douglass, Frederick. *The Life and Times of Frederick Douglass, An American Slave, Written by Himself.* New York: Gramercy Books, 1993.

——. *My Bondage and My Freedom.* 1855. Urbana: University of Illinois Press, 1987.

——. *Narrative of the Life of Frederick Douglass, an American Slave.* 1845. New York: Penguin, 1982.

Du Bois, W. E. B. *The Souls of Black Folk.* 1903. New York: Penguin, 1989.

duCille, Anne. *The Coupling Convention: Sex, Text, and Tradition in Black Women's Fiction.* New York: Oxford University Press, 1993.

Edwards, Thomas. "Ghost Story." *New York Review of Books,* November 5, 1987, 18–19.

Eilberg-Schwartz, Howard. "Freud as a Jew." *New York Times,* January 9, 1994, sec. 7, 30.

Elliot, Patricia. *From Mastery to Analysis.* Ithaca: Cornell University Press, 1991.

Ellison, Ralph. *Invisible Man.* New York: Vintage, 1952.

Eng, David. *Racial Castration: Managing Masculinity in Asian America.* Durham: Duke University Press, 2001.

Fanon, Frantz. *Black Skin, White Masks.* Translated by Charles Lam Markmann. New York: Grove Press, 1967. Originally published as *Peau noire, masques blancs.* Paris: *Éditions du Seuil,* 1952.

——. *The Wretched of the Earth.* Translated by Constance Farrington. New York: Grove Weidenfeld, 1991. Originally published as *Les damnés de la terre.* Paris: François Maspero, 1964.

Faulkner, William. *Absalom, Absalom!* New York: Vintage, 1990.

Felman, Shoshana. *Jacques Lacan and the Adventure of Insight.* Cambridge: Harvard University Press, 1987.

——. "Rereading Femininity." *Yale French Studies* 62 (1981): 19–44.

Felman, Shoshana, and Dori Laub, M.D. *Testimony: Crises of Witnessing in Literature, Psychoanalysis, and History.* New York: Routledge, 1992.

Franchot, Jenny. "The Punishment of Esther: Frederick Douglass and the Construction of the Feminine." In *New Literary and Historical Essays on Frederick Douglass,* edited by Eric J. Sundquist. Cambridge, England: Cambridge University Press, 1990.

Freud, Sigmund. "'A Child Is Being Beaten,' A Contribution to the Study of the Origin of Sexual Perversions" (1919). In *The Standard Edition of the Complete Psychological Works of Sigmund Freud,* edited and translated by James Strachey, in collaboration with Anna Freud and assisted by Alix Strachey and Alan Tyson. Vol. 17. London: Hogarth 1961.

——. "The Dissolution of the Oedipus Complex" (1924). In *The Standard Edition of the Complete Psychological Works of Sigmund Freud,* edited and translated by James Strachey, in collaboration with Anna Freud and assisted by Alix Strachey and Alan Tyson. Vol. 19. London: Hogarth 1961.

——. "Fetishism" (1927). In *The Standard Edition of the Complete Psychological Works of Sigmund Freud,* edited and translated by James Strachey, in collaboration with Anna Freud and assisted by Alix Strachey and Alan Tyson. Vol. 21. London: Hogarth 1961.

——. "From the History of an Infantile Neurosis" (1918). In *The Standard Edition of the Complete Psychological Works of Sigmund Freud,* edited and translated by James Strachey, in collaboration with Anna Freud and assisted by Alix Strachey and Alan Tyson. Vol. 17. London: Hogarth 1961.

——. "Group Psychology and the Analysis of the Ego" (1921). In *The Standard Edition of the Complete Psychological Works of Sigmund Freud,* edited and translated by James Strachey, in collaboration with Anna Freud and assisted by Alix Strachey and Alan Tyson. Vol. 18. London: Hogarth 1961.

——. "On Narcissism" (1914). In *The Standard Edition of the Complete Psychological Works of Sigmund Freud,* edited and translated by James Strachey, in collaboration with Anna Freud and assisted by Alix Strachey and Alan Tyson. Vol. 14. London: Hogarth 1961.

——. "Some Psychical Consequences of the Anatomical Distinction between the Sexes" (1925). In *The Standard Edition of the Complete Psychological Works of Sigmund Freud,* edited and translated by James Strachey, in collaboration with Anna Freud and assisted by Alix Strachey and Alan Tyson. Vol. 19. London: Hogarth 1961.

——. "Totem and Taboo" (1913). In *The Standard Edition of the Complete Psychological Works of Sigmund Freud,* edited and translated by James Strachey, in collaboration with Anna Freud and assisted by Alix Strachey and Alan Tyson. Vol. 13. London: Hogarth 1961.

——. "The Uncanny" (1919). In *The Standard Edition of the Complete Psychological Works of Sigmund Freud,* edited and translated by James Strachey, in collaboration with Anna Freud and assisted by Alix Strachey and Alan Tyson. Vol. 17. London: Hogarth 1961.

Funderburg, Lise. *Black, White, Other: Biracial Americans Talk about Race and Identity.* New York: William Morrow and Company, 1994.

Fuss, Diana. *Essentially Speaking.* New York: Routledge, 1989.

——. *Identification Papers.* New York: Routledge, 1995.

——. "Interior Colonies: Frantz Fanon and the Politics of Identification." In *Identification Papers.* New York: Routledge, 1995.

Gaines, Jane. "White Privilege and Looking Relations: Race and Gender in Feminist Film Theory." *Cultural Critique* 4 (1986): 59–79.

Gaines, Kevin. "Black Americans' Racial Uplift Ideology as 'Civilizing Mission.'" In *Cultures of United States Imperialism,* edited by Amy Kaplan and Donald E. Pease. Durham: Duke University Press, 1993.

Gallop, Jane. *The Daughter's Seduction.* Ithaca: Cornell University Press, 1982.

——. "The Monster in the Mirror: The Feminist Critic's Psychoanalysis." In *Feminism and Psychoanalysis,* edited by Richard Feldstein and Judith Roof. Ithaca: Cornell University Press, 1989.

——. *Reading Lacan.* Ithaca: Cornell University Press, 1985.

——. *Thinking through the Body.* New York: Columbia University Press, 1988.

Gates Henry Louis, Jr., ed. "Binary Oppositions in Chapter One of the Narrative." In *Frederick Douglass's Narrative of the Life of Frederick Douglass,* edited by Harold Bloom. New York: Chelsea House, 1988.

——. *Black Literature and Literary Theory.* New York: Routledge, 1984.

——. "Critical Fanonism." *Critical Inquiry* 17, no. 3 (1992): 457–70.

——. "Criticism in the Jungle." In *Black Literature and Literary Theory,* edited by Henry Louis Gates Jr. New York: Routledge, 1984.

——, ed. *"Race," Writing, and Difference.* Chicago: University of Chicago Press, 1986.

Genovese, Eugene D. *The Political Economy of Slavery.* 2d. ed. Hanover, New Hampshire: Wesleyan University Press, 1989.

Gilligan, Carol. *In a Different Voice.* Cambridge: Harvard University Press, 1982.

Gilman, Sander. *The Case of Sigmund Freud.* Baltimore: The Johns Hopkins University Press, 1993.

——. *Freud, Race, and Gender.* Princeton: Princeton University Press, 1993.

——. *Jewish Self-Hatred.* Baltimore: The Johns Hopkins University Press, 1986.

Gilroy, Paul. *The Black Atlantic.* Cambridge: Harvard University Press, 1993.

Godden, Richard. "*Absalom, Absalom!*" Haiti and Labor History: Reading Unreadable Revolutions." *English Literary History* 61, no. 3 (1994): 685–720.

Goldberg, David Theo. "Taking Stock: Counting by Race." In *Racial Subjects: Writing on Race in America.* New York: Routledge, 1997.

Goldman, Anne E. "'I Made the Ink': (Literary) Production and Reproduction in *Dessa Rose* and *Beloved.*" *Feminist Studies* 16, no. 2 (1990): 313–30.

Graham, Jessica. "Mixed Reaction to Census." *New York Post,* March 15, 2000, 22.

Grosz, Elizabeth. *Jacques Lacan, A Feminist Introduction.* New York: Routledge, 1990.

Hall, Stuart. "The After-life of Frantz Fanon: Why Fanon? Why Now? Why *Black Skin, White Masks?*" In *The Fact of Blackness: Frantz Fanon and Visual Representation,* edited by Alan Read. Seattle: Bay Press, 1996.

Henderson, Mae G. "Speaking in Tongues: Dialogics, Dialectics, and the Black Woman Writer's Literary Tradition." In *Reading Black, Reading Feminist,* edited by Henry Louis Gates Jr. New York: Meridian-Penguin, 1990.

——. "Toni Morrison's *Beloved*: Re-Membering the Body as Historical Text." In *Comparative American Identities,* edited by Hortense J. Spillers. New York: Routledge, 1991.

Hirsch, Marianne. "Maternal Narratives: 'Cruel Enough to Stop the Blood.'" In *Toni Morrison,* edited by Henry Louis Gates Jr. and K. A. Appiah. New York: Amistad, 1993.

——. *The Mother/Daughter Plot.* Bloomington: Indiana University Press, 1989.

Hoffman, E. T. A. "The Sandman" (1816), in *Tales of Hoffman,* translated by R. J. Hollingdale. Harmondsworth: Penguin, 1982.

Holloway, Karla F. C. "Beloved: A Spiritual." *Callaloo* 13, no. 1 (1990): 516–25.

Holmes, Steven A. "The Confusion over Who We Are." *New York Times,* June 3, 2001, sec. 4.
——. "The Politics of Race and the Census." *New York Times,* March 19, 2000, sec. 4.
hooks, bell. *Black Looks: Race and Representation.* Boston: South End, 1992.
Howe, Samuel G. "Letters on the Proposed Annexation of Santo Domingo" (1871). In *Racial Determinism and the Fear of Miscegenation Pre-1900,* edited by John David Smith. New York: Garland, 1993.
Hughes, Langston. "Cross." In *Quicksand and Passing* by Nella Larsen. New Brunswick, N.J.: Rutgers University Press, 1986.
Hurston, Zora Neale. *Their Eyes Were Watching God.* Urbana: University of Illinois Press, 1978.
Irigaray, Luce. *This Sex Which Is Not One.* Translated by Catherine Porter. Ithaca: Cornell University Press, 1985.
Irwin, John T. *Doubling and Incest/Repetition and Revenge.* Baltimore: The Johns Hopkins University Press, 1975.
Jacobs, Harriet. *Incidents in the Life of a Slave Girl Written by Herself* (1861). Edited by Jean Fagan Yellin. Cambridge: Harvard University Press, 1987.
Jacoby, Jeff. "The Absurdity of Question 6." *Boston Globe*, August 12, 1999, sec. A.
Jehlen, Myra. *Class and Character in Faulkner's South.* New York: Columbia University Press, 1976.
Johnson, Barbara. "Apostrophe, Animation and Abortion." In *A World of Difference.* Baltimore: The Johns Hopkins University Press, 1987.
——. *The Feminist Difference: Literature, Psychoanalysis, Race, and Gender.* Cambridge: Harvard University Press, 1998.
Johnson, James Weldon. *Autobiography of an Ex-Colored Man* (1912). Toronto: Dover, 1995.
Jordanova, Ludmilla. *Sexual Visions.* Madison: University of Wisconsin Press, 1989.
Kaplan, Amy, and Donald Pease, eds. *Cultures of United States Imperialism.* Durham: Duke University Press, 1993.
Kaplan, E. Ann. *Looking for the Other: Feminism, Film, and the Imperial Gaze.* New York: Routledge, 1997.
Karl, Frederick R. "Race, History, and Technique in *Absalom, Absalom!*" In *Faulkner and Race,* edited by Ann J. Abadie and Doreen Fowler. Jackson: University Press of Mississippi, 1987.
Kartiganer, Donald M. "The Role of Myth in *Absalom, Absalom!*" *Modern Fiction Studies* 9, no. 4 (1963–64): 357–69.
King, Richard. "The 'Simple Story's' Ideology: *Gone with the Wind* and the New South Creed." In *Recasting Gone with the Wind in American Culture,* edited by Darden Asbury Pyron. Miami: University Press of Florida, 1983.

Lacan, Jacques. *Écrits.* Translated by Alan Sheridan. New York: Norton, 1977.

——. *The Ethics of Psychoanalysis 1959–1960: The Seminar of Jacques Lacan, Book 7,* edited by Jacques-Alain Miller, translated by Dennis Porter. New York: Norton, 1992.

——. "The Mirror Stage as Formative of the Function of the I." In *Écrits,* translated by Alan Sheridan. New York: Norton, 1977.

Laclau, Ernesto, and Chantal Mouffe. *Hegemony and Socialist Strategy.* London: Verso, 1985.

Ladd, Barbara. "'The Direction of the Howling': Nationalism and the Color Line in *Absalom, Absalom!*" *American Literature* 66, no. 3 (1994): 525–51.

Lane, Christopher, ed. *The Psychoanalysis of Race.* New York: Columbia University Press, 1998.

Larsen, Nella. *Quicksand.* In *Quicksand and Passing.* New Brunswick, N.J.: Rutgers University Press, 1986.

Lauretis, Teresa de. *Alice Doesn't: Feminism, Semiotics, Cinema.* Bloomington: Indiana University Press, 1984.

——. "Feminist Studies/Critical Studies: Issues, Terms, and Contexts." In *Feminist Studies/Critical Studies,* edited by Teresa de Lauretis. Bloomington: Indiana University Press, 1986.

Lemire. Elise. *"Miscegenation": Making Race in America.* Philadelphia: University of Pennsylvania Press, 2002.

Lévi-Strauss, Claude. *The Elementary Structures of Kinship.* Translated by James Harle Bell and John Richard von Sturmer. Edited by Rodney Needham. Boston: Beacon Press, 1969.

Leverenz, David. *Manhood and the American Renaissance.* Ithaca: Cornell University Press, 1989.

Lewis, David Levering. *W. E. B. Du Bois: Biography of a Race.* New York: Henry Holt & Company, 1993.

Loomba, Ania. *Colonialism/Postcolonialism.* New York: Routledge, 1998.

Lubiano, Wahneema. Foreword to *(Dis)Forming the American Canon,* by Ronald A. T. Judy. Minneapolis: University of Minnesota Press, 1993.

Malinowski, Bronislaw. *Sex and Repression in Savage Society* (1927). Chicago: University of Chicago Press, 1985.

Mama, Amina. *Beyond the Masks: Race, Gender, and Subjectivity.* London: Routledge, 1995.

Mannoni, O. *Prospero and Caliban: The Psychology of Colonization.* New York: Praeger, 1964.

Maran, René. *Un Homme pareil aux autres* (1947). Paris: Albin Michel, 1962.

Markowitz, Norman. "William Faulkner's 'Tragic Legend': Southern History and *Absalom, Absalom!*" *Minnesota Review* 17 (1981): 104–17.

Marshall, Cynthia. "Psychoanalyzing the Prepsychoanalytic Subject." *PMLA* 117, no. 5 (2002): 1207–16.

Mathieson, Barbara Offutt. "Memory and Mother Love in Morrison's *Beloved*." *American Imago* 47, no. 1 (1990): 1–21.

Matthews, James W. "The Civil War of 1936: *Gone with the Wind* and *Absalom, Absalom!*" *Georgia Review* 21, no. 4 (1967): 462–69.

McBride, James. *The Color of Water: A Black Man's Tribute to His White Mother.* Berkeley: Berkeley Publishing Group, 1997.

McDowell, Deborah E. "In the First Place: Making Frederick Douglass and the Afro-American Narrative Tradition." In *Critical Essays on Frederick Douglass,* edited by William L. Andrews. Boston: G. K. Hall, 1991.

——. Introduction to *Quicksand and Passing,* by Nella Larsen. New Brunswick, N.J.: Rutgers University Press, 1986.

Meacham, Jon. "The New Face of Race." *Newsweek,* September 18, 2000, 38–41.

Milloy, Courtland. "U.S. Census Cultivates Fiction of Race." *Washington Post,* 19 March 2000, sec. C.

Mitchell, Juliet. *Psychoanalysis and Feminism.* New York: Vintage, 1975.

Mitchell, Margaret. *Gone with the Wind.* New York: Warner Books, 1999.

Mobley, Marilyn Sanders. "A Different Remembering: Memory, History and Meaning in Toni Morrison's *Beloved*." In *Toni Morrison,* edited by Harold Bloom. New York: Chelsea, 1990.

Moglen, Helene. "Redeeming History: Toni Morrison's *Beloved*." *Cultural Critique* (Spring 1993): 17–40.

Moon, Michael, and Cathy N. Davidson, eds. *Subjects and Citizens: Nation, Race, and Gender from Oroonoko to Anita Hill.* Durham: Duke University Press, 1995.

Morrison, Toni. *Beloved.* New York: Knopf, 1987.

——. *Playing in the Dark.* Cambridge: Harvard University Press, 1992.

——. "Unspeakable Things Unspoken: The Afro-American Presence in American Literature." *Michigan Quarterly Review* 28 (1989): 1–34. Reprinted in *Within the Circle: An Anthology of African American Literary Criticism from the Harlem Renaissance to the Present,* edited by Angelyn Mitchell. Durham: Duke University Press, 1994.

Murdock, Deroy. "Separation of Race." *Washington Times,* March 11, 2001, sec. B.

"My Shoes." http://myshoes.com/MSMembership.html. April 30, 2003.

Niemtzow, Annette. "The Problematic of Self in Autobiography: The Example of the Slave Narrative." In *Frederick Douglass's Narrative of the Life of Frederick Douglass,* edited by Harold Bloom. New York: Chelsea House, 1988.

Obeyesekere, Gananath. *The Work of Culture, Symbolic Transformation in Psychoanalysis and Anthropology.* Chicago: University of Chicago Press, 1990.

O'Brien, Kenneth. "Race, Romance, and the Southern Literary Tradition." In

Recasting Gone with the Wind in American Culture, edited by Darden Asbury Pyron. Miami: University Press of Florida, 1983.

Olney, James. "'I Was Born': Slave Narratives, Their Status as Autobiography and as Literature." In *The Slave's Narrative,* edited by Charles T. Davis and Henry Louis Gates Jr. New York: Oxford University Press, 1985.

Pabst, Naomi. "Blackness/Mixedness: Contestations over Crossing Signs." *Cultural Critique* 54 (Spring 2003): 178–212.

Parry, Benita. "Problems in Current Theories of Colonial Discourse." *Oxford Literary Review* 9, no. 1–2 (1987): 27–58.

Parsons, Anne. "Is the Oedipus Complex Universal?" *The Psychoanalytic Study of Society* 3 (1964): 278–328.

Pellegrini, Ann. *Performance Anxieties: Staging Psychoanalysis, Staging Race.* New York: Routledge, 1997.

Porter, Carolyn. "*Absalom, Absalom!*: (Un)Making the Father." In *The Cambridge Companion to William Faulkner,* edited by Philip W. Weinstein. Cambridge: Cambridge University Press, 1995.

Project Race. www.projectrace.com/aboutprojectrace/. April 14, 2003.

Pyron, Darden Asbury. "*Gone with the Wind* and the Southern Cultural Awakening." *Virginia Quarterly Review* 62, no. 4 (1986): 565–87.

"Race and the Census." *Boston Globe,* April 1, 2000, sec. A.

Radhakrishnan, R. "Ethnic Identity and Post-Structuralist Difference." In *The Nature and Context of Minority Discourse,* edited by Abdul R. JanMohamed and David Lloyd. New York: Oxford University Press, 1990.

Rampersad, Arnold. *The Art and Imagination of W. E. B. Du Bois.* New York: Schocken, 1990.

——. "Du Bois's *The Souls of Black Folk.*" In *Slavery and the Literary Imagination,* edited by Deborah E. McDowell and Arnold Rampersad. Baltimore: The Johns Hopkins University Press, 1989.

Retamar, Roberto Fernandez. *Caliban and Other Essays.* Translated by Edward Baker. Minneapolis: University of Minnesota Press, 1989.

Roberts, Diane. *Faulkner and Southern Womanhood.* Athens: University of Georgia Press, 1994.

Rodriguez, Cindy. "Civil Rights Groups Wary of Census Data on Race." *Boston Globe,* December 8, 2000, sec. A.

Roediger, David R. "White Skins, Black Masks: Minstrelsy and White Working Class Formation before the Civil War." In *The Wages of Whiteness.* New York: Verso, 1991.

Rogin, Michael. "Blackface, White Noise: The Jewish Jazz Singer Finds His Voice." *Critical Inquiry* 18 (1992): 417–53.

Rony, Fatimah Tobing. *The Third Eye: Race, Cinema, and Ethnographic Spectacle.* Durham, Duke University Press, 1996.

Root, Maria P. P. "Bill of Rights for Racially Mixed People." *Interracial Voice,* May 26, 2003, www.webcom.com/~intvoice/rights.html.

Rose, Jacqueline. *Sexuality in the Field of Vision.* New York: Verso, 1986.
Rubin, Gayle. "The Traffic in Women." In *Toward an Anthropology of Women,* edited by Rayna R. Reiter. New York: Monthly Review Press, 1975.
Rushdy, Ashraf H. A. "Daughters Signifyin(g) History: The Example of Toni Morrison's *Beloved.*" *American Literature* 64, no. 3 (1992): 567–97.
Sabiston, Elizabeth. "Women, Blacks, and Thomas Sutpen's Mythopoeic Drive in *Absalom, Absalom!*" *Modernist Studies* 1, no. 3 (1974–75): 15–26.
Saldivar, Ramón. "Looking for a Master Plan: Faulkner, Parades, and the Colonial and Postcolonial Subject." In *The Cambridge Companion to William Faulkner,* edited by Philip W. Weinstein. Cambridge: Cambridge University Press, 1995.
Santner, Eric. *My Own Private Germany: Daniel Paul Schreber's Secret History of Modernity.* Princeton: Princeton University Press, 1996.
Schapiro, Barbara. "The Bonds of Love and the Boundaries of Self in Toni Morrison's *Beloved.*" *Contemporary Literature* 32, no. 2 (1991): 194–210.
Sedinger, Tracey. "Nation and Identification: Psychoanalysis, Race, and Sexual Difference." *Cultural Critique* 50 (Winter 2002): 40–73.
Segura, Denise A., and Jennifer L. Pierce. "Chicana/o Family Structure and Gender Personality: Chodorow, Familism, and Psychoanalytic Sociology Revisited." *Signs* 19, no. 1 (1993): 62–91.
Senna, Danzy. *Caucasia.* New York: Riverhead Books, 1998.
Seshadri-Crooks, Kalpana. *Desiring Whiteness.* New York: Routledge, 2000.
——. "The Primitive as Analyst: Postcolonial Feminism's Access to Psychoanalysis." *Cultural Critique* 28 (Fall 1994): 175–218.
Sharpley-Whiting, T. Denean. "Fanon and Capécia." In *Frantz Fanon: Critical Perspectives,* edited by Anthony C. Allessandrini. New York: Routledge, 1999.
Siemerling, Winfried. "W. E. B. Du Bois, Hegel, and the Staging of Alterity." *Callaloo* 24, no. 1 (2001): 325–33.
Silverman, Kaja. *Male Subjectivity at the Margins.* New York: Routledge, 1992.
——. "White Skin, Brown Masks: The Double Mimesis, or With Lawrence in Arabia." *Differences* 1, no. 3 (1989): 3–54.
Smith, Lillian. *Strange Fruit.* New York: Reynall & Hitchcock, 1944.
Smith, Valerie. "'Circling the Subject': History and Narrative in *Beloved.*" In *Toni Morrison,* edited by Henry Louis Gates Jr. and K. A. Appiah. New York: Amistad, 1993.
——. "'Loopholes of Retreat:' Architecture and Ideology in Harriet Jacobs's *Incidents in the Life of a Slave Girl.*" In *Reading Black, Reading Feminist,* edited by Henry Louis Gates Jr. New York: Meridian-Penguin, 1990.
——. *Self-Discovery and Authority in Afro-American Narrative.* Cambridge: Harvard University Press, 1987.

Smith, William Benjamin. "The Color Line: A Brief in Behalf of the Unborn" (1905). In *Racial Determinism and the Fear of Miscegenation Post-1900,* edited by John David Smith. New York: Garland, 1993.

Snead, James A. "The 'Joint' of Racism: Withholding the Black in *Absalom, Absalom!*" In *William Faulkner's Absalom, Absalom!* edited by Harold Bloom. Chelsea: New York, 1987.

——. "Light in August and the Rhetorics of Racial Division." In *Faulkner and Race,* edited by Ann J. Abadie and Doreen Fowler. Jackson: University Press of Mississippi, 1987.

Somerville, Siobhan. *Queering the Color Line: Race and the Invention of Homosexuality in American Culture.* Durham: Duke University Press, 2000.

Spillers, Hortense J. "'All the Things You Could Be by Now If Sigmund Freud's Wife Was Your Mother': Psychoanalysis and Race." In *Female Subjects in Black and White: Race, Psychoanalysis, and Feminism,* edited by Elizabeth Abel, Barbara Christian, and Helene Moglen. Berkeley and Los Angeles: University of California Press, 1997.

——. "Interstices: A Small Drama of Words." In *Pleasure and Danger,* edited by Carole S. Vance. New York: Routledge, 1984.

——. "Introduction: Who Cuts the Border? Some Readings on 'America.'" In *Comparative American Identities,* edited by Hortense J. Spillers. New York: Routledge, 1991.

——. "Mama's Baby, Papa's Maybe: An American Grammar Book." *Diacritics* 17, no. 2 (1987): 65–81. Reprinted in *Within the Circle: An Anthology of African American Literary Criticism from the Harlem Renaissance to the Present,* edited by Angelyn Mitchell. Durham: Duke University Press, 1994.

——. "'The Permanent Obliquity of an In[pha]llibly Straight': In the Time of the Daughters and the Fathers." In *Daughters and Fathers,* edited by Lynda E. Boose and Betty S. Flowers. Baltimore: The Johns Hopkins University Press, 1989.

——. "'The Tragic Mulatta': Neither/Nor—Toward an Alternative Model." In *The Difference Within,* edited by Elizabeth Meese and Alice Parker. Philadelphia: John Benjamins, 1989.

Stone, Albert E. "Identity and Art in Frederick Douglass's *Narrative.*" In *Critical Essays on Frederick Douglass,* edited by William L. Andrews. Boston: G. K. Hall, 1991.

Sundquist, Eric J. "*Absalom, Absalom!* and the House Divided." In *William Faulkner's Absalom, Absalom!* edited by Harold Bloom. Chelsea: New York, 1987.

——. "Faulkner, Race, and the Forms of American Fiction." In *Faulkner and Race,* edited by Ann J. Abadie and Doreen Fowler. Jackson: University Press of Mississippi, 1987.

Swift, Mike. "A Fresh Face on Race." *Hartford Courant,* 13 March 2001, sec. A.

Tate, Claudia. *Psychoanalysis and Black Novels: Desire and the Protocols of Race.* New York: Oxford University Press, 1998.

Todd, Jane Marie. "The Veiled Woman in Freud's '*Das Unheimliche.*'" *Signs* 11, no. 3 (Spring 1986): 519–28.

Travis, Molly Abel. "Speaking from the Silence of the Slave Narrative: *Beloved* and African-American Women's History." *Texas Review* 13, no. 1–2 (1992): 69–81.

Trent, Sydney. "'Multiracial' Category Is a Mixed Blessing." *Newsday,* 28 March 2001, sec. A.

Vergès, Françoise. "Chains of Madness, Chains of Colonialism: Fanon and Freedom." In *The Fact of Blackness: Frantz Fanon and Visual Representation,* edited by Alan Read. Seattle: Bay Press, 1996.

Wald, Priscilla. "Becoming 'Colored': The Self-Authorized Language of Difference in Zora Neale Hurston." *American Literary History* 2, no. 1 (1990): 79–99.

Walker, Rebecca. *Black, White, and Jewish: Autobiography of a Shifting Self.* New York: Putnam, 2000.

Wall, Cheryl. *Women of the Harlem Renaissance.* Bloomington: Indiana University Press, 1995.

Walton, Jean. *Fair Sex, Savage Dreams: Race, Psychoanalysis, Sexual Difference.* Durham: Duke University Press, 2001.

Washington, Mary Helen. *Invented Lives: Narratives of Black Women 1860–1960.* New York: Doubleday-Anchor, 1987.

Waugh, Patricia. *Feminine Fictions.* New York: Routledge, 1989.

Werner, Craig. "Minstrel Nightmares: Black Dreams of Faulkner's Dreams of Blacks." In *Faulkner and Race,* edited by Ann J. Abadie and Doreen Fowler. Jackson: University Press of Mississippi, 1987.

West, Cornel. *The American Evasion of Philosophy.* New York: MacMillan, 1989.

———. "Black Culture and Postmodernism." In *Remaking History,* edited by Barbara Kruger and Phil Mariani. Seattle: Bay Press, 1989.

———. *Prophesy Deliverance.* Philadelphia: The Westminster Press, 1982.

White, Walter. *A Man Called White: The Autobiography of Walter White.* Athens: University of Georgia Press, 1995.

Wiegman, Robyn. "Intimate Publics: Race, Property, and Personhood." *American Literature* 74, no. 4 (2002): 859–85.

Williams, Gregory Howard. *Life on the Color Line: The True Story of a White Boy Who Discovered He Was Black.* New York: Dutton/Plume, 1996.

Wyatt, Jean. "Giving Body to the Word: The Maternal Symbolic in Toni Morrison's *Beloved.*" *PMLA* 108, no. 3 (1993): 474–88.

Yellin, Jean Fagan. Introduction to *Incidents in the Life of a Slave Girl* by

Harriet Jacobs. Edited by Jean Fagan Yellin. Boston: Harvard University Press, 1987.

Zamir, Shamoon. *Dark Voices: W. E. B. Du Bois and American Thought, 1888–1903*. Chicago: University of Chicago Press, 1995.

Žižek, Slavoj. *The Sublime Object of Ideology*. New York: Verso, 1989.

Zwarg, Christina. "Du Bois on Trauma: Psychoanalysis and the Would-Be Black Savant." *Cultural Critique* 51 (Spring 2002): 1–39.

INDEX

Gwen Bergner is associate professor of English at West Virginia University.